Praise for *Chang*

Change Your Stars is essential reading written by a transformational leader—Michele Weslander Quaid—who encourages us to change our "stars" of circumstance, removing every limit from our lives.

No matter your belief system, this powerful book is a definitive guide that can and will change your life. It has for me.

Michele is one of the most courageous people I have ever known. It is a rare privilege to be in the presence of a human whose compassion, commitment, and conviction to serve and protect others is so great that it outweighs any concern of personal repercussion, consequence, or danger.

It is an honor to know Michele, and I greatly enjoy her friendship. Our family met her in 2015 when she was the keynote speaker at a community event, and we became inspired by her genius. When Michele moved to Santa Barbara, we served on the board of directors for an educational start-up. Her contributions helped to make the project an extraordinary success.

Through her story, Michele will inspire you with how she outperformed all expectations despite enormous obstacles in her early life. She used her growing influence to destroy corruption, fight fiercely for the protection of others, and eliminate any ceiling people sought to impose.

Not only does Michele share the dynamic, riveting adventures of rising from being underestimated to achieving greatness, she also teaches us to change our stars no matter our circumstances.

Change Your Stars is a must-read for all. *Change Your Stars* will change your life.

Kathy Ireland
Chair and CEO
kathy ireland ® Worldwide

How does someone start life with humble beginnings—born to a single mom, raised below the US poverty level—to truly become a success story, rising to some of the highest levels in our government and technology sectors? You do it by refusing to accept that those circumstances will limit your potential. That's exactly what Michele Weslander Quaid did, and she defied the odds. Her life is a testament to who she is and shows that in this great land of opportunity, if one determines to take risks, pursue great things, challenge oneself, and get outside of one's comfort zone, there is no telling where one can go.

I believe God has made each of us for a unique purpose and that we glorify Him by pursuing that purpose. In that pursuit, we often walk by faith, never entirely sure what comes next. Yet, by being faithful and having the courage to take one step and then another, we can one day look back and realize we accomplished things that we thought might never have been possible at the onset. That is Michele's life as laid out in *Change Your Stars*, an inspiration for anyone to shoot for the stars and become who God intended you to be.

Ned Ryun
Founder and CEO
American Majority

Michele's book, *Change Your Stars,* is one of the most refreshing and captivating stories that I have read of what life in America is like. It reads like a movie, pulling you into the smallest details because they make you feel like her story could be yours too.

At a time when social media has overwhelmed our attention and warped our view of the world around us, Michele's book is a gentle and beautiful reminder that life is far more complex, lessons are all around us, and most families have to work hard to live. Most importantly, we can all change our stars no matter where or to whom we were born.

As a single mother, I resonate with Michele's story. It inspires, encourages, and gives me hope for my daughter's future. I'm positive that it will do the same for many others. It is a reminder of all that makes America great for everyone who lives here, regardless of color or class.

And as someone who works internationally, I wish everyone who wants to understand the American spirit better would read this book. It captures all that DeTocqueville expressed about our great country through the life of a child and the beautiful woman she has become. Her story is relatable, attainable, and captivating.

Tina Ramirez
Founder and President
Hardwired Global

What an inspiration *Change Your Stars* is, especially for those from humble beginnings! Michele's tremendous success didn't come without pain and hardship, but she worked through the difficulties, overcame them, and succeeded beyond anyone's wildest expectations.

Michele has made significant contributions to society and has used her gifts for the greater good. As an innovator, she envisions how things could be better and takes action to make it happen. She has the courage of her convictions to speak truth to power, even at personal cost. Her story will encourage and motivate you to lead a life of significance.

As the CEO and President of Tremblay Financial Services, I have led our organization to the Top Large Branch award for our broker/dealer, Centaurus, for ten years in a row. *Change Your Stars* has been an inspiration for me, our employees, and business associates. I highly recommend *Change Your Stars*. It is a must-read for all!

Timothy N. Tremblay
President and CEO
Tremblay Financial Services

CHANGE YOUR STARS

Live Your Purpose and Achieve Your Dreams

Michele R. Weslander Quaid

MICHELE R.
WESLANDER QUAID

Capucia LLC, 211 Pauline Drive #513, York PA 17402
www.capuciapublishing.com; support@capuciapublishing.com

Paperback ISBN: 978-1-954920-63-7
eBook ISBN: 978-1-954920-64-4
Library of Congress Control Number: 2023904920

Cover Design and Layout: Ranilo Cabo

Printed in the United States of America

Capucia LLC is proud to be a part of the Tree Neutral® program. Tree Neutral offsets the number of trees consumed in the production and printing of this book by taking proactive steps such as planting trees in direct proportion to the number of trees used to print books. To learn more about Tree Neutral, please visit treeneutral.com.

This book is dedicated to my beloved Chris and our darling daughter, Sophia.

CONTENTS

PREFACE	1
CHAPTER 1	
Significant Life Events	5
Against the Odds	8
CHAPTER 2	
In the Beginning	13
Hard Times	16
Fun Times	17
Historic Tour	18
CHAPTER 3	
Big Changes	23
The Evergreen State	25
CHAPTER 4	
Influencers	33
Choices	36
Inspiration	38
CHAPTER 5	
College	41
CHAPTER 6	
Philly	49
CHAPTER 7	
Grad School	57
Long Weekend in Europe	65

CHAPTER 8
National Security Space 71
Living out of a Suitcase 77

CHAPTER 9
Mission Operations 81
Rapid Prototyping 88

CHAPTER 10
Reputation 91
Personal Crisis 93
Free to Thrive 103

CHAPTER 11
The Rebel Outpost 105
Leadership 108

CHAPTER 12
Collaboration 113
A Vision for the Future 117
Rocky Mountain High 121

CHAPTER 13
Another Day That Will Live in Infamy 123
Life of a Change Agent 131
Love to America 132
The Land Down Under 134

CHAPTER 14
The Briefing 137
The Call 139

CHAPTER 15
Oath of Office 143
The Bureaucracy 145
Back in the Beltway 147

CHAPTER 16
Mission Impossible 151
Horizontal Integration 155

CHAPTER 17
CAPSTONE 161
Jointness 171

CHAPTER 18
Rock Stars 173
Oorah 174
GEOINT 175

CHAPTER 19
Boots on the Ground 177
Warrior Goddess 185

CHAPTER 20
Ambassadors and Movie Stars 187
EXCOM 190
Remembering D-Day 191

CHAPTER 21
Sweden 195
Special Ops 196
The Last of the Titans 205

CHAPTER 22
ODNI 207
Diplomatic Dining 211
Tippy Top Secret 213

CHAPTER 23
Tackling Policy Barriers 215

CHAPTER 24
Life Partners 225
Joy and Sorrow 230
Wedding 232

CHAPTER 25
Deployment 239
Office Dynamics 242

CHAPTER 26
Integrated Ops 251
Under the Tuscan Sun 253

CHAPTER 27
Changes 257
CXO 260

CHAPTER 28
Family 263
Ultrasound 267
Reality Check 269
That Sunday That Summer 270

CHAPTER 29
Federal Innovation 273
SecDef Task Force 274
Rolling Stone 277
The Last Straw 282

CHAPTER 30
G2G 285
The Force 288
Our House 290
Promotion 292

CHAPTER 31
Keynotes 295
Outreach 299
Google Ambassador 301

CHAPTER 32
Building Trust 303
Medallion Award 307
Speakers Bureau 309

CHAPTER 33
Transition 317

CHAPTER 34
New Beginnings 327

EPILOGUE 335
GLOSSARY 339
ACKNOWLEDGMENTS 345
ABOUT THE AUTHOR 347

PREFACE

You were created for a purpose. You will never find more fulfillment than when you are doing exactly what you were meant to be doing at any point in time in your life.

Since childhood, I had an idea of what I wanted to do, but while in graduate school, I was recruited to do something else. Looking back, I realize I was meant to go down that different, though related, path. Though I could never have predicted my career, throughout my journey, I have known with certainty at some point in each position I held that I was where I was meant to be at that given time to make a positive difference. Many people told me, "You are here for a time such as this." My career has been unique and uncomfortably exciting at times, and I would not change it.

No one would have predicted my life's trajectory, given my humble beginnings. So many who have heard parts of my story have told me that I must write this memoir about my life and career and how I changed my stars to encourage others in their life journey. I hope that anyone who reads this book will be inspired, particularly young people who are finishing their schooling, planning their future, or just getting started in their careers. I hope my story motivates you to dream big, *shoot for the stars*, and stay true to yourself and your convictions.

As someone with the courage of her convictions and the personal initiative to take on difficult challenges, even things others considered impossible, I have had the opportunity to serve at very senior levels—both in corporate America and the United States government—at a relatively young age. The work that my colleagues and I did in the national security community helped to protect people serving in harm's way who were defending our freedom so that they came home safely to their families.

So many young people have asked how I planned my career path. My response is always the same. There was no planning involved. I just did what I saw needed to be done, followed my gut instinct, acted with integrity, and had the strength of my convictions and the courage to speak the truth to powerful people. Sometimes others were so threatened by the new things I was proposing that they did everything they could to stop me. Eventually, someone saw in me the vision and leadership qualities they wanted and recruited me into a new opportunity to effect positive change.

Most of the positions I served in did not previously exist, so I created the role, which often involved establishing something new or transforming something existing. Once I had things up and running in the new direction, I eventually transitioned the role to someone else and headed off to tackle the challenges in the next role I was called to do. Such is the life of a change agent—you must know when to let go of what you've helped create and move on.

After being sworn in as a senior executive in the United States government the day before my thirty-third birthday, some people said, "You are too young to be in a leadership position." In reality, age has nothing to do with leadership ability. It is who you are and how you conduct yourself that matters.

Change is not easy. It involves risk. If we are not willing to take intelligent risks, we risk never becoming who we are meant to be and never doing what we are meant to do. People thought I was crazy given the career changes I made—when I left a senior leadership position in the private sector to go into government after the terrorist attacks of 11 September 2001, and then when I left a senior executive position in government to go back to the private sector, and especially when I left a lucrative job at one of the most innovative companies in the world to start my own business. I felt called to make each of those transitions, including starting my own company, Sunesis Nexus, and charting my own course to make a positive difference in other people's lives.

So many times throughout the years, but especially after my return to the private sector after serving in the public sector, people approached me after a meeting or presentation and told me they would like me to consult with them, partner with them, help them implement the things I talked about, coach them to innovate, grow, transform, reach their potential and be their greatest selves. The only way I could do that was to leave a secure job working for someone else and become my own boss. When I took the leap of faith, opportunities came, and I never looked back. My work is fulfilling because I'm doing what I was created to do and making a positive difference.

I desire to encourage and inspire others, especially the next generation. I trust you will not be the same person after reading this book. I hope you will be positively impacted and motivated to pursue your dreams. As you will see through my story, you are never too young to lead, and it is never too late to change your stars and become the person you are meant to be.

Sincerely,
Michele R. Weslander Quaid

Pursue your Passion. Live your Purpose.
Engage the Culture. Change the World!

CHAPTER 1

What is your purpose in life? You are beautifully and wonderfully made with unique talents and passions. The most joy you can experience is using your gifts to make a positive difference in the lives of others and the world around you. It is incredible to know you are right where you are meant to be, doing what you are meant to be doing. I am blessed to have had those moments in my life. I hope my story will inspire you.

Significant Life Events

Some dates become indelibly marked in your mind because they represent significant life events. Three dates in my life are 11 September 2001, 11 June 2002, and 26 August 2002.

On 11 September 2001, terrorists attacked the United States of America (USA). I was in the Washington, DC, area at the time—Central Intelligence Agency (CIA) headquarters, to be exact. The CIA does human intelligence (HUMINT). My colleague Gary and I had flown to Virginia from Colorado to present some intelligence-related activities of interest.

We were sitting in the CIA headquarters lobby when the first two planes hit the Twin Towers in New York City. The CIA doesn't allow electronic devices in the building, so we had to leave our mobile phones in the car. We had no other information source, so we were unaware this had happened.

When our escort took us to the conference room, we noted people seemed distracted. During our presentation, people kept going in and out of the room. Then someone came into the conference room and said, "A plane has hit the Pentagon." Mayhem ensued. Gary and I were surprised and didn't have the full context, but we quickly learned what had happened earlier that morning in New York City.

I immediately thought I had to call my mom to tell her I was okay. She knew I worked in defense and intelligence and didn't know where I was working that day, and I wanted to inform her I was not at the Pentagon and assure her I was alright. The staff at the CIA was so panicked they would not allow me to use the phone. They wanted everyone out of the office suite so they could lock it up and hurriedly ushered us into the hallway.

As Gary and I walked out of CIA headquarters and surveyed the chaos outside, I turned to him and said, "Usama Bin Laden," and he nodded. That was not a name well known by our fellow Americans or the world at the time. However, if you worked in the national security sector, as I had for nearly a decade, you knew who he was, and my gut told me he was the instigator of this horrific event. Gary agreed. We discussed what this event could mean for our country, our way of life, and even our work. Things would undoubtedly change.

Once we made it to the parking lot, people were frantically rushing to their cars, all wanting to leave a secure facility not set up to enable people to enter or exit quickly. I told Gary I didn't see any point in getting in that line of cars idling and would prefer to stand outside until the lines cleared. He agreed.

We grabbed our mobile phones out of the car and tried to make phone calls, but the cellular network I was on wouldn't let me make a call. This went on for at least forty-five minutes before someone getting their calls through overheard me fretting about how worried my mother would be and offered to let me use their phone. I was very grateful, and when I got through to my mother, she was relieved to hear my voice.

We eventually got in our rental car and headed to our hotel near Washington Dulles Airport. Traffic was terrible everywhere. Once we were on the Dulles Toll Road, we observed how badly the lines for the exits were backed up. When we got to our exit, people were driving on the shoulders of the road around the toll booth to get where they wanted to go. We couldn't believe they hadn't raised the toll bars during this national emergency and let traffic flow uninhibited.

Once we were inside the hotel, we noted that all the news stations on the TVs were covering the event. Most didn't have anything new to say after a while. I don't usually fall asleep quickly—I don't have an off switch for my brain—and it was tough to sleep that night.

Early the next morning, I heard someone drop the newspaper outside my hotel room door. I got up, opened the door, and looked down at the cover page. Upon seeing the horrific images, tears started streaming down my face. I still have that newspaper. The events of that day would change the course of my career in so many ways and life in America forever.

Another related date is 11 June 2002, which was exactly nine months since the terrorist attacks in the USA on 11 September 2001. On that day, I gave a presentation to the director of the National Imagery and Mapping Agency (NIMA), now known as the National Geospatial-Intelligence Agency (NGA), and the director of the National Security Agency (NSA) at their joint quarterly meeting. NGA and NSA are America's eyes and ears. NGA does the geospatial intelligence mission (GEOINT), and NSA does the signals intelligence mission (SIGINT).

So much had happened leading up to that point. For those fighting the war on terrorism, especially those in harm's way, what I had to share with those directors was critical. The actions that I, on their behalf, would ask these directors to take would be transformative in helping us execute integrated counterterrorism operations more effectively and save lives. Despite that fact, so many people did not want me to give that presentation and had tried everything they could think of—leading up to the meeting and even during the meeting—to prevent me from giving it.

What I was to present drove home the fact that change—in policy and in how they did business—was required for the good of America and those who served our country in harm's way. Many people fear the unknown and what they do not understand. The people who opposed the proposed actions to affect necessary change were comfortable with the status quo. The way we had done business to date had ultimately failed the nation and put people's lives at risk—the lives of the warfighters, the military members defending our country; the first responders, like police officers and firefighters; and thousands of civilians.

The fact that the change could result in something better did not matter to them; they would fight it. Those people—most of whom were bureaucrats who had not been in harm's way—had gone so far as to try and get my national security clearances revoked and get me fired from my job. They wanted to shoot the messenger. There was much at stake for me, the national security community, the warfighters, and our allies.

Lastly, 26 August 2002 has a dual meaning for me. It was my thirty-third birthday. It was also the day I officially transitioned from being the youngest chief engineer in Scitor's history to become one of the youngest people ever sworn in as a senior executive in the US government. A senior executive is considered equivalent in rank to general and flag officers in the military. I had gone from having senior executives try to get me fired for proposing a change to becoming a senior executive with the charter to lead that change. While I considered my life experiences up until that point to be unique, the experiences after that were extraordinary. They would help me discover what I was made of and my purpose in life. I am happy to share them with you in the hope that you will find insight, encouragement, and inspiration for your life journey.

Against the Odds

Sometimes it's the very people who no one imagines anything of, who do the things that no one can imagine.
~ Alan Turing, mathematician

Many see the future for someone born in "less fortunate" circumstances or raised in "disadvantaged" demographics as a fait accompli, meaning something that has already been determined, leaving that individual with no option but to accept it. I can say with certainty that is not the case, especially not in the land of opportunity that is the United States of America as our founders envisioned it.

Throughout my childhood, people's expectations of me were mixed. Many could not see past the circumstances into which I was born and assumed I would never amount to anything. Some were tactless enough to say this within my earshot. While it hurt me to hear people say things like this, rather than embracing a victim mentality, I became all the more determined to be an overcomer and prove them wrong. Thankfully, others looked past my circumstances and saw my character and potential. They believed I could do great things if I set my mind to it and worked hard to achieve my goals.

Some people did not think the prospects were good for someone who fit the following demographics: child of a single mother; father was not in the picture; mother never earned a college degree; mother's income was below the US-defined poverty level; mother had to work multiple jobs to make ends meet; the child was female. Statistically speaking, a child in a single-parent household is far more likely to experience violence, commit suicide, parent a child out of wedlock at a young age, continue a cycle of poverty, become drug dependent, commit a crime, or perform below his or her peers in education. But it doesn't have to be this way.

What you may not expect from a child with these demographics is the following: high school valedictorian and science award winner for the senior class; bachelor of science degree in physics and engineering science—a double major with honors; master of science degree in optics; youngest chief engineer and second-ever female chief engineer in the history of Scitor Corporation; one of the youngest people ever sworn in as a senior executive in the US government; served as a senior executive across the Department of Defense (DoD) and the Intelligence Community (IC) in various precedent-setting leadership roles; served as Google's Chief Technology Officer for Public Sector and Chief Innovation Evangelist.

Those are some of my accomplishments, which demonstrate that the circumstances into which you are born do not predetermine what you can accomplish in life, especially if you have a strong work ethic and are blessed to live in the USA. My life doesn't match up with the statistics or stereotypes, and I believe that we are all individuals who can chart our own destinies. While we cannot choose the cards we are dealt, we can decide how to play them. Rather than play the victim because we lack the resources, we can overcome and be resourceful and discover what we can achieve.

The circumstances into which you are born do not predetermine what you can accomplish in life.

As documented in the 2001 movie, *A Knight's Tale* starring Heath Ledger, directed by Brian Helgeland (Columbia Pictures), many societies have a class system where a person's social status is primarily determined by the family into which he or she is born. In the movie, a young boy named

William longs to be a knight, but he is the son of a poor thatcher. While watching a parade of knights go by, he says, "Someday, I'll be a knight."

A member of the public starts laughing and says, "A thatcher's son, a knight? You might as well try to change the stars!" The boy then asks, "Can it be done, father? Can a man change the stars?" His father replies, "Yes, William. If he believes enough, a man can do anything."

William's father gets him an apprenticeship with a knight while he is still a boy. Though it is painful for them to part ways, his father tells him, "It's all I can do for you, son. Now go change your stars and have a better life than I have."

Years later, when William is a young adult, the knight he is serving dies right before a tournament. William decides to wear the deceased knight's armor and do the joust. His friends say it can't be done because he is not of noble birth. William replies, "A man can change his stars, and I won't spend the rest of my life as nothing." They tell him, "You're a knight in your heart but not on paper, and paper is all that matters to them." William is not deterred. When he takes his mount and prepares to joust, he says, "I've waited my whole life for this moment."

A Knight's Tale is one of my favorite movies, and it's where I first heard the phrase "change your stars."

If you are fortunate as I was to be born in America—the land of opportunity—you have a chance to change your stars and live the life you want to have. In America, you are not stuck where you started. You can chart your own course, and with a love of learning, a good work ethic, and some innovation, you can change your status in life—you can change your stars. Many who immigrate to the USA to become citizens recognize this and take advantage of the opportunities afforded them in America that they did not have in their countries of birth. So many immigrants have made tremendous contributions to American society and the world.

One unique aspect of America is that once you become a citizen, you are seen as 100 percent American. America doesn't have an ethnic identity—it is truly a melting pot—so anyone who strives to become an American, upholds traditional American values, and achieves citizenship is truly one of us. If you were to immigrate to any other country, while you could become a citizen, you would never be considered "one of us" by the native-born. As an immigrant, you'd always be seen as somewhat of an outsider.

Too often, people are judged by the circumstances into which they were born. We should not let past experiences or unconscious bias affect our expectations of others. Don't let someone's low expectations of you limit your potential. I firmly believe that where you start does not define where you will go, but it may influence the character traits that help you get there. As you will see, that is true in my life story.

Where you start does not define where you will go, but it may influence the character traits that help you get there.

CHAPTER 2

In the Beginning

How did I get to where I am today? That's an interesting story. I don't imagine anyone could have ever dreamed of my unusual and exciting career, especially given my humble beginnings.

Many kids dream of becoming doctors, nurses, firefighters, police officers, teachers, athletes, actors, or musicians. Some envision being in the military, but typically not beyond the stereotypical roles you hear about when you are a kid—certainly not the gamut of careers to be found in the national security sector, which is a broad, overarching term I will use for defense and intelligence. As for me, I wanted to be an astronaut and travel into space, "the final frontier."

My life began in my hometown of Santa Barbara, California, where I was fortunate to live for my first fourteen years. I was born to Shirley Lynne Weslander on 26 August 1969. My mom raised me as a single parent. She was the daughter of Reverend Glenn Allen Weslander and his wife, Edna Ruth (Goodman) Weslander, who went by Ruth.

Shirley was the third of four children. She had an older sister, Jeanette, an older brother, Robert, and a younger brother, Kenneth. They were all born within four years of each other, so my grandparents quickly had their hands full raising a young family.

My grandpa Glenn was an ordained minister and a master carpenter employed in one of the two professions at any given time, sometimes both. My grandma Ruth played the piano and organ at church and led ladies' Bible studies. Even after all their kids graduated from high school and started their adult lives, they all stayed in close contact.

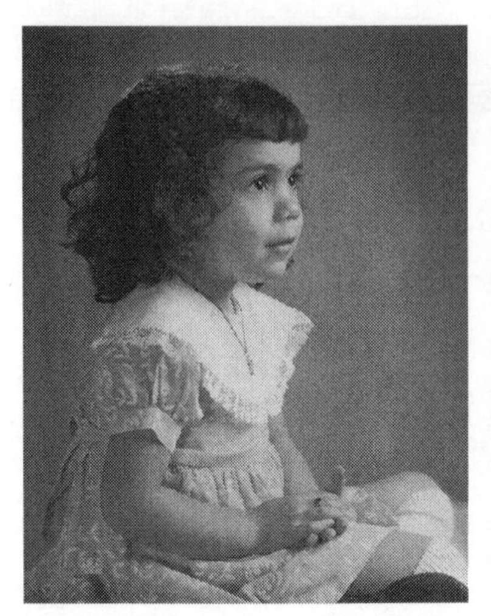

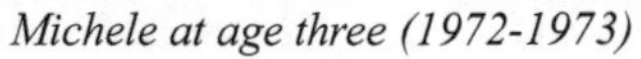

Michele at age three (1972-1973)

Michele at age seven prepares to lead her baton group in a parade (1976-1977)

A testament to my grandparents' strong faith in God and efforts to instill that faith in their children, my mother, and her siblings remained strong in their Christian faith as they started their own families. Growing up in a Christian family and attending church regularly, I accepted Jesus Christ as my personal Lord and Savior at a young age. I have been blessed to have a relationship with Jesus my entire life.

My mom had been attending classes at Santa Barbara City College (SBCC) when she met my father, an international student from Israel. She was very much in love with him. Sadly, when she found out she was expecting me, my father reportedly denied that I was his and wanted nothing to do with her or me. He returned to Israel not long after that, and there was never any communication from him or financial support.

My mom dropped out of SBCC before finishing a degree and got a job to support us. She found it hard to make ends meet because job opportunities were limited for those who only had a high school education.

My uncles Bob and Ken were strong male figures in my life. They were very good to me and treated me like one of their kids and included me in their family adventures when we had the opportunity. Though I did not have siblings, I was close to my cousins.

Believing that education was important and something worth investing in, my mom did her research and enrolled me in the best school in the county—Santa Barbara Christian School (SBCS)—starting in kindergarten. My experience at SBCS was great, and I know it laid a solid foundation of academic excellence and character that has carried me through my schooling, career, and life. A building can only go as high as the foundation will support it, and this foundation built early in my life enabled me to excel.

While they were never well off, my grandparents were generous to provide support where needed, whether it was helping out with payments for SBCS tuition or piano lessons. My grandmother is the one who encouraged me to take piano lessons, which was something I started when I was seven years old and continued for the next seven years until we moved from California to Washington.

Theater became something I enjoyed, and my mom enrolled me in a group called Peanut Gallery that did children's theater productions. While I was never given a lead role, I was regularly the understudy for a lead role and had other supporting roles. As an adult, I realize the lead roles likely went to kids whose families were wealthy donors to the program. Though my family did not have money to donate, I was a good enough actress to merit being the lead's understudy.

My mom made up for what she lacked in financial resources with her love and enthusiasm for sharing life with me. She did her best to create a home. We lived in various apartments around town, including a place by the freeway and another near the railroad tracks, which I vaguely remember. The first place I remember well was a nice apartment we moved into when I was in early elementary school. The apartment complex was a large, rectangular shape with a central courtyard where the shared laundry facilities were located. Our apartment was on the second floor and had two bedrooms, one bath, a living room, and an eat-in kitchen.

We would have been happy living there indefinitely, but the rent started increasing by fifty dollars per month every six months. That was when the minimum wage was less than three dollars an hour, so that rent increase was a lot of money. Many of the renters who could not afford these rent increases got together and staged a peaceful protest, and my mom was one of them. Local reporters took notice, and video footage of a group of us was on the nightly news. Then everyone who was a part of that protest was evicted from the apartment complex, including my mom and me. After that, we moved in with my grandparents for a while.

My mom and I had great fun together. We went roller skating on the beach path, took hikes in the local area, and listened to the Santa Barbara symphony practice sessions that were open to the public. Though we didn't have a lot of resources, we were resourceful with what we had.

My mom was always listening to the radio or records—primarily oldies from the 50s and 60s—and she would sing along and want to dance with me. The most memorable song she sang was "Let Me Be There" by Olivia Newton-John. Even today, when I hear that song, it makes me emotional thinking of the happy times we had together when I was a kid.

Hard Times

While I had a great relationship with my grandparents and enjoyed living in a house with a yard, my mom and grandmother did not get along well. A particular tension was over parenting me. My mom did not feel my grandmother honored her role as my parent because my grandmother would make decisions about me without consulting my mom. Unbeknownst to me, my mom started looking for work in Santa Maria, where her sister, Jeanette, and her family lived. That was when times got tough for us.

When my mom found a job in Santa Maria in the summer of 1980, she located an attic to rent. We had to enter through a ground-floor door and immediately walk up a steep stairway. At the top of the stairway was a small bedroom to the right and a bathroom to the left. Straight ahead was a large main room with a kitchen. My mom put her bed and furniture in the large room. She gave me the bedroom, but I did not have a bed or furniture. I slept on a cot and used empty printer paper boxes to store my clothes and other belongings. I covered the boxes with white printer paper to make them look nicer.

While we had a kitchen with a refrigerator, cooktop, and oven, my mom quickly learned that she had to turn the oven on before she cooked anything so that the cockroaches would die first. We were so sad to have food wasted when she forgot to do that.

This was a time in my life when I remember being hungry. Grocery stores would not take credit cards, so it was a regular occurrence for my mom and me to count change to see what fresh food we could buy until her next paycheck. When we ran out of cash, there was no way to buy fresh food, so we had to choose from whatever canned or boxed food we could find at a general store or drug store. We were always grateful when people brought fresh produce from their gardens to church, which supplemented our limited diet.

A very unscrupulous man ran the travel agency where my mother worked in Santa Maria. He treated the employees poorly and stole the perks they earned by selling vacation packages. While my mom enjoyed engaging with customers, her boss was unethical and created an unhealthy work environment.

My mom enrolled me in a private Baptist school in the area that was very legalistic. The girls were only allowed to wear dresses, even on field trips. The sixth-grade teacher was a wheelchair-bound, cranky old woman. She had a sick obsession with shipwreck stories. We not only had to listen to these terrible tales, such as the sinking of the *Titanic*, but she also required us to memorize the facts, which she would quiz us on. The stories gave me nightmares.

The only saving grace was that I made one good friend at school. She and I were seated across the classroom from each other. Passing notes was not allowed, so we taught ourselves the American Sign Language alphabet and would sign to each other. In time, the teacher forbade that as well.

After just half a year in Santa Maria, my mother realized she was miserable at her job, and I was unhappy at my school. So, we moved back to live with my grandparents in Santa Barbara and resided there from the middle of my sixth-grade year through my eighth-grade year.

Fun Times

I was excited to return to Santa Barbara and SBCS in January 1981. The sixth-grade teacher was Mr. Kaji, a native of Hawaii. He was so much fun and the polar opposite of my other sixth-grade teacher.

My best friend, Janell, and I had great fun together. Janell lived in Hope Ranch, a community with large estates; her house was the biggest I had ever seen. The fact that I came from a family of a different socioeconomic status did not mean anything to her or her family—they accepted me for who I was. Her mother was a pianist and once told me if I was interested in pursuing piano, she thought I had the talent to become a professional pianist. While I enjoyed piano, I knew there were other things I wanted to do in life, but her faith in me meant so much.

Sixth-grade graduation in June 1981 was a special day. I was wrapping up my elementary school years and looking forward to junior high. I had some fantastic teachers and fun experiences at SBCS.

My grandparents gave me a Bible with a wooden cover made from Israeli olive trees to commemorate this milestone in my life. Inside they wrote Proverbs 3:5-6. In the NIV, those verses state: "Trust in the Lord with all your heart and lean not on your own understanding; in all your ways submit to him, and he will make your paths straight."

In SBCS junior high, I had a math teacher, Bill Paulsen, who was quite a character. He was a Vietnam War vet, wore his hair in a crew cut, and told great stories about his time in combat. I remember one story about him being congested and having to go on a sortie, a combat mission. When he inverted the plane, all his sinus congestion drained into his oxygen mask. Yuck!

Mr. Paulsen was a favorite teacher of mine and my friends, and he made it clear he believed in me. My mom said that he once told her, referring to me, "I'm betting on the winning horse." Mr. Paulsen's encouragement was an inspiration to me.

He was also one of the physical education (PE) teachers. We had three PE tiers depending on how you scored during the fitness tests. Usually, I was in the highest tier, but depending on how I scored compared to others, I might drop down to the middle tier until the next round of testing. One of the tests was the fifty-yard dash. I was paired against a boy in the highest tier for the test, and I beat him. Mr. Paulsen told me, "I loved the look on your face when you beat that boy!" He was one of my biggest cheerleaders in junior high.

Historic Tour

One of the highlights of my junior high years was the eighth-grade historic tour to Washington, DC, in March 1983. Our high-spirited principal, Mrs. Tirzah Riley, led it. I was so excited to visit our country's capital city and the surrounding areas to learn more about America's history and see the historical sites. It was a sacrifice for my mom to send me, as she had to earn extra income to cover the trip, but she really wanted me to go, and I truly appreciated her doing this for me.

To help manage the class and hotel room assignments, they broke us up into small groups with a chaperone. Mrs. Pamela Anderson, my good friend Joanna's mom, was our chaperone and room mom. Previously, I had stayed with the Andersons for a week when my mother was away on a trip, and they had been like family to me ever since. So, I was pleased to be a part of her small group, and she made our time together fun.

We visited the United States Naval Academy in Annapolis, Maryland. This was my first exposure to a military academy. The brother of one of the boys in my class was a midshipman—a naval cadet enrolled there—and we got to meet him. He was sharply dressed in his uniform, like the other midshipmen on campus.

Then we traveled to Williamsburg, Virginia, a highlight of the trip. It was so much fun to glimpse what life was like in the colonial days. From there, we traveled to Thomas Jefferson's Monticello in Charlottesville and then to George Washington's estate in Mount Vernon. It was interesting to see the residences of these American leaders. Thomas Jefferson was the primary author of the Declaration of Independence and America's third president. General George Washington led the American Army in the Revolutionary War against the British and became America's first president.

From there, we traveled to Philadelphia, Pennsylvania, to visit Independence Hall and see the Liberty Bell. Independence Hall is called the birthplace of America because the Declaration of Independence and the US Constitution were debated and signed there.

As Benjamin Franklin left the Constitutional Convention in 1787, he was asked what type of government America's founders had created. He replied, "A republic, if you can keep it." America was founded as a constitutional republic, and the Constitution outlines the federal government's role. America's founders wanted a small federal government and big individual liberty.

The Liberty Bell originally rang in the bell tower of Independence Hall. It gained iconic importance when abolitionists fighting to end slavery in America in the 1800s used it as a symbol. It cracked sometime during this period, but its famous zig-zag crack occurred in 1846 when the bell was rung in honor of George Washington's birthday. After that, it was taken from the bell tower and displayed.

We also visited Betsy Ross's house. George Washington commissioned her to sew the first American flag in 1776.

Next, we visited Gettysburg, Pennsylvania, where we toured the battlefields and memorials. The National Park Service (NPS) has an excellent visitor center with an impressive cyclorama depicting the battle. Gettysburg was one of the Civil War's bloodiest and most decisive battles. President Abraham Lincoln considered it significant that the Union victories at Gettysburg and Vicksburg under General Ulysses S. Grant occurred on the same day, 4 July 1863, the anniversary of the signing of the Declaration of Independence.

President Lincoln gave his famous Gettysburg Address in November 1863 at the official dedication ceremony for the national cemetery. It always struck me that Lincoln said, "The world will little note, nor long remember what we say here," for he couldn't have been more wrong. Lincoln's Gettysburg Address is one of his most famous speeches. I read and memorized it in school and was glad to do so, for it represents a seminal moment in American history.

The Republican Party was created to abolish slavery, and Abraham Lincoln was the first Republican president. Lincoln was morally opposed to slavery and made it his mission as president to abolish it once and for all in America. Following his election, slave-holding southern states started seceding from the Union. The Civil War was fought to end slavery and preserve the USA. It is important to note that slavery was common around the world at the time, and America is the only country in modern history that has fought a war to end slavery. President Lincoln signed the Emancipation Proclamation and championed the Thirteenth Amendment to the US Constitution, abolishing slavery.

The remainder of our time was spent in downtown Washington, DC, and it was exciting to be in our country's capital city. We visited the White House, the Capitol, the Washington Monument, the Jefferson Monument, the

Lincoln Memorial, and the Smithsonian museums. My favorite was the Air and Space Museum, given my life-long dream of becoming an astronaut!

The president at the time was Ronald Reagan, sworn in as the fortieth president of the United States (POTUS) in January 1981. He is one of my favorite presidents. Ronald Reagan loved America and was a champion of individual liberty and the free market. He has so many great quotes, but one from 1981 that succinctly summarizes his philosophy is this: "Government's first duty is to protect the people, not run their lives." Ronald Reagan understood that a just government protects the liberty of its citizens.

We were required to write in a daily journal during the historic tour. When we returned to school, we had to submit a written summary of the trip and a photo album, which I still have. In my summary, I wrote, "Going on the trip made our country's history become real and interesting because I was standing right where it happened. The most important thing I learned on the trip was how interesting history could be. Reading history isn't as meaningful or interesting as learning about it where it actually happened."

Little did I know that I would spend most of the first twenty-five years of my career in the greater Washington, DC, area! On my first business trip to Washington, DC, I marveled at the fact that I could never have imagined as an eighth grader that I would someday work in our nation's capital city. Spending most of my career working in and around Washington, DC, has afforded me a unique perspective.

CHAPTER 3

Big Changes

Knowing how much I enjoyed SBCS, my mom committed to letting me attend through eighth grade. After that, the option was to stay for ninth grade, the final grade they offered, or start ninth grade at the local high school.

I did not realize my mom was planning to make a move from Santa Barbara after I completed eighth grade. She took me on vacation to cities in Northern California. I later found out that she was looking into jobs and housing options there.

In the summer of 1983, we made a road trip to Seattle, Washington, with my aunt Karen and my cousins Lynelle and Jennifer. Karen had married my mom's older brother Bob when he returned from the Vietnam War. They later divorced, and he moved to Seattle. The girls were looking forward to seeing their dad, and I was looking forward to seeing my uncle. We drove up to Seattle in our respective VW Bugs—my mom's Bug was red, and my aunt Karen's was green. It was fun to make the trip together.

My cousins and I were in for a big surprise after we arrived. Our mothers informed us that we had just moved to Seattle. As you can imagine, we were in shock and very upset. We loved Santa Barbara and didn't even get to say goodbye to our friends. My mom realized how upsetting this surprise move was for me. She bought me a plane ticket to travel back to Santa Barbara so I could have one last birthday party with my friends in August and get a chance to tell them goodbye before the next school year started.

The realization I was in a new state and would have to make new friends caused me to make a crucial decision. I told myself I had to learn to overcome my shyness. While I was friendly with everyone in my class and school, I only really talked to my close friends. Generally, I wouldn't initiate a conversation with someone outside that close-knit group but would always happily engage in conversation if someone reached out to me.

To give you an idea of how shy I was, I sat next to a guy I liked in eighth-grade history class. His name was Erik. One of his friends, Sean, sat behind me in one class and would taunt me by singing Adam Ant's "Goody Two Shoes" and throwing spit wads in my hair, but Erik was always kind to me. I looked forward to history class because I got to sit next to Erik and longed so much to talk to him but was too afraid to initiate conversation myself.

Erik was intelligent and a good athlete but was soft-spoken and humble. He would always smile at me, and when he would talk to me, it would make my day. We were usually in the top-tier PE class together, and I could tell he respected me for that. I had hoped we would end up at the same school in ninth grade, and I would gain the courage to talk with him more and build our friendship. When I discovered my mom had moved us to Seattle, it pained me that I had never mustered the courage to talk more with Erik, as I valued his friendship.

The SBCS yearbooks were delayed and were not delivered until after I had officially moved to Seattle, but my friends who returned to SBCS for ninth grade were able to sign mine before the school mailed it to me. Erik was one of them, and he wrote, "Stay cool. Miss you." That touched my heart when I read it. I missed him too, and at that moment, I told myself I did not want to live with the regret I had for not engaging more in our friendship when I had the chance.

I decided to focus on reaching out to others who tended to be shy like me. By doing this, I made new friends, learned to overcome my shyness, and built my confidence in just being me.

Using my understanding of what it was like to be shy, I decided to focus less on my inhibitions and focus instead on reaching out to others who tended to be shy like me. By doing this, I made new friends, learned to overcome my shyness, and built my confidence in just being me.

The Evergreen State

When we moved to the Seattle area, we found an apartment in a suburb called Mountlake Terrace. My mom enrolled me in Mountlake Christian School (MCS), and my cousins also enrolled there. I made good friends at MCS and had great experiences in choir and drama, and also as a cheerleader and athlete.

As someone who enjoys theater, I looked forward to being in the school plays. I consistently got lead roles. The drama teacher's daughter was a grade ahead of me, and sometimes the star roles went to her, but I had a blast with the supporting roles. One such role was as a very arrogant fashion designer. After the performance, people said I did a great job and remarked that the character I played was nothing like me. In another role, I played an eccentric old lady. The makeup startled some friends, who said they didn't recognize me. Though it was not the star role, I played my heart out in that one too, and people later remarked that I stole the show by making them laugh.

To those who had known me since childhood, my love for acting would not come as a surprise, as I was the one who would always get my cousins together at family gatherings, write a script, practice it with them, and then we would perform it for the adults. However, when you realize how shy I had been, you can recognize that theater was a great outlet for me. I was able to become another character and live that role to the fullest.

My mom liked to run for exercise, and I have always enjoyed running. I competed well as a sprinter from elementary through high school. The 100-meter and 200-meter races were my best personal events. In addition, I was a part of teams for the 4 x 100-meter and 4 x 200-meter relays.

One day at a track meet, our coach had the idea to put together a 4 x 400-meter relay team on the spur of the moment. He wanted me to be the one to start out of the blocks. Our coach remarked that the look on my face said, "You have got to be kidding," which was accurate because that was what I was thinking. Sprinting a quarter to halfway around the track is one thing, but racing entirely around the track is another, and I had not trained for that. I gave it all I had, and my energy was spent by the time I completed the lap and handed off the baton. Our relay team did well.

Ultimately, our 4 x 100m relay team competed in the Washington State B league championship that year. Unfortunately, my teammate, who started out of the blocks, dropped the baton as she was in the zone to hand it off to me. I had to stop and turn around and pick it up. While I made up a lot of ground before handing it off to the next runner, it was not enough. We came in fourth place. Had the baton not been dropped, we would have placed as one of the top three relay teams. That was a huge disappointment, but it was still pretty amazing to be a part of the state track meet. Though track is generally an individual sport, the relays are a team sport, and I thoroughly enjoyed being a part of the relay teams.

While I had always been good at track and field because I was a fast sprinter, I had never learned ball handling. Growing up as the child of a single mom, I didn't have a dad playing catch with me. The first ball sports I played were at SBCS junior high. I was not thrilled with the idea of a ball coming at me fast in softball, and I had to learn to catch and connect a bat with the ball. When the bat did connect with the ball, I was great at running the bases because I was very fast. I also played soccer in eighth grade. As a runner, I could sprint and play the entire game and not get winded. I enjoyed soccer and was very disappointed I only had the chance to play for one season.

At MCS, I played basketball and volleyball. Though I was not a high scorer in basketball, I was able to beat anyone down the court. I won my team's best defensive player award, which meant a lot to me. In one season, I scored my first basket at an away game. Everyone on the bench rose to their feet and cheered, and all my teammates on the court congratulated me. The other team was wondering what the big deal was, but everyone on my team knew the significance of that basket, and we laughed about it later.

In volleyball, I never quite had the arm strength to serve well overhand, but I had a very consistent underhand serve that would go high and then drop, frequently earning an ace for my team. The other team likely thought it was a joke that someone on varsity was serving underhand, and then they would watch in surprise as the ball dropped in the middle of their court.

When cheerleading tryouts came along, I competed and made the squad. We did well in cheer camp and scored higher than the squads from other schools. We were a first-rate squad and earned top grades academically. Our schedules were hectic because the schools we competed against were often far away on the San Juan Islands, which required a ferry boat trip. We rode the bus with the boy's football team for their away games. When it was basketball season, I would play in the girls' game. Then after I was all sweaty from that, I'd have to change into my cheer uniform for the boy's game. That may seem a bit crazy, but I enjoyed playing sports and cheering for those playing, and I understood what it took to be an athlete and a part of a team.

In my sophomore and junior years, my class elected me to be their homecoming princess and elected Gavin Fysh to be the homecoming prince. We were both excellent students, played varsity sports, became good friends, and remain friends to this day. It meant a lot to me to be selected by my class to represent them in the homecoming court. Often the most popular boy and girl are selected for homecoming court, but our classmates did not vote for who was the most popular; they voted for who they wanted to represent them—two classmates they respected and valued as friends. That was special to both of us.

As my junior year of high school approached, I felt drawn into leadership and decided to run for student body vice president. My slogan was "Michele Wes for Vice Pres." I won! That was a huge vote of confidence from the entire student body. They saw me as a leader and someone they trusted and respected.

Unfortunately, the academics at MCS were not on par with SBCS. I was acing all my classes and had a grade point average (GPA) over 4.0. By the middle of my junior year, I realized I needed to transfer to a public school to be more prepared for college, particularly in math and science. This was a tough decision for me, as I would leave my friends and go to a school where my class was larger than the entire MCS student body. Though I was able to complete the cheerleading season and basketball and volleyball seasons, I would not be able to fulfill my entire term as student body vice president. I was also very aware that many in the MCS student body looked up to me, and if I made a move from MCS, others might as well, and some did.

Gavin Fysh and Michele as the homecoming prince and princess for the sophomore class (1984-1985) [left] and junior class (1985-1986) [right] at Mountlake Christian School

When I changed schools in early 1986, my mom and I were renting space at my uncle's house in Bothell. It was a culture shock going from a small Christian school environment to a public school. Whereas my MCS class was under thirty students, my Bothell High School (BHS) class had over 300 students, most of whom had been in school together since kindergarten.

I arrived on campus the week before the cheerleading tryouts. Though I was a newcomer, I was good enough that the student body voted for me, and I made the squad. Little did I realize that, historically, the BHS cheerleading squad did not have a good reputation. However, we made some significant changes when I was on the squad, resulting in a positive trend that continued for years. I also went out for track, but competing at the AAA level was very different compared to the B level. While I was good, I would not make it to the state competition at that level, and I was okay with that.

One aspect I found to be very different at public school was a bias against people of faith exhibited by the faculty and staff members. In honors English, I did a report based on Francis A. Schaeffer's book *How Should We Then Live?* Following my presentation, my classmate and friend, Amy, a star 400-meter sprinter on the track team, approached me and said, "That was an excellent presentation, Michele. Be prepared to be graded down because you referenced a Christian author." That statement shocked me, and I asked how that could be. She replied that was just how things were, and she was correct.

That English teacher had a severe bias against me. Then again, this was the same person who read gory excerpts from Steven King's horror books in class. I have never read a horror story or watched a horror movie in my life because I am sensitive to things like that, and I told the teacher so, but she read the book out loud to the class anyway. I'm guessing she read those stories partially because of the shock value to people like me.

In stark contrast to my English teacher, my history teacher, a product of the late 1960s hippy generation, had no issues with me whatsoever. On the surface, we were on opposite ends of the spectrum, and one might think he would have had a bias against me, but that was not the case.

One of my gifts is remembering numbers; I could remember dates better than anyone in the class. That ability, combined with being a good student, enabled me to ace every one of his tests. He told me he had to pull my grade out of the group before he did the curve for the class. Though we were very different, he respected me. When he wanted to play The 5th Dimension's "Age of Aquarius" music in the classroom, I asked if I could go to the library to study because it was hard for me to concentrate with that playing in the background; he would always let me go.

As we approached the last few weeks of our senior year in the spring of 1987, my history teacher told the class, "Some members of your class of 310 students will drop out of high school right before graduation." That statement was astonishing to me. Why would anyone do that? Didn't they realize life would be hard enough if they only had a high school education, but options were even more limited if they never graduated? To my shock and amazement, he was right.

Being involved in many extracurricular activities meant long nights doing homework. My mom often told me it was late and that I needed to go to bed. My response would always be that I had to stay up and finish my work—I wanted to maintain my high GPA. I had set a very high bar for myself long ago and wanted to prove that I could do it. Furthermore, I knew it was critical to get high marks to increase my options for college, including scholarships.

That diligence paid off. I was the valedictorian of my graduating class, and there were four salutatorians. Some BHS administration members were unhappy that an outsider, i.e., someone who did not grow up in the public school system, was the valedictorian. They tried to change the grading scale, but I still came out on top no matter how they ran the numbers.

Every other school I knew had the valedictorian give a speech at graduation. The BHS administration did not offer me the chance to speak for whatever reason; I had to ask. They knew I was a Christian, and one thing that was very clear though unspoken was that I was not supposed to bring God into my remarks. So, after much thought and prayer, I figured out a way to deliver the message I wanted to share with my class and the audience without mentioning God or giving a Scripture reference.

Michele's high school senior year photo (1986-1987)

The Seattle Center was packed for my high school graduation ceremony in early June of 1987. This would be the biggest crowd I'd ever spoken in front of, but I was not nervous. As I stood at the lectern to give my valedictory remarks, I first congratulated the four salutatorians of our graduating class. Then I talked about setting goals and pursuing dreams.

I finished with the following quote: "Love is patient, love is kind. It does not envy, it does not boast, it is not proud. It does not dishonor others, it is not self-seeking, it is not easily angered, it keeps no record of wrongs. Love does not delight in evil but rejoices with the truth. It always protects, always trusts, always hopes, always perseveres. Love never fails."

Those familiar with Bible Scripture recognized this as an excerpt from 1 Corinthians 13, though I did not quote the reference. My purpose for reading that Scripture was to remind the audience—my classmates and those gathered to honor them—of the definition of love. We all long to be loved. True love looks like that, and Christians are called to exhibit such love. If everyone demonstrated love like this, the world would be much different and a better place for all living beings. We are all imperfect and make mistakes, but if we strive to love like this and choose those who share these values as our friends, our relationships will be blessed.

Michele giving her valedictory address at BHS senior class graduation (1987)

CHAPTER 4

Influencers

I was fortunate to have positive influencers in my life—family members, teachers, and others. They believed in me and told me to aim high—*shoot for the stars*—pursue my dreams and achieve my goals. As I like to say, "Sometimes you achieve more than you thought you could because someone who believes in you thought you could."

Sometimes you achieve more than you thought you could because someone who believes in you thought you could.

The first was my mother, Shirley. In my school years, she was my biggest cheerleader. My mom said I could do anything if I set my mind to it. She told me to focus on my studies, as I would work the rest of my life; my present job was to be a good student. My mom also encouraged me to pursue extracurricular interests. If I wanted to do something, she would work to save money to enable me to do it.

The day I got my driver's license, my mom handed me the keys to the car and the checkbook. From that time forward, I started shopping and cooking for our family because she had to commute a long way to and from work. That was a good experience for me because I learned life skills, including managing a household.

My grandfather, Glenn, was a great role model and the cornerstone of our family. In the absence of my father in my life, he was my father figure. His parents were immigrants—his mother from Denmark and his father from

Sweden. Tragically, my grandfather's mother died when he was eight years old, and his father died when he was sixteen, so he was orphaned. A couple of motherly ladies took him in so that he could finish school, and he was always grateful to them. Though life was never easy for him, and he never had financial wealth, my grandfather was the most generous person I've ever known. He was humble, unflappable, a loyal friend, and a steadfast provider for his family.

Grandpa Glenn was kind and had a great sense of humor. A fun story highlighting my grandfather's good nature occurred when I was in fifth grade, and we were living with my grandparents. At the time, my grandfather was working full-time Monday through Friday as a carpenter for Bailey Construction. He was also the full-time senior pastor of a local church, Cathedral Oaks Assembly, which he had been asked to step in and save from being permanently closed. He preached on Sunday mornings, Sunday evenings, and Wednesday nights, and he also served as the church groundskeeper, maintenance man, and all-around handyman. That was two full-time jobs, and he had to be exhausted.

On Sundays, after preaching at the morning service and eating lunch, my grandfather would lie down for a nap. He had a very loud and interesting snore you could hear throughout the house. This particular day he fell asleep on the couch in the living room. When he started snoring, I got my new cassette tape recorder and recorded him. After my grandfather woke up, I played it back to him, and we laughed. There was such merriment in his eyes. He had never heard what he sounded like snoring, and it struck him as funny. My grandfather was a great storyteller and loved a good joke, and this truly amused him.

Looking back now, I don't know how he did it all as he was about sixty years old and working almost every day of the week to cover those two full-time jobs. While he earned a good income as a carpenter, he received no income or compensation for his work at the church—an inconceivable fact I did not learn until I was an adult. Grandpa Glenn had what we call the Weslander Work Ethic, and I learned it from him.

My grandparents and I had a special bond. They had four children. Many people remarked that I was like their fifth child—we were that close.

I learned so much from my grandfather through the way he lived, the way he treated other people, and the things he said. He lived generously, though he did not have much material wealth. Grandpa Glenn truly cared about people, and his love and compassion were evident. He made friends easily, even with those who were not like him and did not share his viewpoints. His faith in God was strong. A great storyteller, my grandfather delivered very informative and insightful sermons from the Bible that kept his audience engaged. Though soft-spoken and humble, he was a great public speaker with wisdom and insight.

Michele at age two with Great Papa Morgan Goodman, Grandma Ruth, Grandpa Glenn, and cousins Mark and Lynelle (1971)

My grandmother encouraged me to take notes during his sermons, which might be one reason I've always been a habitual notetaker—it helps me remember things, and it's always nice to have notes to refer to later. I often joke that though my grandfather was a reverend, my grandmother was the religious one. I never considered my grandfather to be religious. He lived his faith. His love for God was evident, and he led people to God by the way he lived. The slogan—Loving People to God—is printed on a placard that hangs in the sanctuary of the church he once pastored, which is now called SouthCoast Church. Every time I see it, I think of him.

Because of his compassion for his fellow man, my grandfather started a juvenile hall ministry. He went alone to minister to the kids, and many came to faith in God through his efforts. That faith gave them hope, and they turned their lives around. In time, a young couple, Mike and Mary Ann Solodon, joined him. When he retired from juvenile hall ministry after thirty-eight years of service, the Solodons took over the ministry, which they now call The Juvy Project. My grandfather's legacy lives on through their work.

Specific teachers also made a positive impact on my life. Bill Paulsen had the most significant impact at SBCS because he clearly believed in me.

In 2013, SBCS merged with a high school named Providence Hall; the school's name was changed to Providence, a Santa Barbara Christian School.In January 2015, the Head of School called me and asked me to be the keynote speaker at their annual auction banquet in April. It was wonderful that Bill could be at that event. He and his wife, Sue, sat at a center table facing me. I looked right into Bill's eyes when I talked about the significant positive impact he had on my life. He was nearing eighty years old then and had a big smile and that characteristic twinkle in his eye. I guessed Bill thought he had indeed bet on the winning horse. It was very gratifying for me to be able to publicly acknowledge what a positive influence he had been in my life.

My physics teacher at BHS, Mr. Sherm Williamson, also positively impacted me. Physics was complex, but I was determined to learn, and he recognized and appreciated that. I would come to his classroom after school for help. There was a lab section in his classroom, and he would go to the paper towel dispenser and roll out a bunch of paper (this was long before the automatic dispenser days). Then he would diagram the problems for me on that paper so I could better understand them. He is the one who nominated me for the senior class science award that I won, and he is the reason I chose to study physics in college. After earning my Bachelor of Science (BS), Physics and Engineering Science, I returned to BHS to thank him. He was pleasantly surprised and told me I was one of only two students in his teaching career who had come back to thank him. That made me all the more glad I did.

Choices

Choices are the hinges of destiny.
~ Pythagoras, philosopher

Reflecting on my formative years, I see many choices that influenced the path I took in life. One big one was after we moved from California to Washington. I realized if I was going to make new friends, I had to learn to overcome my shyness. That is when I intentionally decided to do things that would force me to build my confidence to lead and the courage to speak publicly, including sports, cheerleading, choir, drama, honor society, and student council.

Though I never identified with any particular group in school, the members of various groups accepted me. One of my MCS teachers remarked to my mother, "Michele likes everyone, and everyone likes Michele." To be clear, that did not mean I was considered one of the popular kids. Although I was admired and well-respected by the members of different groups, they often did not think of including me when they did something together. Regardless, my classmates appreciated the qualities they saw in me. They voted for me to represent them in the homecoming court two years in a row, and the entire student body elected me vice president my junior year.

Though it was tough to transfer to public school in the middle of my junior year of high school, I had to do it for academic reasons because I had always intended to attend college. In public school, I was also a cheerleader, played varsity sports, and was in the choir and the honor society. My classmates respected me, but I did not identify with or feel like I belonged to any particular group.

I see this in a different context as an adult, as I have always been my own person and a leader, not a follower. As a mother, I see those same traits in my daughter, Sophia. She has had similar experiences at school, being well-regarded but not included in any particular group. I know it is hard for her when she's not part of the "in" crowd at school, but I recognize she has wisdom beyond her years and thinks at a higher level than most and takes an interest in topics—like liberty and global affairs—that likely never cross the minds of her classmates. Though we never fit into a particular group of our school peers, she and I felt comfortable in groups of adults at a young age. It still amuses me when Sophia speaks up to share her perspective with a group of adults who are then speechless, not expecting someone her age to be so articulate and have such wisdom and insight. Sophia means "wisdom," so her father and I named her appropriately.

If you are an individual who chooses not to follow the crowd, that is not a bad thing, though people might try to convince you otherwise through peer pressure. They likely cannot relate to your individualism, which makes them uncomfortable. Remember, you are never too young to lead and make a positive difference within your sphere of influence.

You are never too young to lead and make a positive difference within your sphere of influence.

There is a verse I often share with young people, which has become one of my daughter's favorites. "Don't let anyone look down on you because you are young, but set an example... in speech, in conduct, in faith, and in purity" (1 Timothy 4:12, NIV).

Inspiration

My inspiration to pursue a science, technology, engineering, and mathematics (STEM) education in college came from various sources—world events, personal interests, pop culture, and influencers in my life.

Astronomy has fascinated me since I was a kid, and I have always dreamed of being a part of the US space program and traveling in space. On 20 July 1969, Neil Armstrong became the first man to walk on the moon. I was born a month later, so I grew up at the end of the space race that had begun in the early 1960s.

Because of my interest in space and astronomy, my mom took me to Griffith Observatory in Los Angeles. It was a memorable experience to look through the Zeiss telescope at the stars and planets in the night sky. Today, apps enable you to raise your mobile phone to the sky and see the constellations and stars plotted before your eyes.

Another source of inspiration was popular culture—specifically, *Star Wars*. I saw the original *Star Wars*: *Episode IV - A New Hope,* written and directed by George Lucas, at the Arlington Theater in Santa Barbara when it came out in 1977. To this day, I remember my mom talking to the person in the small box office along the sidewalk underneath the theater overhang. The conversation went something like this: "How much are the tickets? Five dollars?! Michele, the tickets are five dollars! Are you *sure* you want to see this movie?" I was very sure. She bought the overpriced tickets. Later she said it was some of the best money she had ever spent because it became my favorite movie of all time.

Star Trek was another significant influence, along with space-related shows on TV at the time, like *Battlestar Galactica* and *Buck Rogers in the 25th Century*. I always thought it was fun that Buck Rogers supposedly launched in 1987, which was the year I was to graduate from high school.

As soon as I met the qualifications to apply for the National Aeronautics and Space Administration (NASA) astronaut program, after earning my master's degree and gaining the required years of work experience, I applied. I still have my first rejection letter from NASA, dated 13 May 1996. That did not deter me. I continued to apply each year.

Subsequently, after talking with a few astronauts, I learned there are approximately twenty-five slots and typically over 2,500 applications. NASA doesn't look at an application unless the person has a doctorate (PhD) or is a military fighter pilot. As a person with a master's degree who had never been in the military, let alone a fighter pilot, the chance of someone looking at my application was slim to none. At that point, I realized perhaps God had other plans for my life and career. Ultimately, I was recruited into America's other space program.

CHAPTER 5

College

Choosing the right college is essential; nothing beats visiting the campus and meeting with faculty, staff, and students to determine whether a place is right for you. Though I always imagined I would return to California for college, it was only after visiting all my colleges of interest in California that I decided to visit Seattle Pacific University (SPU). After my visit there, I knew that was where I was meant to be.

In the summer of 1987, I worked as a counselor in a day camp program and continued that line of employment every summer after that. The only exception was the summer between my junior and senior years when I did an internship and co-op at the Applied Physics Lab (APL) at the University of Washington, where my mom worked. This provided excellent work experience relevant to my career that I could put on my resume.

At the start of each new summer day camp program, it was always fun to go around the room the morning of the first day and listen as each counselor said what they were studying in school. Everyone else's major was education related; they were always surprised I was studying science and engineering. Invariably, someone asked, "Why are you doing this?" I always responded, "I love kids, and I grew up going to day camps because my mom worked full time, so it is a natural fit for me."

As I packed up my belongings and drove to college, I wondered about my roommate, but after arriving on campus, I learned that person had not shown up. That was fine with me, as it was someone I didn't know.

Another girl on my dorm floor was in a similar situation. Her roommate had not shown up, but she did not want to live alone. Her name was Barbara, and she came to me and asked if I would be her roommate. That was a big decision for me, but in the end, I decided I would room with her, as she seemed nice, and having a roommate was part of the college experience. We quickly became the best of friends.

Barbara was studying to be a teacher while I was studying science. We had no courses in common. She saw how much I studied and how hard I worked to solve physics problems, often realizing after hours of effort I had yet to learn the math required to solve the problem. I took calculus for the first time in college, whereas all the rest of my classmates had taken calculus in high school.

How did that happen, you wonder? I was registered for pre-algebra in seventh grade at the start of junior high. However, when I started the school year, my mom was told the pre-algebra class was full, so they put me in basic math. Looking back, I wonder if some students registered late, and their parents insisted they needed to be in pre-algebra. So, someone in a position of authority determined that the student least likely to need higher math in life was the daughter of a single mom who only had a high school education. Was there any consideration that I excelled academically, was ready for pre-algebra, and would not be challenged in basic math? Apparently, not. They took me out of the pre-algebra class to make room for another student.

This event in junior high had a substantial negative impact on me later. As it turned out, I was the student who went on to major in physics and engineering science in college. Had I not been so determined to get those degrees, I would have quit and changed to a different major because it was difficult for me, given my math and science were out of sync.

That decision by someone at my junior high school to move me out of pre-algebra in seventh grade due to class capacity issues got me off the math track required to be prepared to pursue science and engineering in college. To support their college studies, students interested in STEM careers must be on the proper math track in junior high.

My personal experience is one reason I am a big advocate for STEM outreach in schools and why I believe we need to do that when students are in fifth and sixth grade. If a student does not get into the right math track by seventh grade, it can negatively impact their ability to pursue fields of study that require higher math in college.

If I had an advocate—someone who recognized my interest in science and knew I needed to be in pre-algebra my seventh-grade year to be prepared for STEM studies in college—perhaps the school would have let me remain in the class; instead, they bumped me to create space for someone else. Fortunately, I had teachers and classmates in college who were understanding once they realized I had not yet learned the math to solve a science problem and were willing to teach me the required math at that moment so I could ultimately solve the science problem.

Tests are generally stressful for anyone, but recognizing I had gaps in my education made me all the more anxious before tests. Like many college students, I would often stay up until the wee hours of the morning studying and only have a few hours of sleep before going to class to take the exam. Usually, I would go to bed exhausted but could not turn off my thoughts, which meant I couldn't sleep, so I did not get a good rest.

One such instance was before a calculus test. While I had studied for a long time and was as thorough as possible, I was anxious. Though I slept a few hours before the exam, I did not get much rest. When I was handed the test in class, I blanked out. Never before or never since has that happened to me, but it happened then.

When I talked to the professor afterward, he was reasonable, recognizing that I was a good student, as reflected in my homework and other tests. He told me how I could make up for my low score on that test with additional coursework. This experience helped me realize how you can psych yourself out negatively. I held myself to very high standards and was my own worst critic. This taught me that each of us needs to guard our thoughts, as the narrative you tell yourself can impact your results.

When I shared the story about the exam with Barbara, she was empathetic and sympathetic. She thoughtfully listened and told me, "Remember, Michele, this is not relevant to your salvation." Barbara continued to say that to me every time I had a test, and her statement has stuck with me to this day. When I get stressed out about something, I try to step back and take a strategic look and remind myself that it is not relevant to my salvation.

I've shared this story with high school and college students to help them have a more balanced perspective. Grades are a measure taken in a moment in time. They do not define you. What matters is who you become. Good grades help you get into college, grad school, and acquire a job; however, in time, they will only be a memory. Things that cannot be so easily measured are the character traits that cause you to pick yourself up after being beaten down and keep going. That is what separates merely successful people from the resilient ones who can be world changers.

Grades are a measure taken in a moment in time.
They do not define you. What matters is who you become.

Barbara also gave me an excellent book recommendation that afforded me a new perspective on life—Frank E. Peretti's *This Present Darkness*. The name was inspired by the Bible verse, "For we do not wrestle against flesh and blood, but against the rulers, against the authorities, against the cosmic powers over this present darkness, against the spiritual forces of evil in the heavenly places" (Ephesians 6:12, ESV).

The characters in the book include angels and demons—those operating in the spiritual realm that we cannot see but whose actions influence the physical world. Outside the Christian faith, and even inside some Christian communities, the term "spiritual warfare" is rarely heard or spoken, let alone understood. That is to our detriment for we are spiritual beings, and spiritual warfare is real. This book helped to make it more real for me.

The next verse says, "Therefore take up the whole armor of God, that you may be able to withstand in the evil day, and having done all, to stand firm" (Ephesians 6:13, ESV).

The book also helped to emphasize the power of prayer. Some people only pray when they are in desperate situations. Others pray every day. God is always present, ready, and waiting to hear from us.

Regardless of where you are in that spectrum or your thoughts on these subjects, this fictional story will give you a new perspective and challenge your thinking. I was fortunate to be in the audience when Frank Peretti visited our church. He said he was going to "read" from the book. Frank immediately started acting out a scene, becoming each character in it as he did, which made the characters in the story come alive.

This was such an important book to me that years later, I asked my combat-veteran husband to read it shortly after we were married. Then when our daughter Sophia was eleven, she overheard me talking about it with someone and told me she wanted to read it. I wasn't sure, thinking it was pretty heavy material for an eleven-year-old. So, I told her she might want to wait until junior high or high school. After Sophia persisted, I realized she could probably handle it as she was more mature than most eleven-year-olds and had wisdom and insight beyond her years.

After Sophia finished the book, she told me she was glad to read it. She had the same insights I had and said it gave her a new perspective on the spiritual realm that interacts with our physical world. I'm glad she read it too.

I highly recommend reading the book. It might get you thinking about things you haven't given much thought to, like what is going on behind the scenes in the spiritual realm, and cause you to look at life and the world in a new and different way. If nothing else, it will keep you in suspense for a long weekend.

At SPU, I had an excellent physics professor named Dr. James "Jim" Crichton. He got to know each student personally, including facts about their hometown, family, and interests. Many times someone would walk into his class just before it started, and he would greet them with something like this, "Troy from Moses Lake, how are you today?" Given my initials were MW, he nicknamed me "Mega Watt," and would greet me that way.

Professor Crichton was always good-natured. It was clear he loved what he did for a living. He felt called to teach physics and inspire young students to do great things. His caring nature extended beyond the classroom time that he was required to give. Professor Crichton was always personally available for office hours and would also lead Friends of Physics hikes on the weekends. The greater Seattle area had beautiful areas to hike, and it was a favorite pastime of mine. Given the perpetual drizzle, this California girl learned to hike in the rain with a raincoat and umbrella—a little moisture would not deter us.

At the start of my sophomore year in the fall of 1988, I met Curt. We were the same age, but he was a freshman. Curt was from a small town in Idaho. He had taken a year to study abroad in Germany during his high school years, which is why he was a year behind me in college.

He was an electrical engineering (EE) major, so we saw each other in the Science and Engineering Building. Curt was also in the US Air Force (USAF) Reserve Officers Training Corps (ROTC), run through the University of Washington. He was upbeat, had a great sense of humor, and we quickly became friends.

Eventually, we started dating and had so much fun together. We both enjoyed the great outdoors, including hiking in the mountains and kayaking on Lake Union. Curt did sweet things like singing to me one night outside my dorm room window and writing me notes and cards. We were also a part of some of the same study groups.

The standing joke among female science and engineering students was that our male classmates outnumbered us, but none of them wanted to date a girl in science and engineering. That was not the case with Curt. He appreciated my intelligence; it was not threatening to him.

As someone who did not attend her senior prom, I was excited when Curt invited me to his Air Force military ball. That was a high-class formal event with the military members in their mess dress. We had such a blast.

By the end of my sophomore year in physics, we were learning about things that seemed very esoteric, like quarks. I wanted to apply the science, not study the theory. As it turns out, all my study buddies were majoring in EE, a.k.a. "double E." No one in my family had a technical background, and I previously had no exposure to engineering.

So I asked my engineering classmates to tell me about their classes. Their engineering descriptions piqued my interest; this sounded like something I would like to do. So, at the end of my sophomore year, I decided to add a second major—engineering science. That was effectively the EE degree without the senior design courses.

My EE coursework started at the beginning of my junior year in the fall of 1989. My professor was Don Peter. He did not have a PhD but had practical work experience, and I found his insights tremendously valuable. He would start each class with a devotional and share his life experiences.

Professor Peter also took a personal interest in his students and showed no bias. He did not cut me any slack because I was female, but he was sure proud when I scored the highest grade in the class on an exam. I knew he was rooting for me.

Every semester at SPU, I carried over the full credit load—in STEM courses, no less—requiring sign-off by my academic advisor. It was intense, and I had very little time for the social side of college, but I graduated with a double major in physics and engineering science, with honors (cum laude), in four years.

Before my senior year, Curt and I decided it would be better to stop dating and just be friends. We realized that while we enjoyed sharing life together immensely, the timing was not right to make a life-long commitment to each other. We were still so young and getting to know who we were as individuals, our priorities, and what God wanted us to be. We cared a lot for each other and were committed to remaining friends. Our classmates were shocked when we broke up, as almost everyone assumed we would marry.

Some of my happiest memories from college are the fun times Curt and I shared. Curt cheered for me when I graduated with honors in the spring of 1991. When I went away to grad school across the country, we stayed in touch for a while, but then the communications dropped off.

It wasn't just classmates who I stayed in touch with after graduation but also professors Jim Crichton and Don Peter, who had become my friends. Sadly, Jim was diagnosed with melanoma a few years later. I called to speak with him in November 1999, a month before he died, and told him all the amazing things I had been able to do in my career and reiterated his positive impact on my life.

Professor Dr. James "Jim" Crichton and Michele at Seattle Pacific University graduation (1991)

Don and I have stayed in touch via letters, emails, and in-person visits when we happen to be in the same place at the same time. He and his wife, Jo Ann, a physical therapist, have always been good about including me in the distribution of their annual holiday letters. When I did volunteer work in inner-city Philadelphia the summer between my college graduation and grad school, Don sent me care packages with Dave Berry clips from the Seattle newspaper that would always make me laugh.

It takes more than excellent academics to make you successful in life. The healthy learning environments and character development that both SBCS and SPU provided, along with excellent academics, have served me well in my life and career.

When I graduated from college in 1991, the economy was such that many potential employers were not hiring. I visited a few, all of whom said they'd like to hire me but had no job openings. So, I decided it was an excellent time to pursue grad school. I was still in academic mode, and I might as well check that off my list.

As I researched and thought about what course of study I should pursue in grad school, I recognized that optics was an up-and-coming field and something that would likely be of interest to NASA. So I chose that topic for my senior project, and my SPU professors were very supportive. However, when people asked me what I planned to study in graduate school and I told them I planned to study optics, most would cock their head to one side, look thoughtful and then reply, "Well, I suppose we always need more people to make eyeglasses." No one would say that today, as the general populace is aware of many amazing things that are going on in the field of optics. Still, at the time, those technologies were relatively unknown or not yet discovered.

When considering graduate schools, I decided to apply to the schools with the top optics programs in the country—the University of Arizona and the University of Rochester—as well as four other colleges with respected optics programs. All the universities I applied to granted me admission, but of the top two, Rochester offered me more financial aid than Arizona. Having put myself through college with scholarships, grants, part-time work, and student loans, I opted to take the graduate school offer with the most financial assistance.

CHAPTER 6

Philly

During the summer of 1991, between my college graduation and grad school, I volunteered to run day camp programs and tutor kids in the federal housing projects of inner-city Philadelphia, Pennsylvania. College students from across America and all over the world came to volunteer. During our first week in Philadelphia, which we called Philly, the program leaders gave us situational awareness training, recognizing that most of us had little to no exposure to the inner city and lacked street smarts.

Immersed in a predominately black community, we all stood out because we did not fit that demographic. The program leaders told us never to carry our wallets and if we were lost to always look like we knew where we were going, as otherwise we would be a target. It's funny that years later while on a business trip, a colleague remarked that I looked like I knew where I was going even though we were lost and trying to figure out where we were going. I replied that I learned that skill in Philly.

This summer program had run for years, and the people in the community where we worked appreciated us dedicating our summer to serving them and their children. We ran camp programs during the day for the kids and offered tutoring after camp. We also planned family activities on the weekend. We got to know the kids and their families through these outreach efforts.

This was an eye-opening experience for me. Many people think that to do a mission trip they must travel to a foreign country, but there was a need in our own country. When I spoke to people back home, they would ask me to describe my experience, and I told them there was no way I could describe it in a context that they would understand; they would have to see and experience it for themselves. This was a microcosm of America most people did not think about, let alone understand.

Groups of volunteers were stationed in different areas around Philly and in Camden, New Jersey. My group lived in a converted orphanage in southwest Philly without air conditioning. I would step out of the shower in the morning and start sweating before I could dry off. We were constantly sweating all day in the sweltering heat and high humidity. Growing up on the West Coast, I had no real concept of East Coast heat and humidity until Philly.

At our house, we had teams that took turns shopping and cooking for the entire group each week. I became the lead for my team. The group enjoyed the meals we made our first week and asked us to be cooks for the rest of the summer, but we decided it would be better if everyone took turns in that capacity to share the workload. As a vegetarian, I focused on providing healthy meals with fresh produce. Unfortunately, other teams chose to go the easy route with things like canned pork and beans, which were unhealthy and not vegetarian. I had to buy food for myself, so I would not go hungry those weeks.

Living in close quarters like this and working all day together, we got to know each other and built friendships. There was a guy from England and two gals from Canada in my group; we laughed at the differences in our respective versions of the English language. After eight years of living in the state of Washington, which borders Canada, I picked up saying "Eh?" at the end of some sentences. After living for a summer with two Canadians that stuck.

Eric Pajdak, a native of Hawaii, became one of my good friends. His dad, who unfortunately died, was an American military serviceman, and his mom was Japanese. Eric was a bodybuilder, and I convinced him to be my running buddy so I could safely run on the streets of Philly. He agreed and asked me to wake him up the mornings I wanted to go for a run. His thick black hair would often stick straight up on the top of his head when he woke up. Those mornings I would call him King Kamehameha, and he would grin. King Kamehameha united the Hawaiian Islands into one kingdom in 1810, and he wore a hat with something resembling a mohawk on top of it. Eric saw the humor and took it in stride.

The day before everyone was scheduled to leave Philly, I realized I needed to do laundry. I was very conscientious about never taking my wallet with me all summer. Usually, we always went anywhere with at least one other person, but no one was willing to go with me as they were busy packing and saying their goodbyes. The laundromat I had gone to all summer was some distance away, and someone suggested a closer one and gave me directions to get there. So, I grabbed my backpack, packed with my wallet and other things, and my laundry, and headed to the laundromat.

When I arrived, there were no customers, but the manager and a group of friends were talking. As I went to a washing machine and started preparing my laundry, a man approached and offered to show me how things worked, including how to add the coins. I thanked him and then turned to open my backpack to get my change for the machine. My backpack was wide open, and another man was standing next to it with his hands rolled up in his shirt. I knew he had opened my backpack, taken my wallet, and had it hidden in his hands, wrapped up in his shirt.

My heart started racing. I had a decision to make. They had set up that tutorial to get me to turn away from my backpack so they could steal from me, and I realized it was not worth risking my life to get my wallet back. I stated, "My wallet is missing. Without it, I have no money to pay to use the washer and dryer." I looked at the man I knew had my wallet, and he shrugged. I packed up all my belongings and left the laundromat.

On my walk back, with my heart still racing, I thought about the irony of what had just happened to me. For one, I had been so careful all summer not to take my wallet with me—only to carry the money I needed in my pocket. In a hurry, I grabbed my bag with my wallet and forgot about this safety measure. Furthermore, while other college grads had spent their summer doing something fun such as vacations and world travels, I had spent my entire summer volunteering in a sweltering and dirty inner city, living in a building with no air conditioning, to support children and families in this community.

Those men in the laundromat had no idea who I was or what I had done for their community. Even if they did, they might not have cared. These black men likely saw me as a stereotype—a "rich, white girl"—never realizing that I had worked my way up from a disadvantaged start and that I used my savings to pay my way so I could do volunteer work in their community that summer. I did not stereotype the people, but these men had stereotyped me. Stereotypes are destructive.

This was also an example of something else the program leaders had warned us about that summer, a phenomenon they called "getting over." They told us that some people in the community would expect you to pay their way and try to manipulate you to do so rather than pay their own way, though they had the means. That was an anathema to me. Thankfully, none of the families I had worked with exemplified that attitude, but those men did—they took advantage of me. While those men only saw me as someone they could rob, I am sure the people in the community whose lives I touched that summer would have been upset with those men for doing that to me.

When I got back, I shared the story with my teammates. I was concerned that I had no identification, ATM card, or credit card. What's worse, I had gone to the ATM the day before to withdraw $100 in cash to help cover expenses for my trip and had no other money.

Eric offered to loan me money and told me there was no rush to pay it back. He knew I would pay him back when I could, and he felt awful about what had happened to me. That is a good friend.

It was an incredible hassle to call my bank and credit card companies to cancel the cards; even then, some did not follow through promptly. Because they did not take appropriate action immediately, they hassled me for months about fraudulent charges for all sorts of items, including furs. As an animal lover, I would never buy or wear fur, which I told the credit card company when they called me about that charge. I again pleaded with them to cancel the card and block further charges.

I took the train from Philly to Rochester, New York, without incident. This was in 1991, a decade before the government implemented all the strict ID requirements following the 11 September 2001 terrorist attacks. Travel would be difficult, if not impossible, now without an ID.

Eric's loan got me home, and I paid him back. Our friendship has lasted a lifetime. We invited each other to visit our respective hometowns before we parted ways in Philly. I visited him in the garden island of Kauai right after I completed finals following my first year of grad school. Eric showed me wonderful hospitality, and I got a glimpse of what it was like to be a *Kama'aina*, a native of Hawaii. Eric went on to have a career in the Kauai Fire Department.

Michele with Eric Pajdak at the Kauai Fire Department Engine 4 (1999)

Reflecting on my experience working in the federal housing projects, that was my first exposure to government assistance programs. It made me realize that we, as a country, had a challenge. Our welfare system was broken, and though I didn't know exactly how we could fix it, I knew it required attention. Furthermore, while some people truly needed the assistance, others took advantage of it. I'll give some examples.

One day, I escorted some kids back to their home after camp, and they invited me inside. I was shocked they had every tech gadget you could imagine—TV, stereo and entertainment system components, etc. As far as I could tell, it was the latest and greatest equipment. My mom and I could not afford these things, and she never once took government assistance, so how could a family on government assistance afford all this?

Something was not quite right. Welfare was supposed to be a temporary support mechanism for people who had fallen on hard times, but the government was now making it comfortable to stay on welfare, removing the natural incentive for people to support themselves.

In another case, a young single mom who was pregnant with her third child confided in me that she wanted to break out of the welfare system and move away from the federal housing projects. She desired a better life for her children and wanted to provide for them independently. However, that was very hard to do.

The current program seemed to trap people in the system and keep them a slave to their master—the government. Once a person started making a certain income, all the government assistance disappeared—the safety net was gone. If they couldn't make it through that difficult transition to self-sufficiency, they would give up and resort to taking government assistance again. The government effectively penalized them for trying to become independent and control their own destiny.

This mother in the federal housing projects wanted freedom for herself and her children, but, to use a rocket science term, she lacked the escape velocity to break out of the gravitational pull of the welfare state and kept falling back into the cycle of dependency on the government.

The idea of a "free" handout from the government may sound good, but nothing is ever free—it's either paid for by higher taxes or increased national debt. This is because the government does not make money—it either takes it in the form of taxes from those earning money or prints it, thereby causing inflation. Furthermore, there are always strings attached, and people dependent on the government lose their freedom and are not in control of their destinies.

Our freedoms are eroded as the government's power grows. Big government proponents perpetuate this cycle of dependency, as the more people rely on the government for handouts, the bigger and more powerful the government becomes. I've never understood why anyone would want to control someone else's life, but too many career politicians and people in government crave power, particularly over other human beings.

America's founders understood this and established the USA on the principle of individual liberty and the freedom of individuals to live their lives as they wish and to pursue what brings them happiness. They defined a just government as one that preserves the natural God-given rights of individuals. Using their God-given wisdom and discernment, they sought to create a governmental structure that would transcend time.

Having experienced tyranny and understanding the natural tendency of man to abuse power, they intentionally crafted America's founding documents to limit the power and reach of the federal government so as not to unnecessarily infringe on individual liberty. The US Constitution precisely circumscribed the government's power and was written to protect every individual's natural rights from government overreach. It was carefully crafted to enable a free market economy, where the voluntary exchange of goods and services and the laws of supply and demand provided the sole basis for the system—without government intervention.

The founders wanted to provide a safety net for people in dire need who could not provide necessities for themselves while at the same time not discouraging people who could get jobs from supporting themselves. The original welfare system required recipients to stay in poor houses and work. In stark contrast, today's welfare system creates a dependency on the government without an objective to get people self-supporting again.

It is frightening that some people promote socialism, which should not be confused with social programs. In Marxist-Leninist theory, socialism is the intermediate stage between capitalism and communism, where the means of production are collectively owned by a centralized government that plans and controls the economy. Examples throughout modern history have shown that socialism always fails to deliver on the promise of equal outcomes and ultimately makes life worse for everyone. Socialism is never better than a free market society, which enables individuals to create a better life for themselves and their families through hard work and innovation.

Throughout America's history, people from many different backgrounds have risked so much, sacrificed everything, fought, and died to preserve our liberty. The freedom we enjoy was hard won. We should not be willing to surrender it to the government.

Most people long for independence—to be free to chart their course and destiny—but the current welfare system works against them. This experience reminded me that most people want a hand-up, not a hand-out. By lifting people up, you help them get on their feet so that they can support themselves, and they can genuinely change their stars if they take advantage of what America and the free market offer.

CHAPTER 7

Grad School

Upon arriving at the Institute of Optics at the University of Rochester (U of R) for orientation in September 1991, one of the professors greeted me with the statement, "Welcome to the second cloudiest city in the nation." He knew I had moved from Seattle, known for overcast skies and drizzling rain. That gave me pause—I'd moved from California to Washington to New York, each with progressively worse weather. This was not a good trend for someone who truly appreciated sunshine.

However, I was determined to have a positive attitude and make the most of my new environment. Rochester has rich cultural offerings, and I attended art festivals in the community and free performances at the Eastman School of Music, within walking distance from my studio apartment downtown.

The fall colors were gorgeous. Growing up in California—the Golden State—with abundant sunshine, beaches, and palm trees, and having attended high school and college in Washington—the Evergreen State—I had never seen anything like the East Coast fall colors. They are spectacular. People back home on the West Coast would ask me to describe the colors, and I said there was no way; you had to see them for yourself. The ivy on the buildings and the leaves on the trees were a symphony of color. Those colorful memories would help carry me through the gray days.

Rochester gets snow from October through May; most is lake-effect snow coming off of Lake Ontario. Digging my car out of the snow each day during those months, I tried to appreciate the beauty of the individual snowflakes—something I had never seen before moving to Rochester—and sang "Jingle Bells" to pass the time. We could go nearly two weeks without seeing the sun, which was depressing.

When it first started snowing, I recall remarking out loud in a room full of classmates that I guessed I would have to start taking the bus. One immediately said, "No, you need to learn to drive in the snow." I told him that in Seattle, everyone knew how to drive in the rain, but just an inch or two of snow put the whole city out of commission, with accidents everywhere.

It was different in New York, where they were equipped to handle the snow; they'd effectively shut down for half of the year if they weren't. I had to marvel that, though they knew how to drive in the snow, there were invariably accidents all over town when there was rain in Rochester. Later, I would remark, "People are good at driving in whatever weather they are accustomed to—in Seattle, it is rain, and in Rochester, it is snow." I am sure glad that I learned to drive in both!

A year later, when my mom came to visit for Christmas, we made plans to drive to Niagara Falls on Christmas Eve. As it turned out, there was a blizzard that day, and my mother, who lived in Seattle, marveled at the fact that people were out driving and getting to where they needed to go despite there being over a foot of snow on the ground and more accumulating. I informed her that if there was that much precipitation in the form of rain, it might be a different story.

We stayed overnight in Buffalo and drove to Niagara Falls the following day. It was negative 17 degrees Fahrenheit, negative 27 Celsius, with wind chill. We did not make it across the parking lot before running back to the car because we were shivering so badly. We were indeed not accustomed to that bone-chilling cold and had a good laugh. Never fear, we made it to Niagara Falls another time, and I would take other people to visit while I lived in Rochester, but in warmer weather.

Once I started the master's program at the Institute of Optics, I quickly realized I was in an accelerated program designed for students who earned their bachelor of science in optics at U of R to earn a master's degree quickly. They had the same teachers and textbooks but worked at a more advanced level and faster pace. Someone like me—who had no prior experience in optics other than a self-directed senior project—was at a significant disadvantage. Though I studied diligently to master the coursework, I could never solve problems as fast as those who had been doing this for four years.

Though I would get A's on exams, some professors would decide they could not give everyone A's, so they did a curve. I once had an A grade turned into a C because of this. When I asked the professor why he would do this, he replied, "I cannot give everyone an A. Not everyone can earn an A in my class." I reminded him that they had seeded this program with students who were at the top of their classes across the nation—students who had earned A's in their previous collegiate coursework. So how was it fair to take the A's they earned in his class and artificially lower them by forcing a curve?

It became clear that this was not about being fair, it was about appearances, and he didn't think it reflected well on him if everyone got an A in his class. As a consistently high-performing student, the C on his exam was hard for me to take, especially since an A had been my original score. As I've learned, life throws you curveballs, and you must stay on your feet and keep moving forward. Furthermore, an academic grade is only one person's measure of where you are at a given time in your life.

One professor had a thick Indian accent, and we all found it hard to understand what he was saying. He treated it as an affront when I asked questions and was always very condescending to me. He rarely listened to what I had to say. If he bothered to respond, it was often with a basic statement about something that was already obvious to me and did not answer my question. So, I would ask my question again but differently, and he would cut me off and dismiss it. In these instances, a doctoral candidate classmate would often turn to me and say that they understood my question and would answer it after class. Many of my classmates remarked that this professor had a bias against me.

It eventually got so bad that I went to my academic advisor. I told him my fellow students witnessed how badly this professor treated me and said I should file a complaint. My advisor told me to hold off on that. He would deal with it. The next semester they announced the professor was now tenured. It was clear I was asked not to raise an issue because they did not want anything to interfere with that professor getting tenure.

My only previous interaction with a man of Indian descent was at SPU; he was the father of one of my senior-year roommates. He treated me well and thought it was great that I was pursuing science and engineering. His daughter and our other two roommates were liberal arts majors, and he cheered when he heard I got the top grade in my engineering class. Because of my experience with my roommate's father, I did not conclude that my professor's bias was cultural, as many of my friends suggested. I recognized his treatment of me reflected his personal bias.

Fast forward to many years later, when I was in the midst of a successful career. The new Dean of the School of Engineering and Applied Science at the U of R, Robert Clark, reached out to me and asked if he could meet with me while he was in Washington, DC. I agreed.

After Rob briefly introduced me to how he came to be dean, he asked me point blank, "How was your experience at the Institute of Optics?"

I said, "Do you really want to know?"

He said, "Yes."

I told him, "It was not good."

Rob asked me to elaborate, so I told him stories from my experience to back my statement. I did caveat that one professor, Thomas Brown, stood out as really caring for the students, but he was the exception. Most of his peers were more focused on their Optical Society of America presidency, their side business, or their latest book, and rarely showed up for office hours. So, it was clear that teaching and investing in the students were not their priorities.

He thanked me for sharing and then told me I was not alone. Rob said he had met with others who had similar experiences; he wanted to change that. He then asked if I would serve as an advisor to him on the Dean's Visiting Committee, composed of business people and alumni who volunteered their time to support the school. I said I would willingly do so, hoping that future students would have a better experience than I did.

Rob was true to his word and worked diligently to take the recommendations that I, and other advisors, gave him to transform the program and the teaching for the better. One of our recommendations was integrating communication skills training, including writing and public speaking, into the curriculum. You can be the most brilliant person or have the most brilliant idea. Still, if you cannot effectively communicate it to others—particularly those who do not share your educational background and expertise—it will limit your ability to be successful. As I have always liked to joke, being an engineer and scientist with communication and social skills is great job security. But in all seriousness, those skills should not be so rare in people getting technical degrees.

To their credit, the School of Engineering and Applied Science, with Rob's leadership, implemented a great program, empowering graduates to have the technical expertise and communication skills necessary to enable broader success in their careers. Rob went on to become the U of R Provost, the senior academic administrator at the university. As I was finishing this manuscript, I was pleased to learn that the U of R leadership had the foresight and good sense to appoint Thomas Brown as the Director of the Institute of Optics.

A few years after joining the Dean's Visiting Committee, I was surprised to learn that the same professor who had shown such bias against me in grad school had won an award for teaching. Upon hearing this news, I was in disbelief. Rob did his best to convince me that the professor had indeed transformed; he had been nominated by the students for the award. This shows that anyone can change and that we need to keep an open mind about people even if we've had a bad experience in the past.

It was tough for me to move across the country, thousands of miles away from my family and friends, to a place where I knew no one. The winter weather in Rochester was brutally cold, the graduate program was intense, and I had not-so-positive experiences with some professors.

In circumstances like this, you discover what you are made of and what you can do. Being true to myself, I decided to persevere even though it was difficult, setting the trend for my life.

When I would share my experiences with my mom via phone, she would tell me I didn't need to stay; I could come home. I told her I would not let any of this beat me; I would stay the course, keep working hard, and see it through. In circumstances like this, you discover what you are made of and what you can do. Being true to myself, I decided to persevere even though it was difficult, setting the trend for my life.

I felt so very alone in Rochester, and my refuge was Bethel Full Gospel Church, located in the city and within walking distance from my apartment. Though I never developed any close friendships there, I benefited from the Bible teaching of the pastor, Ron Domina. He and the church as a whole focused on ministering to the community. I volunteered in various outreach ministries, including clothing drives and providing Thanksgiving dinners for the homeless. It was a reminder that no matter how tough things seemed for me, someone else always had it worse. They say it is more blessed to give than to receive, and I was fortunate to be able to bless others through service and grow my faith in the process.

During that time alone in New York, I spent much time in prayer. I knew that even if there was no one else for me to talk to, God was always available and interested in listening. At that time, I also realized that God answers the little prayers so you can believe in him for the big ones. My faith certainly became my own at this time when there was no one there for me but God.

God answers the little prayers so you can believe in him for the big ones. My faith certainly became my own at this time when there was no one there for me but God.

I felt God's protection one night after I parked my car in the lot and walked to the entrance of the apartment building in the dark. Three men approached me who looked suspicious and like they were up to no good. At that moment, I prayed to God, asking for his protection. The men suddenly changed course a moment later and walked away from me. I was surprised but relieved. Years later, I heard stories from missionaries and others about how they were protected and then heard from their would-be assailants that they decided against harming them when they saw large men standing next to them. I wondered if God had sent angels at that moment to protect me.

Though the first semester was pretty lonely, I made an unexpected friend in the second semester, and ours has been a life-long friendship. One day I was working in the computer room at school and met an international student, Wolfram Ragg, who was in the same program. He was from Germany, and when I learned that, I remarked, "This program is hard enough with English as your first language, so I cannot imagine how hard it must be with English as your second language. That's impressive." I meant it as a compliment, but I would later find out through an American mutual friend that Wolfram had taken it as an insult. That friend told Wolfram he was sure I had meant it as a compliment. When our mutual friend introduced us again, we discussed that dialog, and once we realized the misunderstanding, we laughed.

Later, Wolfram wrote us a very long email in German. Neither of us read or spoke German, and I decided it would be fun to translate it phonetically, i.e., sounding out the German words and coming up with something that sounded similar in English. When I sent my reply, our American mutual friend read it. We laughed until we cried because it was amusing to an English speaker. Wolfram did not know why it was so funny, but he took it in stride.

Wolfram loved American culture, and I would call him a German cowboy. He was a fan of Clint Eastwood and invited me and some other friends for a showing of *The Good, the Bad, and the Ugly*. Wolfram also had a great sense of humor. One night after he hosted a group of us for a showing of *The Godfather*, we went out to dinner at an Italian restaurant. Wolfram walked up to the hostess and said, "Yes, we would like a table for the Corleone family." The surprised hostess quickly realized he was joking.

Wolfram's sweet girlfriend, Claudia, now his wife, would come to visit him often. Claudia and I quickly became friends. While earning his master's degree, Wolfram took a job at the U of R Laser Lab, and he and Claudia took full advantage of the opportunity to explore America. They took epic vacations together during his breaks, driving around the USA in his VW van. They likely saw more of the USA—including our amazing national parks—in their short time in America than many Americans see in their lifetimes.

My U of R financial aid package included part-time work for the Institute of Optics. I was a laboratory teaching assistant (TA) for the undergraduate program. This meant my fellow TA, Eric from Pittsburgh, and I had to work through each of the labs ourselves to understand how to do them successfully to help the undergraduate students. We took turns—one of us would do the lab while the other would take notes for reference.

When Eric was doing a lab, and I was taking notes, the head of the laboratory gave a tour to some emeritus professors and alumni. Observing us, one of the men in the group remarked how cute it was that the young man's girlfriend was taking notes. The laboratory manager was horrified and quickly tried to remedy the situation by informing the man that both Eric and I were graduate students in optics serving as TAs in his lab. This surprised the man, who was not expecting a woman to be studying optics, let alone at the graduate level.

After the tour, the laboratory manager returned and apologized profusely to me. I told him not to worry about it. The incident reflected that one man's attitude, not his. However, that was yet another exposure to bias, which appeared to be generational in this case. Still, many men his age would never have made that assumption and would likely have applauded a woman in the optics program.

Michele at University of Rochester graduation (1992)

Doctoral and master's students were in the same classes at the U of R. The master's students would talk about how we got the short end of the deal. We got half the student aid as the doctoral students, who got a full ride, and part of our financial assistance package required us to work part-time, whereas the postgraduate students got a stipend, so they didn't have to work.

There was a class system there, and we would joke about how we would outdo each other by getting various doctorates. Wolfram topped us all by saying that he was going to be Dr. Dr. Dr. Ragg. On graduation day, I went to pick up my laminated name tag for the reception and noticed that someone had crossed out "Ms." and written "Dr." in sharpie on my badge. I knew who had done that and caught Wolfram's eye across the room, and he gave me a wink. Various members of the faculty and staff observed my nametag during the event and gave me a look, but I didn't care. They weren't in on the joke.

Before Wolfram returned to Germany in late 1992, he said, "You must come to visit me."

Long Weekend in Europe

Continental Airlines ran a "long weekend in Europe" promotion the following year. I called my mom and told her I could fly to visit Wolfram in Germany for less than I could fly to visit her in Seattle.

International calls were more complex in those days and more expensive. After calculating what time it was in Germany to be sure I called at a reasonable hour, I phoned Wolfram to tell him about the airline promotion and ask when would be a good time to visit. His father answered the phone in German, I replied in English, and after us going back and forth this way briefly, I said, "Wolfram," and shortly after that, Wolfram got on the phone. He told me I was a little off in my time calculation as it was late there (oops!), but he welcomed me to visit. I was excited for many reasons, not the least of which was the fact that this would be my first international trip.

When I arrived in Munich, Germany, in the spring of 1993, Wolfram and Claudia came to meet me, and we walked through a big plaza. I noticed what looked like a biergarten with a large gathering of people decked out in red, white, and blue, with their faces painted the same colors. When I asked Wolfram what that was all about, he said, "Why don't you go ask them?"

I walked up to a group and said, "Sprechen Sie Englisch?" which means "Do you speak English?" in German. When they replied yes, I told them I had just arrived from America and was curious to know why they were dressed in red, white, and blue. They were excited to have an American visitor and told me they were celebrating their local football (soccer) team that had done very well. They insisted that I sit with them to get a picture. They put a red, white, and blue knitted hat on my head and scarf around my neck, and a huge beer stein in my hand for the picture. So my first picture in a foreign country was taken with people I didn't know who were friendly enough to welcome me to join them. That's hospitality!

Michele with some hospitable German football fans at a biergarten in Munich, Germany (1993)

Wolfram's family graciously welcomed me to stay at their house in Bavaria. His parents did not speak English, and I did not speak German, so we made a lot of hand motions and facial expressions. I tried to pick up key terms and get through some basic sentences using my English-German dictionary.

While Wolfram was at work during the day, I would go on my own adventures or tour around with his parents. They quickly learned I liked postcards and would exclaim, "Postcard!" when they saw some. In turn, I would utter *sholoss* (castle), *schon* (beautiful), and *essen* (eat).

I have been a vegetarian since high school because I am an animal lover and realized I could be healthy eating a vegetarian diet and no animal had to die for me to survive. The German diet was not very vegetarian-friendly. One day, Wolfram's family made sauerkraut and something else that was red and resembled a sausage. His younger brother, who knew a little English, was home at the time, so I asked him what it was. He pondered for a moment and then proceeded to get a knife and pretend that he was cutting his arm. A bit shocked by the demonstration, I had no idea what he could mean. So when Wolfram got home, I asked him. After querying his brother, he told me they had eaten blood sausage. Hence the knife demonstration.

The German *brezel* (a baked pretzel) is something that I enjoyed. Wolfram's parents were so kind to get some fresh from the bakery one day and serve them with the meal. Wolfram was at work, but his brother was home, so I asked him if they had any mustard. He wasn't sure what I was saying, so I told him it was yellow, and you spread it on bread, but it wasn't butter. He diligently went through the cupboards and refrigerator until he found something in what looked like a toothpaste tube. I realized it was mustard and said that was it.

"*Senf!*" he exclaimed, "This I have never heard!" The family looked at me in disbelief. When I asked how they ate their pretzels, his brother told me they used butter. When Wolfram got home and heard the story, he affirmed that it was considered odd to request mustard for pretzels, as that was not how Germans ate them.

One day Wolfram dropped me off at a train station in Tuttlingen on his way to work so that I could make a day trip to Heidelberg. We had practiced what I would need to say—in German—to the person selling tickets. I needed a round-trip ticket with a departure on the next train out and a return by a specific time so he could pick me up. The man at the ticket booth took my money but refused to sell me the round-trip ticket; he would only give me a one-way ticket. While we were discussing this, the train arrived, stopped briefly for a couple of minutes, and departed the station.

The next train would not come for a long while, and even if I caught it, I would have no time to walk around in Heidelberg. So that plan was a bust. I asked for a refund, but the man refused. Then I asked where I could find a phone, and he just sent me away.

As I walked out of the train station, I saw a lady coming in and said to her, "Sprechen Sie Englisch?" She replied, "Yes," and asked how she could help. When I explained what had happened, she got agitated. She said that man was her father and she would speak to him. Per the animated dialog that ensued, she appeared to give him a good lecture and got him to give me a refund. Then she sent me in the direction of the post office, which was where I could find a payphone.

This was a small town, and the buildings looked similar, and I was wondering if I was going in the right direction when some high-school-age girls approached me. I said, "Sprechen Sie Englisch?" One of the girls looked at me startled and said, "Yes, a little." Then she asked where I was from. When I told her I came from New York in America, she asked what I was doing in this little town. I briefly explained the story to her and asked if she could help to point me in the direction of the post office, where I could find a payphone, and she did.

The staff at the post office greeted me in German. When I said, "Sprechen Sie Englisch?" someone replied, "Yes." I explained that I needed to call my German friend at work and asked for instructions on how to do that, and the person showed me.

When I placed the call, someone other than Wolfram answered the phone in German. When he realized I was American, he switched to English, and I explained what had happened and that I needed to talk to Wolfram to see if he could get his parents to pick me up. Wolfram was upset and wanted to give the man at the station a talk, but I told him that the man's daughter had already done that. He said he would contact his parents and have them come pick me up.

While waiting for Wolfram's parents, I worked very hard to put together sentences in German, using my English-German dictionary, to express how thankful I was to see them and how much I appreciated them coming to get me. I have no idea how good my German grammar was, but his parents gave me a big smile after I said it. They ended up taking me to the Black Forest. The tourist area would not open up for visitors until later in the month, but they told the proprietor that I had traveled from America, and he let us walk around.

By the way, I made it to Heidelberg on a different day and had a great time walking around. Given my limited German and the fact that cappuccino is universal, I ended up drinking a lot of coffee at various cafes. I've probably never been so caffeinated as I was while roaming around Germany. Thankfully, the Germans had delectable coffee.

When I went inside churches, I often was fortunate enough to hear someone playing the organ. I found a stained-glass window in one church with Einstein's $E=mc^2$ etched on it. As a science major, I thought that was interesting, so I took a picture and told Wolfram about it later. The castle on the hill was lovely. I also found a student's prison, where unruly university students were sent from the late 1700s to the early 1900s. Can you imagine?

Wolfram and Claudia took me on grand adventures in the evenings and on his days off. We toured Bavaria and visited Neuschwanstein Castle. The poster I got there now hangs framed on my daughter's wall all these years later. I told her, "That's the real castle that inspired Walt Disney World's Cinderella castle."

I had always wanted to travel internationally, and that trip only solidified that desire. Furthermore, I realized the importance of getting out of your comfort zone, leaving the safety and security of your home country, and traveling the world to meet new people, see new places, and experience new things. Since that time, I have had the opportunity to take many international trips, and every one of them has shaped me in some way for the better—broadened my horizons and helped me see things from a new perspective. I appreciate that there may be many different ways to approach something, and no one way is necessarily better than another.

Wolfram and Claudia have remained dear friends to this day and have hosted me for many great adventures in Germany and Switzerland, where they now live. I have them to thank for the fact that I enjoy red wine.

In the early 2000s, I came to visit them after they married and moved into a flat in Switzerland. When I arrived, Wolfram proclaimed, "To celebrate, we must open a fine bottle of red wine!" I told him not to waste a fine bottle of red wine on me as I had only recently started drinking wine and didn't care for red wine. He responded, "Then you haven't had a good bottle of red wine." Wolfram opened a bottle of Rioja from Spain, and I enjoyed it. He was right—I liked good red wine, not the cheap stuff. Quality in wine and other things makes a difference. Since then, I have regularly kept at least one bottle of nice Rioja at my house and enjoy introducing others to it.

CHAPTER 8

National Security Space

While in my first year of graduate school at the U of R, Eastman Kodak tried to recruit me to be an image scientist with their government programs team. Kodak was an Industrial Associate of the Institute of Optics, so they received the graduate students' resumes. My stated objective at the top of my resume was "Work for NASA on the US Space Program."

My initial responses to Kodak's efforts to entice me were, "I do not intend to stay in Rochester. I'm going back to the West Coast after I graduate." I also remarked about how bad the Rochester weather was, but they were persistent.

Finally in the spring of 1992, I agreed to visit and do interviews. I met people who would become my first professional work colleagues during my visit. Many were my age and straight out of college or grad school. They kept telling me, "We cannot tell you what we do because it's classified. Nonetheless, given your interests, we think you would enjoy the work." To my previous statement that nothing beats visiting a prospective college, the same applies to a prospective employer and meeting the employees. You get a feeling for the culture during the process.

It was a big decision to not just move to Rochester for grad school but to stay there to start my career. The economy was such that the employers of interest out west were still not hiring. So, after much consideration and prayer, I decided the responsible thing to do was to accept the offer from Kodak, get started with my professional career, and start paying off my student loans.

That news hit my mother hard as she wanted and expected me to move back to Seattle. She told me I could live with her while I searched for a job.

It was difficult for me too; it meant that this move to the East Coast—so far away from anyone who knew or cared about me—was going to be permanent for now.

Furthermore, I would work full-time while I finished my remaining coursework for my master's degree. As it turned out, that was a blessing. Once I started applying what I had learned at my job, it all made more sense because I could see real-life applications of my schoolwork in this context. This is one reason why I am a firm believer in experiential learning. It makes all the difference to apply a math equation to real life. That's when it clicks.

During the employment negotiation process, Kodak management informed me that they would offer me higher pay, except that I had not yet finished my master's degree, and that would not be "fair" to those who had already finished their master's degree. In retrospect, I do not believe that for a minute. For one, they did not increase my pay automatically once I earned my degree. In addition, some managers are notorious for trying to hire good people for as little pay as possible. I know this because later in my career, I heard firsthand the discussions of hiring managers in both the private sector and government and was appalled that they wouldn't just pay people what they were worth. I think employers should compensate people based on their value; the amount should not be determined based on factors like age, gender, marital status, number of dependents, etc.

Regardless, my starting income was more than my mother had ever made in her entire life, and she told me so. That sparked a change for us as a family financially, as I was completely supporting myself and paying off my student loan debt, and my mom could focus her income on her needs alone.

Despite my success in school—high school valedictorian, bachelor's degree with a double major in physics and engineering science with honors, and a master's degree in optics—I was a bit nervous when I officially started my first professional job. Would I be able to apply all I had learned to be successful in my career?

I started work in June 1992, and my first day was challenging because it started early. The Kodak Hawkeye building had a legacy work schedule dating back to when there used to be shift work for manufacturing, and the team had kept it. They started just after seven a.m. This was an early start for someone who tended to stay up later into the evening. It took some getting used to and a focused effort to adjust my evening schedule so I could get to bed earlier and was not so tired in the morning.

Michele at her temporary office with the Kodak ColorSense Calibrator team (1993)

The management told me it could take awhile to get my national security clearance. In the meantime, they assigned me to a commercial project team working on the ColorSense Calibrator. Our goal was to ensure the colors you saw on your computer screen were the same as those you saw on the paper printout of that image. We used a calibrator to help ensure that "What You See Is What You Get" (WYSIWYG). This was an issue in the imaging business, as what you saw on the screen was not always what you would see in the printed product.

Kodak's core business was film production, and they made big bucks on silver recovery from film processing. Silver halide is used in photography because it is photosensitive and reacts with light to form the image. The exposed silver halides are chemically reduced to elemental silver during the development process. People would drop off their rolls of film in pouches at drug stores, and the film would be processed and made into prints on photo paper. If any image processing was to be done on the images before they were made into prints, it was important that what you saw on the screen was what you would get in the finished product. Hence, the need for calibrators.

That was a fun first job and would be relevant to my future work on satellite imagery as an image scientist.

As it turned out, I got my clearances by September 1992; the process took only three months. Many of my colleagues were amazed I got my clearances so fast, as it had taken them up to a year to get cleared. They joked that my life must have been relatively uneventful while they had been much more adventurous, so it took longer for their backgrounds to be investigated and for their clearances to be processed. Who knows, but I was excited to start the real work.

Michele in front of the Eastman Kodak Company Hawkeye Building (1993)

There are various security levels when you work on classified government programs. The basic levels are Secret (S), Top Secret (TS), and Top Secret/Secret Compartmented Information (TS/SCI). There can also be a compartment, but we won't get into that. When you work at the TS/SCI level, you have to work inside a Secret Compartmented Information Facility (SCIF) or "skif."

On the first day I arrived at my desk inside the SCIF, I found a plaque. It read, "My job is so secret I don't know what I am doing." I laughed. Someone had a good sense of humor in welcoming me to the team.

They wasted no time throwing me into the thick of things, which included attending all the meetings. In those meetings, I quickly realized I was hearing a whole new dialect of English because they spoke in acronyms.

Soon I would learn that "acronym speak" was a way of life in the national security world. Each intelligence discipline had its unique terms, as did the military services. Some of the terms overlapped, but others were unique.

I started writing down all the acronyms I heard or saw in presentations and then would talk with my colleagues after the meetings to find out what they meant. I created a glossary of terms for my reference. Then I found out another new hire had been doing the same. She and I combined our notes and published a glossary of terms that subsequently was given to all the new hires.

Here I will point out that from now on, there will be some of this acronym speak, which is simply a way of life in the national security community. I have created a glossary for you to reference if you need a refresher about the meaning of a particular acronym. Stick with me; by the end of this journey, you will have basic fluency in the language of the IC and DoD.

That fall of 1992, my grandparents flew from California to visit and helped me get set up in my new apartment. Grandpa Glenn did handyman work, like hanging pictures, and Grandma Ruth organized my kitchen. This would be the first of many times they helped me to get settled after a move.

When I wasn't at work, I took them for drives to see the fantastic fall colors. We toured the Finger Lakes region and took a luncheon cruise on the *Canandaigua Lady*. They served us white wine made with Niagara grapes. My grandmother refused to drink hers and offered it to my grandfather, who obliged.

This was the first time I'd ever seen my grandfather drink an alcoholic beverage. I had grown up in a pretty "dry" family, not because anyone was against it but because nobody chose to drink alcoholic beverages except on rare occasions. Aside from the glass of white zinfandel wine I had when my Italian-heritage grad school classmate took me out for dinner on my twenty-third birthday, which was the first alcoholic beverage I had ever tried, this might have been my second. The wine was light and sweet, and we both enjoyed it.

We were inspired to tour some of the scenic wineries in the area during their other visits. I kept thinking, "Who'd have thought I would go on wine tours with my grandparents?" They were great adventurers and world travelers, so this came with the territory.

When my mom came to visit, I was excited to treat her to a live performance of *The Nutcracker* at the Eastman School of Music in downtown

Rochester. Watching her take it all in was a joy for me. She later told me that she felt transported to a wonderful place when the music started. My mom made many sacrifices so that I could get a good education and enjoy enriching experiences in my childhood. It meant so much to me to be able to do something special for her.

At Kodak, I worked with a good team of people, which occasionally included some young military officers who worked jointly on projects with us as part of the Education With Industry (EWI) or "e-we" program. These officers were called "e-wees." There was truly a one-team culture; it didn't matter who your employer was, as we were all working toward the same objective on behalf of our country.

My first boss, Bill Fintel, was great. He was not a micromanager by any stretch of the imagination. Bill was very good at helping me learn the ropes, and then he let me loose on some projects.

One of my first projects was an engineering study report (ESR) that I did in partnership with a more experienced colleague who was a little older than me and whose name was Kyle. He was great to work with and had a good sense of humor. One day, when I asked about the art of the possible, i.e., could we do something a certain way that had perhaps not been done before, he gave me an interesting response.

Kyle pinched his thumb and index fingers together, lifted them to a corner of his mouth, acted like he was inhaling, and then pulled his fingers away and said, "You're smoking dope." I laughed. That was a fun way to communicate, "You're dreaming. That's not realistic. There's no chance that's going to happen." We joked about that often. When I saw him years later, I told him that was one of the things I remembered about our time together, and we had a good laugh.

Though I was relatively new, Bill had faith in me. To his credit, he put me in charge of optimizing the image processing algorithm for one of the new imagery sensors, infrared (IR), that would be launched and initialized. We were responsible for the Image Chain Analysis, and our group was called ICA.

I was responsible for reviewing all types of sample imagery scenes, which I did by looking at rolls of film on a light table—something you can now see at the Smithsonian National Air and Space Museum Udvar-Hazy Center. Then I adjusted the image processing algorithm to optimize the dynamic range, which would help maximize the amount of information we got from the pixels. My work involved a lot of data, which I represented in points and graphs.

When I had my first opportunity to give a presentation at the quarterly meeting with the government customer, I was determined to nail it. So, I booked a conference room, locked myself in it, and ran through my charts repeatedly until I knew them by heart.

The management for many levels above me feared this government official. She was abrupt and abrasive and did not suffer fools gladly. If she felt you did not know your stuff, she would skewer you. I determined this would not happen to me.

When the time came for me to give my presentation, I got on stage and introduced myself. Other than glancing at the screen to ensure the slides had advanced, I never looked at them. I had everything down cold, and I handled the questions with ease.

When I sat down, colleagues near me were mouthing, "Great job!" Afterward, they asked, "How did you do that? You did not look at your slides once!" I told them I had practiced.

The government official came up to me and said I did a good job. She was impressed, which was a big deal because she did not hand out compliments. That set the tone for our relationship. She respected me from the start and treated me with respect. My colleagues and managers who still feared her were amazed. This experience reinforced the importance of being prepared and making an excellent first impression.

This experience reinforced the importance of being prepared and making an excellent first impression.

Living out of a Suitcase

In 1993, the first full year of my career, I traveled thirty-two out of fifty-two weeks on temporary duty assignments, also known as TDYs. That is a lot of travel. Most of the trips were to the Washington, DC, area.

Looking back at my eighth-grade historic tour to Washington, DC, I never dreamed I would return to work in our country's capital city.

Kodak had a large travel budget but was always looking to save money. Given I was single and no one was home missing me while I was away, they asked if I would stay over the weekends when I had to work in the area for two consecutive weeks to save on airfare. Usually, that was fine with me. Often I would work a few hours on Saturdays. On Saturday afternoons and Sunday after church, I would tour the sites in downtown DC, such as the monuments and the Smithsonian museums.

The National Air and Space Museum was one of my favorites. One day, I decided I would read every last placard in the Apollo section. Another time, I got to see a special *Star Trek* exhibit. Through that, I gained insights into how *Star Trek* characters and storylines represented the nation-states and political dynamics at the time, which I never realized while watching the TV show as a kid.

Because of my frequent travels, I got to know the hotel staff, who welcomed me back. The people at the car rental and airline ticket counters got to know me too.

One time after I returned from a trip, our office secretary asked me if I was dating anyone. I looked at her and said that would only be possible if he were a pilot who flew between Rochester and DC, as I was rarely ever home. When I was home, it was often only long enough to unpack my suitcase, do my laundry, open the mail, pay the bills, and then pack for another trip. That part was rough, but I was happy when I could help cover a trip for a colleague with a family and kids at home who missed them when they were away.

Because I spent so much time at the ops facility in the DC area, now known as Aerospace Data Facility East (ADF-E), many people thought I lived and worked there. I got to know the roles of different groups and made friends throughout the ops facility. While I interacted with people across the site, my primary work was with other engineers, image scientists, and imagery analysts, called IAs. I effectively became a part of the team, which meant a lot.

One day during a conversation with someone in another office, I mentioned I was an engineer. Surprised, he said, "You don't look like an engineer!" I laughed and said, "Why, because I'm not wearing thick, black-rimmed glasses with a white shirt and a pocket protector?" No, I didn't look like a stereotypical engineer. I stayed true to myself. I dressed professionally, and I dressed like a lady.

When I was in town, I worked at whatever spare desk I could find in the Product Engineering Branch (PEB). Once when I was in town, my colleagues invited me to the site picnic and teambuilding event, and they recruited me to play on their softball team.

Given my initial experience with softball as my first sport, I wondered how much I would contribute to the team. Playing that day, I found the confidence that comes with maturity, and years of experience with other sports enabled me to perform much better than I had in seventh grade. Their chosen team name was The Powerful Pixel Pushers of PEB. They were engineers with a good sense of humor.

The Exploitation Engineers, called EXEs, whose office was down the hall, also had a good sense of humor. Many were former military and had colorful language and interesting stories. The EXEs did a cursory review of all the imagery that came in from the satellites. They often tipped PEB to apparent anomalies in the imagery, which we would then have to pinpoint and resolve.

One time I was working on a questionnaire and asked one of the EXEs, among others, to take a look at it. His name was Kevin Collins, and he was former military. He was a jovial soul and had great stories to share when we were working long days together in ops. When I received his feedback, I noticed one of the remarks he had written in the margin was "WTFO." I had no idea what that meant, so I walked down the hall to ask him.

Kevin said, "WTFO. You know, Whiskey Tango Foxtrot, Over." I told him that while I recognized the military phonetic alphabet, which I had been working diligently to learn so I could speak like them, I did not know what WTF meant and asked him to tell me. Kevin's face turned red, and he told me he could not tell me. I persisted, and he finally relented. When he explained what it meant, I burst out laughing. Then I replied, "So you mean I could be a little clearer regarding what I am asking?" He nodded. You had to learn the lingo to fit in with this group, and Kevin had just educated me on another term.

One of the most significant events we dealt with, in addition to resolving anomalies, was the initialization of imaging payloads on satellites after launch. Many industry partners would descend upon the ops facility working their part of the process until we could officially declare everything operational. Those were long and intense days but also very gratifying. We were doing something critical to the country's security and came together as one team to do it.

These intense periods always occurred around Christmas and New Year, impacting our personal lives. Later, when I worked with an Air Force officer who had previously done launches, he remarked how they were proud to get the payload up just before the holidays. I replied, "Yeah, and then you stuck me and others with the task of initializing it over the holidays while you were home enjoying time with your family and friends." Somehow, at least three payloads I had to initialize got scheduled that way.

In time, the members of PEB started telling me they wished I was a permanent member of the team as they respected me and valued my contributions. I wished I was, too, because the extensive travel took a toll on me. So, I told my management at Kodak that it made more sense and would save the company a lot of money in travel dollars if they permanently moved me to the DC area. They would not do it. They said they had a big travel budget as part of the government contract and had not considered creating a permanent position in Washington, DC, though we had extensive work there.

Shortly after I requested to move to DC, the Kodak management enabled a colleague of mine, Patty, to go on an extended TDY to work there effectively as a full-time employee in ops for a year. She and I would talk about how they needed to make her role permanent and enable others like me to do the same.

CHAPTER 9

Mission Operations

Other companies had permanent positions in PEB, including Harris Corporation. One of my colleagues from Harris approached me and said he was getting ready to transfer into another role in the DC area, and his position at ADF-E would be open. The Air Force officer, who was the PEB deputy director, indicated he would welcome me to take that position and become a permanent member of PEB. At the same time, Patty asked Kodak to make her role permanent, but they resisted.

When I resigned from Kodak in February 1995 to take the Harris position on site, Kodak asked me to do exit interviews with my boss, his boss, and his boss's boss. Each wanted to know why I chose to leave, as they valued me as an employee. I told them it was unreasonable to make someone spend most of her life traveling and living out of a suitcase when she could move to a location permanently and work there. Shortly after I resigned from Kodak, they made Patty's position on-site permanent. So, in the end, it worked out for both of us to get permanent jobs in PEB, but I had to switch companies to do it.

Before I moved from New York to Virginia, I had some long TDYs to do a big evaluation with analysts. They used the second-generation image data exploitation (IDEX II) softcopy imagery workstation at the National Photographic Interpretation Center (NPIC), where CIA and DoD imagery analysts worked. At the time, IDEX II was a million-dollar highly classified state-of-the-art system. Now you can see one on display at the Smithsonian National Air and Space Museum Udvar-Hazy Center. Chris was the technician who staged all the imagery and reset everything for each new analyst, and we spent long days together for a month. He was older than me, divorced, and had kids. During the idle time, we shared more about our backgrounds.

Through our conversations, he learned I was a Christian. He told me about struggles with his faith and how he didn't feel like he fit in or was welcome at churches. He also thought the Bible was too formal as written and hard to understand. Sadly, too many people have experiences like that, which turn them away from the church and the Christian faith.

I told Chris about my grandfather, a pastor but not religious, and how he truly loved people. He was the example I had of who a Christian was and how to live your Christian faith. Christians are humans and, as such, are fallible due to humankind's sinful nature. So we must keep our eyes on Jesus and live by his example.

In addition, I told Chris there were many different versions of the Bible, some much easier to read than the King James Version, which is what he had. Before the last evaluation wrapped up, I gave him The Living Bible, which, per Bible Gateway, "is a paraphrase of the Old and New Testaments with the purpose of saying exactly as possible what the writers of the Scripture meant, and say it simply, expanding where necessary for a clear understanding by the modern reader."

Chris later told me that the time he spent talking with me prompted him to attend church again and that The Living Bible had made all the difference for him as it was much easier to read and understand. That was one of my first opportunities to share my Christian faith with someone. I didn't preach to him. I told my story. He could tell I cared about him and empathized with his struggles. Because I didn't judge him and openly shared my challenges and insights, he was open to giving the church another chance and ultimately recommitted his life to Christ. I felt so blessed that God saw fit to use me this way.

During those last few long TDYs to DC, I did apartment shopping in the area. I visited one community where someone had a condo for rent. It was a new community, and the sales office was still there, so I asked for more information about the amenities. When the representative realized I was planning on renting, she wondered why I didn't just buy a place. I told her it was because I had recently graduated from graduate school and was still paying off student loans, and I had no savings to make a down payment.

She then told me about the Federal Housing Administration program that allowed first-time homebuyers to have a minimum amount of money for a down payment to buy their first home. I ran the numbers and knew I could make the monthly mortgage payments. The challenge was coming up with the down payment, and I could not take out a loan to do it.

During my weekly call with my grandparents, I mentioned this opportunity to buy instead of rent. They were excited for me and said they would like to help. They gave me $5,000 toward the down payment required, and I became a homeowner for the first time a few months before my twenty-sixth birthday. My mom was so excited for me as I was the first one of the two of us to own a home. It was her objective to get to that point someday soon so she could stop "lining the pockets of a landlord" and start building equity.

That home purchase was a smart move. I paid off my student loans in record time and bought a car. It felt terrific to be debt free, aside from my mortgage and car payment, and I paid off my car in record time. After growing up in a family perpetually in debt, it was my goal to never be in debt as long as I could help it, and I've stuck to that strategy all my life.

Working for Harris enabled me to work with a newer imaging sensor, radio detection and ranging (RADAR), and the associated phenomenology. My colleagues and I worked on different processing algorithms that helped improve image quality. The imagery was not literal, so part of the challenge was getting the analysts to understand how to interpret the image and appreciate its value.

Every contract had a Contracting Officer Technical Representative (COTR) either a military officer or government civilian who supervised the contract and provided approval for contract activities. Given I was doing a lot of new and innovative things, I wanted to be sure that my COTR was aware and approved.

I was fortunate to have a technically astute but easygoing COTR in Major (Maj.) Larry Shand, USAF. Initially, I would call him and leave messages explaining an opportunity and asking for his approval. When he didn't call me back, I switched my tactic and called and told him that I was going to do something I assumed he would be okay with and to contact me if he had any concerns.

Sometime later, when I saw Larry, he told me, "Michele, your method works well for me. I trust you and your judgment and appreciate you giving me a heads-up regarding your activities." He let me have free rein to do good things without his preapproval and ask for forgiveness later if something did not go as planned, as long as he knew what was going on. That was a good modus operandi, a.k.a. MO, that I would use throughout my career.

Do good things; ask forgiveness later. That was a good modus operandi, a.k.a. MO, that I would use throughout my career.

While working in PEB, I was fortunate to be mentored by Maj. Curt Munechika, USAF, the deputy to the civilian in charge. Curt was intelligent, easygoing, and had a great sense of humor. His ethos was "work hard, play hard, and have fun while doing it." This could be due in part to his upbringing in Hawaii. Curt would refer to the leadership as "the big dogs" and how something would be really "hosed" if we messed it up. His facial expressions were priceless and would make me laugh. He saw my potential and invested in me and my career.

There was a diverse group at PEB—military, government, and industry. One of the senior members was a brilliant scientist named Neil, who knew the satellites better than anyone else. He was a national treasure. We all hoped nothing would go wrong with the systems when he took his annual month-long vacation to some exotic place. Neil was also very generous with his time, sharing his knowledge and insight, and I learned a lot from him.

He told me about a meeting he had with a banker one day. The banker described something and said, "It's not rocket science." Neil said matter-of-factly, "I am a rocket scientist." The banker did not hear that very often.

There was also a rather odd guy named Bruce on the team. He had been stationed in various places worldwide and had some interesting stories. Bruce had a tough exterior shell and seemed to like to shock people with his remarks. I looked deeper and heard the compassion he had—for people who were suffering around the world, for animals, and so on. Bruce was one of a few guys I shared an office with, so we interacted almost daily. Somehow

I worked my way into his circle of trust, but I was sworn to secrecy and could not tell anyone that he was a nice guy to protect his facade. Bruce went so far as to stick up for me when other guys got a little inappropriate or unprofessional, and I appreciated that.

I had to frequently interface with a problematic female coworker who also worked for Harris. Though she was not a member of PEB, she visited often. She was highly competitive and likely never played team sports because she appeared to lack understanding of the concepts of teamwork and good sportsmanship as they applied to the workplace. The projects I initiated and ran were very successful. Instead of admiring me for that, she felt threatened. She was envious when I received recognition.

She went so far as to corner me privately one day and tell me that she was jealous of me and wanted to take over a project I had initiated and was leading that had gained recognition. She added that she was entitled to have it because she wanted it. I was stunned upon hearing this as her attitude was shocking to me.

To make matters worse, right after that conversation, we had to join a group of colleagues at a gathering. Still in shock, I was surprised and repulsed that she put on a show and tried to act like she was my best friend. She had not been a friend to me by any stretch of the imagination; she had been an adversary.

In time, I realized her angle was to pass herself off to others as if she was a close confidant of mine so people would believe the misinformation and lies she would tell about me. She continued this duplicitous behavior and became more aggressive. This situation started to cause me a significant amount of stress.

I raised the issue of her behavior with our mutual boss at Harris and told him of the stress it was causing me and the damage she was trying to do to my reputation, but he was unwilling to do anything decisive about it. He recognized that she had issues. However, he would not address the matter and deal with her one-on-one. Any conversation he would have about the issues I raised, he wanted to have with the two of us together. These discussions did not cause her to change her behavior at all. Instead, she thought that she had gotten away with it and that I shared the blame for her actions equally. This emboldened her to continue the behavior that caused me so much stress.

She was hostile to me in private but transformed herself in public and represented to others that she was a good friend, all the while trying to take credit for my work and project her failures on me. This was dangerous to my reputation and career. Because she portrayed herself as my trusted friend, other people would put their guard down and believe what she said. It was apparent she was doing whatever she could to undermine me.

My reputation was very important to me, so I decided to talk with Curt, our government customer. As I started explaining about this very difficult coworker, I could tell Curt was getting concerned. He finally stopped me and said, "Is it Bruce?" I replied, "No, it isn't Bruce. While Bruce is odd and likes to shock people, I see through all that and know he has a good heart. In addition, you never have to guess where Bruce is coming from—what you see is what you get. He's WYSIWYG. He is genuine, not duplicitous." Curt was notably relieved. I told him this had to do with a female coworker, and I'd much rather work with Bruce than with her.

Curt guessed who it was right away. Then he told me something that set my mind at ease. Curt said he knew me and the quality of my work. No one else would change his mind and impression of me. Curt had observed the dynamic between this female coworker and me and saw through her attempt at veiled sabotage. He surmised that she was insecure and threatened by my competence and success. Curt realized that some women see another woman as a threat, as she did, rather than recognizing that success for one of us is beneficial for all of us.

It is a sad reality, but I learned through this challenging work experience that there are generally two types of women. Most women build each other up and see one woman's success as a shared success for all women and something to be celebrated. However, some women think there is room for only one woman on a team or in a workgroup and see any other woman as a threat. They are jealous of another woman's success, as if it somehow makes them look bad. Such women often seek to attack and tear down other women—especially those perceived to be more successful—to make themselves feel better and build themselves up. To all the women out there, don't be like this! We have enough struggles in male-dominated societies and work environments—we must work together and build each other up!

Though Curt could not directly take action to improve my work environment or address the situation concerning this woman and her behavior, which continued to be a source of stress to me, I was relieved that he was wise and insightful and understood what was going on. Many men lack the discernment to see through such conniving behavior. I held Curt in high regard, and I was comforted knowing that my reputation with him was not at risk.

Though my role was in the DC area, Harris Corporation headquarters were in Melbourne, Florida. So, I occasionally traveled there to collaborate with the personnel in the research lab. Dr. Andy Lee was one of those brilliant minds, though he was incredibly humble and down to earth. He was part of the team that developed an algorithm that enabled automated registration and mosaicking of imagery.

Imagery had to be registered, meaning draped over and tied to terrain models, like the World Geodetic System made in 1984, known as WGS-84. Then it had to be mosaicked, meaning stitched together with other imagery to create a bigger picture, as you see in Google Earth and Maps today. The Harris algorithm Andy developed automatically did this, which was a huge deal. Registration and mosaicking of imagery had been a manually intensive process up until then and very time-consuming. This new algorithm changed the game.

That beautiful seamless-looking globe you see on Google Earth was made possible by the innovations of people like Andy at least a decade prior. Always thoughtful and approachable, Andy was my go-to person for any product changes required or new capabilities desired by the government customer.

Harris had quarterly meetings with their customers and sometimes held special project meetings in Melbourne I was required to attend. One such session was on 29 October 1998, the same day the space shuttle *Discovery* (STS-95) was to launch from Cape Canaveral at the Kennedy Space Center. There was to be a special crew member—Senator John Glenn—who, at age seventy-seven, would be the oldest person ever to travel in space. He was a former Marine Corps fighter pilot and in 1962 had become the first American to orbit the earth in *Friendship 7*, part of the Project Mercury mission.

I wanted to be at the launch, and my boss, Steve Boos, knew it. As a resident of Melbourne, he had been to many launches, but I had yet to see a shuttle launch, and it was killing me to be so close yet so far away.

I kept looking at the clock, hoping that the meeting would wrap up early so I could drive to Kennedy and watch the launch from a distance, but as the meeting droned on, that was not likely. Then just as the hour approached where there was no way I could make it there in time to see the launch, Steve walked over and slipped me a causeway pass. I lit up—not only was he dismissing me to see the launch, but the pass allowed me to see it up close. I was ecstatic!

That was a special day for me—my first space shuttle launch with an American legend, John Glenn, on board. Listening to the audio minutes before the launch, I heard Glenn's fellow Mercury astronaut in attendance, Scott Carpenter, say to the shuttle *Discovery* crew, "Good luck, have a safe flight." Then he delivered the same historic send-off he had given before the *Friendship 7* launch thirty-six years prior: "Godspeed, John Glenn."

Rapid Prototyping

While I enjoyed my work in ops, I became increasingly concerned regarding the growing information technology gap between what was available in the commercial sector and what was in use inside SCIFs in the government sector. If we did not figure out a way to rapidly bring in new technology, test it, and get it into ops, the technology gap would expand to the detriment of the country's security. Ironically, the government cited "security concerns" as the reason for not bringing in new technology. So, we had to figure out a way to work around that. Other people on-site shared this concern, and we brainstormed how to address it.

ADF-E was part of the imagery intelligence (IMINT) enterprise. Multiple data feeds—narrowband and wideband—came into the site, and we would need access to all of them to test new technologies.

We devised a concept for the Operational Technology Evaluation Capability (OTEC). This would be a rapid prototyping environment with a certified and accredited space and taps into all the data feeds.

Previously, every time we wanted a new data tap, we had to go through a long and laborious paperwork process to modify the Interface Control Document (ICD) for each interface a new technology might touch. So, we hit up the requirements team with requests for every data tap we could think of all at once, which had never been done before. Once they got their heads around why we were doing this and saw the potential benefit, they approved our request. There was a similar process we had to go through to bring in any new technology, which was why we needed such a testing environment in the first place.

By creating OTEC—a certified and accredited environment with all the data taps—we could host new technology and no longer have to worry about making changes to ICDs. Moreover, we could maintain any technology that proved viable to operations in OTEC until it went through the formal process, with all the necessary documentation and approval, to become a part of the baseline capability.

OTEC was precedent-setting and enabled much more rapid insertion of cutting-edge technology. OTEC ended up proving to be extremely valuable.

Eventually, OTEC transformed into IMINT labs across the imagery enterprise. It proved so valuable it later evolved into Multi-INT labs across multiple intelligence discipline enterprises. Those labs are still a part of the national security enterprise today.

When I started collaborating with colleges at ADF-E to develop the OTEC Concept of Operations (CONOPS), I was still in PEB. I was doing my PEB job and additional work to get the OTEC capability up and running. This confounded the government civilian who ran PEB. When colleagues were talking about the great things I was doing, he remarked, "That Michele Weslander, she not only does her job here, she does all these other things!" He didn't mean it as a compliment. The person who reported this to me was in shock, for what type of boss would complain about an employee doing that?

Harris couldn't quite get their heads around this either. They were not supportive when I told them I wanted to move from doing PEB work to helping get OTEC up and running. A year prior, I had told them I wanted to move out of PEB and onto something else. At that time, I had effectively spent six years in PEB—three years collaborating with the team via Kodak and three years as part of the team via Harris—and felt it was time to move on to other things.

However, the government was pleased to have me as a part of PEB, and the Harris management was content that their government customer was happy. They did not care that I wanted to expand my experience and grow my career. This dialog went on for a year before the OTEC opportunity came up.

CHAPTER 10

Reputation

I have been fortunate to have mentors, and one who stands out is Lee Akridge. It's a funny story about how we met in January 1999. We both knew each other by reputation—I knew he was wicked smart and held in the highest regard in the community, and he had a similar impression of me. Lee heard that the government official leading the stand-up of OTEC wanted me on his staff full-time, and Harris was not supportive of me leaving PEB because it wasn't their typical line of work. His company, Scitor Corporation, was already working with the group that OTEC would be a part of, and their staff on-site knew the government lead wanted to hire me and that I had a good reputation.

Lee approached me and said, "No interview is required. What must I do to hire you?" Lee's words were a pleasant surprise, and I took what he said as a huge compliment. That's one thing you had to appreciate about Lee; he was not a man of many words, but when he spoke, you better listen because his words were meaningful and had an impact.

Until then, I was used to hiring managers playing games and trying to manipulate the situation, even though they were pursuing me. They were always making excuses for hiring me for a salary less than they were paying others—particularly men—in similar roles. Not Lee. His approach was a breath of fresh air. He hired me, gave me more starting pay than expected, and treated me fairly. Never have I been treated so well all around by a boss.

At OTEC, I worked as part of a team led by a government civilian named Bill. He was a Christian and a good-natured, fatherly figure. Bill was a grand champion for our project and worked with Lee to help get me on contract. I already knew some other team members from my past work at the site. One of them was Al Kelly, and he and I and our mutual friend Maj. James "Jim" Long, USAF, had been discussing the need to do something like this for a long time.

Al and I both had a vision of what OTEC needed to be. He was a big idea guy but preferred to talk rather than write things down. Given my writing skills, I was the primary author of the CONOPS. Al was experienced with all the paperwork processes on site and worked to socialize the OTEC concept with the groups whose support we required. We made a good team.

One of my other close colleagues was Sheila Derdeyn, a sharp engineer. She and I were the only two women on the team aside from the secretary, who had a massive chip on her shoulder. This woman tried to make life miserable for us—especially me and Sheila—through the spiteful and petty things she said and did. We used to joke among the group that if you didn't inadvertently knock off that chip on her shoulder by something you said or did that set her off, she would intentionally knock it off, bite your head off, and blame you for it.

The secretary was a government employee and one of those people who had a class system in her head. She believed and acted as if government employees were superior to industry partners; therefore, government employees could treat industry partners however they wanted. This was all the more ironic because she was a black woman and presented herself as very religious.

Many government employees, a.k.a. "govies," believe and act as she did and think they can get away with it. They'll blame the industry partner for any issues that may arise because "the government customer is always right." This was causing me stress, and I was worried that her behavior and the things she said would reflect negatively on me.

One time when I met with Lee, I started to broach this subject. He cut me off, looked me straight in the eye, and said, "Michele, she is jealous of you. You are attractive, smart, and talented; she is overweight, incompetent, and does not aspire to do anything more than make life miserable for everyone else. Your future is bright, and you will move on from this in time, but she will still be here, and she knows it. Don't worry about her." That was such a relief for me. Lee had wisdom and insight and could see through to the heart of an issue. He wanted me to know he saw the reality of the situation and that he had my back. That's a characteristic of a good boss and a great friend.

Personal Crisis

When Lee hired me in January 1999, I was dealing with a crisis in my life. I found myself in an abusive relationship where the abuser was my husband.

Here's the backstory. In March 1995, just about a month into my new job with Harris, I spent two weeks in an intensive training program for the government's satellite collection management system. I met a USAF officer there who was in the middle of a permanent change of station to work at ADF-E. He was eleven years older than me and divorced with two kids who lived with their mom in another state. He owned a home at his last duty assignment and rented an apartment in the local area.

Once we were both settled into our new jobs on-site, we started meeting in the cafeteria for lunch. We would often walk outside on the grounds after lunch before returning to our respective offices. Our colleagues observed this courtship and told us that they thought we made a good couple.

We seemed well suited, sharing our Christian faith and many similar interests. We started attending church together. We were both runners, though I had been a sprinter in school, and he ran marathons. After running with him, I ran my first 5k race and then a 10k race. We spent as much of our free time together as possible, sometimes going on day trips to sites around the greater Washington, DC, area. After two years of dating, we decided to get married and build our future together.

We got married in May 1997. Our relationship was seemingly wonderful for the first two years we dated, so one would expect we would be in a honeymoon phase after we wed. However, once we said, "I do," and started living under the same roof, I discovered a different person–like Dr. Jekyll and Mr. Hyde.

I soon realized that almost everything he had said while courting me was not true. He had told me what he thought I needed to hear to get me to marry him, including the plans we made during premarital counseling. In reality, he didn't want to share life with me. He didn't want to spend time together, buy a house, have kids, or combine finances.

After we were married and he moved into my condo, one would expect that we would have started to integrate our lives. Instead, we lived entirely separately under the same roof. When I brought this up with him, he admitted he did not want the things we had discussed. When I asked why he would tell me that he wanted all these things before we were married when it was now clear after we were married that he didn't truly mean that, he just shrugged it off.

He didn't want to do anything with me when we had time off on weekends and holidays. I planned trips we could take together, but he did not want to go anywhere with me. He wanted me at his work events, but he didn't want to come to mine. When I asked why he wanted to marry me if he did not want to share life with me, he did not respond.

While marriage can be a blessing, developing a mutually edifying relationship takes work. You need a solid foundation of honesty, integrity, shared values, and commitment to building a strong, healthy, trusting relationship. This is why I insisted that we go through premarital counseling to be sure we had the essential conversations and were compatible. But it was all for naught if he hadn't been honest. The foundation of our marriage seemed to be lies, and we had nothing solid to build on.

Though we were married, I felt very much alone. I effectively became a widow to his golf and other activities, though he had never golfed or done the other things before we were married. I tried to join in his pastimes, such as watching golf with him on TV and learning about the game and the key players, even though I wasn't personally interested in the sport, just to have something to share. He was not interested in doing the reciprocal with me.

None of this made sense to me because it contradicted everything he had said and all the plans we had made together before we wed. I was living in a miserable alternate reality.

In 1998, as my husband was approaching retirement from the military after twenty years of service, my career was starting to take off. At first, he seemed to truly appreciate me and not be intimidated by my intelligence or success. I believed this was partly due to him being eleven years older than me and previously married. But then he constantly tried to belittle me, tear me down, and play manipulative mind games. My home environment was becoming increasingly hostile. I put on a good face when we were in public, but I was dying inside.

During all this domestic turmoil, I took the job with Scitor in January 1999. Shortly after that, my mom called me and said that since I had settled in Virginia, she wanted to move closer to me because I was her only immediate family. She flew from Washington to Virginia to look for jobs and stayed with us for a week.

After witnessing how my husband treated me, my mom confronted me one day when he was away and said, "What are you doing?" I asked her what she meant. She said, "He treats you horribly. Why are you staying and taking this abuse?"

I told her that I always believed marriage was a forever commitment, and when I married him, I committed to being faithful to him forever. So, I could not just walk away without doing everything I could to try and salvage the marriage. Ours was not just a dating or living together arrangement; it was a marriage, and breaking that covenant could not be taken lightly. I told her I was trying to get him to join me for counseling; to date, he had refused. Shortly after she flew home, my mom received a job offer and started planning to move to Virginia.

Then one day, my husband made a remark that led to a revelation. He was standing in the living room admiring the awards he received at his military retirement ceremony. When I walked in and found him there, he turned to me and said, "You are one of my trophies."

At first, I was perplexed, as that seemed like an odd thing for a man to say to his wife. Then I realized that I was the proverbial trophy wife! You'll have to excuse the optics reference, but none of the filters I had applied to the situation previously ever made sense. Once I used that filter, it all made sense.

Suddenly I realized that, to him, I was a possession. He did what he felt he had to do to acquire me. Now that he had me, I was just something he could put on the shelf with his other trophies. He could take me out to show his friends when he wanted to; otherwise, he left me on the shelf. I was not a human being of value to him—I was an inanimate object. My hopes, dreams, and desires didn't matter to him.

Not only did my husband consider me his trophy, but he also treated me as his verbal punching bag. It got to the point that he was verbally abusing me relentlessly almost every day. I was desperate to be away from him—to find a safe space. Though I continued to plead with him to go to counseling, he refused.

When he finally consented to go to counseling, the session was surreal. He turned on the charm for the counselor, behaving as he had before we were married, and effectively told the counselor that everything was fine. He had his act together, and all the issues were in my head. When I provided examples, he would rationalize them away. He claimed he did nothing wrong, that his behavior toward me was my fault, and he saw no reason to change.

As I would learn later, after reading some books on domestic violence and verbal abuse, this is the classic behavior of an abuser. Furthermore, in stark contrast to physical abuse, which is often visually apparent, verbal abuse is not. It effectively causes internal bleeding—emotional, mental, psychological—that others cannot readily see, but it is domestic violence nonetheless. Reading these books helped me realize I was in a domestic violence situation and needed to get out. When I suggested we separate and that he find another place to live, he refused.

In desperation, I sought out a lawyer. I told her the situation, and she agreed that this was domestic violence and that I needed to get away from him and file for a divorce. I told her that, if possible, I wanted to do as much as I could on my own to save on legal expenses. She completely understood and offered me a package where I would write the documents, and then she would review them and do the filing. She told me there was a six-month timeline for divorce in Virginia, given we didn't have kids together.

I told the lawyer we were living in a condo that was my property before we were married, and I was afraid that if I left, I would lose it, and he refused to separate by moving out. She said that what mattered was that we lived separately, even if it was under the same roof. I told her that was effectively how our marriage had been from the start.

After that conversation, I moved into the living room to sleep on the futon, which started the living-separately clock. The lawyer provided reference materials, and I reviewed them and drafted a separation agreement. Realizing he was very materialistic, I wrote the document so he would take all the belongings he had before the marriage and all the things we had purchased together since the wedding. I'd only keep my condo and the things I had before we were married. So he would walk away with his property and all our joint property.

As I previously mentioned, he had two kids from a prior marriage who lived with their mom in another state. As someone who loves kids, I welcomed being their stepmom and worked to build a good relationship with them. They knew I was not trying to replace their mom, and they appreciated that. We became friends and enjoyed doing things together. In time, he became jealous of my relationship with them and started excluding me from his plans and limiting my time with them.

We hadn't resolved things before his kids came for another visit in the summer of 1999. To keep up appearances and not make their visit awkward, I moved out of the living room while they were there, even though I knew this would mean restarting the clock for our separation. By then, he had gotten to the point that he did not try to hide his abuse of me from them.

After a particular episode, I pulled him aside and asked him what type of example he thought he was for his children. Did he want his son to think it was okay to treat a woman this way? What's worse, did he want his daughter to think it was okay to be treated this way by a man? Once again, he ignored me and dismissed my concerns. After his kids left, I moved back into the living room to restart the clock for our separation.

Shortly after that, there was an episode at home when my husband started yelling at me and then backed me into a corner and was hostile and threatening me with his face just a few inches from mine. I was scared and pushed him away. He immediately became incensed, accused me of hitting him, and said it was physical abuse. Incredulous, I told him that he could not be serious. He had backed me into a corner and was inches from my face, violently yelling at me. I had merely pushed him aside to get away from him.

He had severe anger management issues, as was reflected in the results of a test we both took as part of premarital counseling. Unfortunately, we did not receive the results until after we were married. On the graph, his plot was far outside the normal bounds for anger. His remark made me think he could do anything—including physical abuse—and lie about it. I was terrified.

Months prior and many times since, I had told him I thought we needed to separate, but he refused to leave, and that was still the case. At this point, I knew that I ultimately needed to divorce him. I had to give him the separation agreement to start the process, but I was afraid of how he would react.

In this context, with all this emotional turmoil, I approached my new boss, Lee, in his office one day in mid-1999. When I asked Lee if I could speak to him for a few minutes, he welcomed me into his office. As I started to explain my situation and the fact that I might have to be away for a while in fear of my safety, depending on how things went when I tried to end the relationship, the emotional weight of it all caught up with me. It was so traumatic to me to realize the end of my marriage that I could not control the tears rolling down my face.

Lee handed me a box of tissues. He was unemotional but expressed his concern, thanked me for letting him know, and said he would support me in whatever I needed to do.

As I got up to leave, Lee handed me one of his business cards with his personal contact information written on the back and told me to reach out to him if I needed help. His act of kindness meant so much to me.

Lee was one of the few people who knew what I was going through in my personal life. The rest of my coworkers were unaware, as I never talked about my personal life at work and maintained the appearance that everything was fine.

Then I came to work one Monday morning, and the OTEC secretary announced, "Bill died." I was in shock. He had gone home on Friday, had trouble breathing, sat in his easy chair, fell asleep, and suffered a heart attack. Bill's death hit me hard because he was my government boss and friend, but probably even more so because my emotional reserves were low given what I was going through at home.

At Bill's funeral, I could not stop crying; though it was inaudible, the tears streamed down my face nonstop. After the service, one of my Scitor colleagues walked over, hugged me, and held me for a while. He had no idea what I was going through at home, but he was distraught at my grief, and his compassion touched me. I felt blessed to work with some people who were not only talented but also compassionate.

Once I had done all the required reading and research to draft the separation agreement and my lawyer had reviewed it, I resolved to take the first opportunity to present it to my husband. While the separation agreement was not well received initially, I asked him to take it to review and consider, pointing out he would get everything, and I would only keep my condo and what I had before the marriage. Our finances had always been separate, so that split was easy.

He used all kinds of fear and intimidation tactics to try and manipulate me to change my mind, but I was resolute. His behavior toward me could change in a moment, and he seemed to display multiple personalities going from friendly to hostile to everything in between. Thankfully, after repeated requests and trying to find people to help him move, he agreed to sign the separation agreement.

In the fall of 1999, he moved out. After he took the last item out of my condo and departed, I shut the door, sat down, and prayed. It felt like an evil spirit had left the place. That was such a huge relief. I told myself that I would learn from this horrific experience and then let it go—forgive and forget about him—and move on with my life. All night, I worried he might come back, but he didn't, and the next morning I had the locks changed. That was the first day of the rest of my life.

After the required six months of living separately, I filed for divorce. As fate would have it, the divorce decree was signed by the judge on the first day of spring in 2000—exactly five years from the day we met and just shy of three years of marriage.

I prayed to God that he would help me to be a better judge of character and to help me heal. I had two serious relationships before my marriage—one while I was in college and one while I was working for Kodak—both with nice Christian men close to my same age. In each instance, most people assumed we would get married, but in time we realized we had more personal growth and discovery to do before making that commitment. Comparing those two relationships to my failed marriage, I realized that had I chosen to marry either one of them, we could have made it work because we had sincerely good intentions, healthy hearts, and shared our Christian faith.

In the case of my ex-husband, his heart was not healthy—it was poisoned with a cancer of lies and manipulation. Though my ex could act like he had it all together and was happy and healthy, deep inside he was not, for no one who is truly happy and healthy would treat another human being as he treated me. Though my ex called himself a Christian, his behavior after we wed demonstrated he was not. Driven by his sinful nature and selfish desires, he was a Christian in name only. Only God can change a heart like that.

We are all spiritual beings, and a person cannot be spiritually whole until they truly surrender their life to Christ and follow Him daily. That's what it means to be a Christian. This involves accepting God's forgiveness and grace to change and extending that same forgiveness and grace to others. You only hurt yourself if you hang on to offense. Unforgiveness will hold you back from realizing your full potential and fulfilling your purpose in life. By forgiving, you find freedom, which is the key to victory.

Unforgiveness will hold you back from realizing your full potential and fulfilling your purpose in life. By forgiving, you find freedom, which is the key to victory.

The Bible says, "By this everyone will know that you are my disciples, if you love one another" (John 13:35, NIV). I realized my ex was genuinely incapable of loving someone else. In a way, I pitied him. We're all flawed people due to our sinful nature. Suppose we truly repent and ask for forgiveness when we fall short of how we should live, constantly work to be the best we can be, and continually strive to edify those with whom we are in a relationship. In that case, we will be true to our calling because life is all about relationships.

God gives his love to us unconditionally. When we receive that gift, we can give it to others through our words and actions. We are to love others as God loves us, which means loving them unconditionally without expecting anything in return. That is not easy, so we must ask God to teach us to love how he does. Once we receive God's unconditional love for us, we can consciously love others.

Jesus said, "It is more blessed to give than to receive" (Acts 20:35, ESV). When we place service to God above service to ourselves, we can demonstrate his love to others by blessing them. Loving someone else, encouraging them, meeting their needs, and helping to improve their life is one of the most rewarding things you can ever do. When we give to others, we are blessed in return. Imagine a relationship between two people who live this way—each focused on blessing and lifting up the other. I believe that is what God intended marriage to be.

Truthfully, it was difficult for me to share this life experience with you. I had buried it all deep in the recesses of my memory for decades as a coping mechanism so that I could forget about him, let go of the pain and suffering, and move on with my life, which I had done successfully. But after much prayer during my writing, I realized I needed to share this part of my life to provide a complete picture of what made me who I am today. All our experiences—good or bad—shape us.

All our experiences—good or bad—shape us.

Furthermore, I shared this harrowing experience with the belief that perhaps it would speak to someone who knows a person in a similar situation or is in one themselves. No one should stay in an abusive relationship. God does not want that for anyone. Abuse prevents you from experiencing God's peace and joy and keeps you from functioning optimally. The abuser will blame you for their behavior, try to manipulate you, tear you down, shatter your defenses, and attempt to trap you in any way they can to stay in the relationship.

While there are godly guidelines given to us regarding how to live our lives, which include making lifelong commitments and not taking them lightly, at the same time, we must recognize we live in a fallen world full of sinners.

Suppose both people in a relationship recognize their sinful nature and constantly work to overcome selfishness and be the best person they can be. In that case, they will be able to have a healthy relationship by striving to edify each other, not tearing one another down, and seeking forgiveness and restoration, not retaliation.

If not, at some point a person has to decide whether they will stay in an unhealthy relationship and lose themselves or whether to recognize the relationship's failure, cut their losses, learn from the experience, and move on.

I believe the enemy of our souls uses abusive situations to try and thwart God's plans. If you live with abuse, you will lose yourself. You'll be unable to become who you are meant to be or to fulfill God's purpose for your life.

Given my healthy family environment growing up, I knew what love was because it was demonstrated to me, and I understood my value as a human being because it was instilled in me. Many are not so fortunate. I learned a lot from this experience, as I had never been in an abusive relationship or witnessed someone exhibit radically different personalities and be so duplicitous. Because of this experience, I was no longer so naive, and I had data points that would cause me to put my radar up when I saw characteristics like that in the future. I've always said that if someone can learn from my painful experiences so they don't have to experience the pain themselves, my pain was worth it.

One of the hardest things about the divorce was losing contact with my step kids. I had a good relationship with them; my ex's daughter and I had become especially close. His daughter sent me an email after she found out we were getting a divorce in which she said she wanted to stay in contact but was unsure how to navigate all this. I replied and said I understood and wanted her to know I would always care about her and wanted to be there for her and be her friend.

In time after the divorce was final, the emails from her dropped off. It was hard to lose contact with the kids but understandable. I imagined their mother supported our relationship as long as I was married to their dad because she knew I treated her kids well. Still, she probably wasn't as supportive of her daughter keeping a relationship with her "ex-stepmom" once we divorced. Regardless, I still think about the two of them. By now, they are adults and may have their own families, and I hope and pray they are healthy and happy.

If there was one good thing besides the new insights that came from this distressing time in my life, it was the fact that I built my first layer of thick skin. The constant beating, bruising, cutting, scabbing, and scarring had done it, but I was determined not to become calloused or cynical. I wasn't born with thick skin and was blessed to grow up in a loving family where I didn't need it. My thick skin was built up through the school of hard knocks and would come in handy later in my career.

Free to Thrive

After I was free from the abusive home environment, I felt more like myself and was able to start the healing process. I was genuinely able to excel and reach my potential. Lee was a great boss and also became a dear friend. He was there for me, believed in and empowered me through it all.

Lee was always there for others—present, helping them out, uplifting them. He was a giver who never thought of himself. At one point after we got to know each other better, I told Lee that I knew I was in his life to help him learn how to take a compliment. He raised his eyebrow and gave me his typical "Really? I'm not so sure" look. I am happy to say that over time he did learn to take a compliment; deep down, I think he truly valued the fact that I cared to tell him what I appreciated and admired about him.

We built a strong trust and became close friends. When I had big dreams of things we could do differently to provide even more benefits for our customers, Lee advocated corporate leaders give it a try. He trusted me and my judgment and believed that whatever I was working on was bound to be good. Time and time again that was proven to be the case.

CHAPTER 11

The Rebel Outpost

My job required me to travel frequently to sites around the country. One such site was known as The SouthWest, now Aerospace Data Facility South West (ADF-SW). The commander was Colonel (Col.) Ted Cope, USAF. This ops site was far from headquarters in Washington, DC, and the crew used that to their advantage to do innovative things for their customers, particularly the warfighters. They called themselves The Rebel Outpost and flew the Jolly Roger flag. One of their mottos was, "Do good. Ask forgiveness later."

Col. Cope was one of those larger-than-life leaders who was brilliant, had a quick wit, and a great sense of humor. He was easygoing and approachable and found a way to make things happen. Col. Cope and his team always welcomed me at ADF-SW and considered me an honorary member of the team, which meant a lot to me.

Here's a story that highlights the ADF-SW mission focus. The Director of the National Reconnaissance Office (DNRO) came to visit the site. That was a big deal. Col. Cope and his team gave the DNRO a tour and provided him with numerous briefings about all the good things they were doing.

They sought his feedback at the end of the day. The DNRO was thoughtful and said, "I realize you did not ask permission for any of these projects that you briefed me on today." The staff was a bit nervous upon hearing that remark. Then the DNRO continued, "It is good that you didn't ask permission from headquarters because we would have likely said no. But everything you have done is good for the mission and the warfighters." He appreciated their MO: "Do good. Ask forgiveness later."

This also drove home another point: no one knows better what needs to be done than those closest to the issue or, in warfighting terms, those closest to the fight. The best bosses recognize that and hire good people and empower them to do great things without requiring them to ask for permission before they do it. True leaders inspire a shared vision and provide the top cover for their team to thrive.

True leaders inspire a shared vision and provide the top cover for their team to thrive.

The government has baseline programs that are acquisition programs of record, which means their funding is part of the regular budget process. If you want to do something innovative outside the baseline program, getting funding can be difficult. The team at ADF-SW saw the value of the world wide web and wanted to prototype a capability for warfighters to access the data holdings at their site via the web.

The only baseline capability to access imagery was a NIMA program called Libraries. It relied on a client-server model, was custom-built, and was very expensive to operate and maintain. Towards the end of the fiscal year, the innovators at ADF-SW pooled leftover funds from various projects to fund an innovative initiative called the Web-based Archive and Retrieval Portal (WARP) via a contract with Harris Corp. Customers could access the WARP interface via a web browser and do searches to discover what imagery was available in their area of interest. Additionally, they could order the imagery electronically via the web browser. This web-based access to satellite imagery was revolutionary at the time.

The COTR for that contract when I started working with them in the late 1990s was Captain (Capt.) Joe Imwalle, USAF. He was quite a character. Joe was a few inches over six feet tall and very buff from his daily two-hour workouts. He had long sideburns that he kept just barely in compliance with USAF regulations. People called him Elvis. Joe was friendly, upbeat, and very sharp. He worked in an office with a few other Air Force officers, and they always did some good-natured kidding of one another.

Joe and I collaborated on enhancements and improvements to WARP and other data-access initiatives to benefit customers. Often when I was in town, Joe would invite me to join him at the gym for a workout, and he was the one who taught me how to do weightlifting.

In the summer of 1999, Joe got ready to transition to his next assignment. He introduced me to Capt. Christopher Quaid, USAF, who had recently arrived on station and would be taking over as the WARP COTR.

Chris had gone through ROTC at Southwest Texas State University, where he majored in psychology. Though he initially had a pilot slot, the USAF decided there were too many pilot slots in his year group, so he was reassigned to space operations. Chris's first assignment in the Air Force had been at Minot, North Dakota, where he worked in a missile silo. I would not want that job!

He was thrilled to have been brought to work in the national security space community by Maj. Regis Baldauff, USAF. Chris was a great communicator and enthusiastic champion for good causes but needed to become fluent in the technical aspects of the project. I had the technical expertise he lacked and trained him on what he needed to know about the systems.

The fact that Chris worked at ADF-SW and I worked at ADF-E, which were across the country from each other, made it challenging to collaborate on teleconferences together, as we couldn't lean over to talk to each other in a sidebar conversation. This was long before we had a chat capability on computer systems. I learned there was a way to send a popup message to someone's computer screen using the Microsoft Disk Operating System (MS-DOS) prompt and a command called "net send." So, we would open Command Prompt windows on telecons and "net send" messages to each other. Chris would send me a message when he had a question, and I would reply.

As the government official leading the project, Chris needed to know the right questions to ask, and the information I messaged him in real time helped him do just that. He would joke that by sharing my technical knowledge and insights with him via this messaging system, I made him look brilliant on calls with his technical prowess and expertise. That was our secret.

Chris also loved to prank his coworkers using this system. You can imagine a coworker's reaction when they received a popup on their screen informing them that the commander wanted to see them in his office immediately! Eventually, the secret got out, and more people started using this system to message each other.

We were great business partners, and it soon became known across the community that Weslander and Quaid were a dynamic duo who made good things happen in support of the warfighters. Chris and I did things that had not been done before and that some considered impossible. Around this time, I got the call sign, Warrior Princess.

The government leadership and the warfighters applauded us for taking the initiative. In time, my corporate leadership recognized these contributions as well.

One example is a concept paper I wrote called Virtual Archive Portal (VAP). There were data holdings in different archives in various locations across the country. Still, there was no way to do a single search of metadata to see everything available throughout the enterprise, let alone retrieve it. WARP only enabled a web search and retrieval for the satellite imagery holdings at ADF-SW. VAP provided that search capability enterprise-wide, as we enjoy with Google and other enterprise search engines today, and the ability to retrieve satellite imagery from a remote archive.

Scitor held an annual Tools, Techniques, and Technologies conference known as T3, and Lee encouraged me to submit a paper on VAP. The feedback I received after presenting the VAP paper at T3 2002 was tremendous. My colleagues saw the value, and so did our government customers.

Chris contracted the VAP capability with Harris Corp. and had it built and implemented. Two decades later, VAP is still considered a mission-critical system, meaning it is an essential service for operations, and the status is briefed at the DNRO's morning meeting each day.

Leadership

I've been fortunate to work with people who embodied great leadership qualities throughout my career. Lee made tremendous contributions in his own right and was also a great manager of people. He had wisdom and insight. Despite Lee's strong presence, you knew he cared and gave credit where it was due.

Chris was similar to Lee in that regard. He was highly competent and surrounded himself with good people. Chris always sought opportunities to praise his team members, let them give presentations on their projects, and publicly credit them for their work.

Speaking of great leaders that I met at this time in my life, two USAF colonels, now retired, had a tremendously positive impact on me. One was David "Sparky" Olsen, and the other was Kris Henley. They were two government officials who saw no badge type and no class system. It did not matter if you were a military member, government civilian, or industry partner, which some people called "contractor." We were all one team, and they focused on who was the best person for the job, regardless of their employer. Furthermore, they welcomed and expected every team member to speak up as peers, irrespective of rank.

Sparky was a commander who set a great example as a leader. He created a one-team culture with a bias to *make it happen*. Always approachable, Sparky was open to hearing new ideas about how to make ops more efficient and effective in supporting our customers, who were the national decision-makers and the warfighters. He also opened the morning ops-intel briefings, previously only given to the commander and site leadership, to everyone who worked on-site. This afforded anyone—whether an engineer, scientist, analyst, secretary, security officer, or janitor—to see the impact of their efforts on the mission, in aggregate with everyone else's.

There were a couple of innovative programs instituted under Sparky's leadership. One was Make It Happen, and the other was Ideas In Action. These programs helped to create a one-team culture.

Make It Happen was a training course open to everyone working on-site. This included the security guards and janitorial staff, analysts and engineers, managers and secretaries, and everyone in between. They ran classes at various times to accommodate different work schedules.

During a session, one of the security guards remarked that he appreciated being included, adding that often people walked past him and never acknowledged his presence, let alone said hello. This shocked me, as I knew all the security guards at the site, always made eye contact with them and said hello. Some had become good friends.

One day, a few coworkers rode with me in my car, returning from a meeting. They were very impressed when, as we entered the front gate, the head guard with JD on his name tag stepped out of the guard shack, took off his hat, and did a ceremonious bow as I drove up. I laughed, and he gave me a big grin.

It was hard to think that some people wouldn't give the guards the time of day, but it was clear the site leadership was intentionally trying to mix us all together to create a one-team atmosphere where no person's role was viewed as more important than another's. The leadership was making it clear we all had a part to play in supporting the mission, and I appreciated that.

To solidify this *make it happen* attitude, they handed out laminated cards at the end of the course with a hole punched so we could hang them on our badge lanyards. One side was in a red/orange/yellow gradient and said, "NO," with a list of the usual reasons people said no. The other side was in a green/blue gradient and said, "YES! Make It Happen." The charge here was that if someone started to tell you no, you were to hold up the NO side of the card and then ask how to get to YES! Make It Happen. Brilliant!

Ideas In Action was complementary to Make It Happen. The site commander wanted to be sure all good ideas had an opportunity to be heard, and he recognized that people doing the day-to-day work knew best what improvements we could make. He also realized that not every manager between him and the person with the idea would support it. So he wanted to provide a way for people to "skip echelon" and get their ideas directly to him anonymously if desired. They created an Ideas In Action website for people to be able to provide submissions electronically and installed Ideas In Action lockboxes around the site for people who wanted to submit their ideas that way.

This initiative led to the implementation of some great ideas that better supported the mission and saved a lot of taxpayer dollars. One such idea ultimately led to the site receiving the Vice President's Hammer Award, created to recognize government efficiency, in stark contrast to "yesterday's government and its $400 hammer."

One example of such out-of-the-box thinking pertained to satellite imagery collection and delivery of imagery products—specifically, how the imagery tasked and collected by the satellites was delivered to the customer. The government had a courier system to transfer and deliver classified documents, including imagery on film flats. The issue was that once a customer requested an image, they could not be sure when it would be collected. Once it was collected, they had no idea when it would be delivered. Furthermore, there was no tracking system, so customers never knew what day their package would show up.

In contrast, the commercial sector shipping companies like FedEx had implemented tracking systems for packages. That system noted when FedEx received a package for delivery and when it was delivered to the recipient. Someone working on this issue daily at the ops site wondered why we couldn't do the same. That's when the idea came—why not use FedEx to deliver the classified imagery film flats?

We all heard the collective gasp of the national security enterprise. Who could propose such a heretical idea?

The site commander didn't think the idea was crazy. He reached out to the head of FedEx, who was open to the concept. They cleared him, and we started shipping classified film flats via FedEx. Genius! This saved the taxpayers a lot of money, and customers knew when to expect their packages.

Col. Kris Henley was the commander at an ops facility, The Blue Cube, in California. He was a friend of Sparky's and very like-minded. One time when I visited the ops site in California, I got stuck in security because they could not "find" my clearances. The government has this highly antiquated process of "passing clearances," often via fax, in advance of a visit. If they genuinely cared about security, they would look up a person's clearance status in real-time via a computer system, but old processes die hard. Many years later, I would be able to effect positive change in this regard.

Once I got through security, I could not reach my contact to escort me to Col. Henley's office. So, I called the front office to let them know I was in the lobby and needed an escort. A few minutes later, Col. Henley, the site commander, greeted me and escorted me to his office. He was so down-to-earth and affable. Kris and Sparky were both that way.

CHAPTER 12

Collaboration

Scitor was a Systems Engineering and Technical Assistance (SETA) contractor for the government. They hired top-notch people and then put them on contract to augment government teams. Scitor didn't build anything. Instead, their people were their business, and they took good care of their employees, all considered individual contributors. Scitor encouraged individual contributors working on related programs to collaborate, so we would have summits on topics of common interest.

At an ops summit in 1999, some of us who supported IMINT operations started talking with people who supported SIGINT operations. We discussed the potential benefit of connecting the two enterprises—America's eyes and ears—to have better situational awareness. It made sense to us though it hadn't been done before.

Our SIGINT colleagues informed us there was a tool on NSA's network called Collaborative Virtual Workspace (CVW). That tool came from an office at NSA led by Justin Wilson. It was the brainchild of a bunch of gamers who thought about how a virtual world might be beneficial to helping people collaborate across NSA's global enterprise.

As the story goes, Justin and his team went door to door in the hallowed halls of NSA at Ft. Meade and asked people what they were working on. If they needed to collaborate with others, they would reply, "Have we got a tool for you!" In time, those people told two friends, and so on and so on. Before you knew it, they reached a tipping point, as described in Malcolm Gladwell's book. It became standard operating procedure (SOP) for NSAers to come into work, log in to the NSA network, and log in to the CVW tool.

We got the idea that enabling IMINTers to access and use CVW would help facilitate collaboration across the intelligence disciplines.

CVW was developed by MITRE, a Federally Funded Research and Development Center (FFRDC), which meant the government paid for and owned the technology. The trouble was that CVW was not web-based. It was developed back in the client-server days, which meant that for someone to have access to the tool, they had to have access to the network where the tool was hosted.

You'd think that extending a network from one classified government facility SCIF to another classified government facility SCIF would not be too complicated, but it was. It took an eighteen-month policy battle to extend the NSA network to our non-NSA ops facility SCIF.

One of the issues was a disconnect between NSA's and NIMA's respective sharing policies. NSA was "five-eyes," an alliance comprising Canada, Australia, New Zealand, the United Kingdom (UK), and the US. However, NIMA was only "four-eyes," an alliance comprising only four of those countries—New Zealand was excluded. That seemingly minor difference caused significant issues, and we could not figure out why there was a difference in policy at that time. Years later, I would figure this out and be able to do something about it.

Once we finally got NSA's network extended into our non-NSA ops facility SCIF in 2000, we could train the staff on how to use CVW. We had identified a Marine Corps Training in Urban Environment Exercise (TRUEX) called Shadow Tracker that would be run later that year and enable us to test our theory. We believed connecting the two intelligence disciplines—their collection managers, engineers, and analysts—via this virtual collaborative environment would enable shared situational awareness. This would afford the national security enterprise insight into the combatant commander's intent. They would be able to task systems to do intelligence collection in a more timely manner, thereby making the national technical means (NTM) assets, meaning the highly classified reconnaissance satellites, relevant to a tactical fight.

First, we had to find some people at NIMA willing to learn the CVW tool and a new way of doing business that could prove beneficial. This was a challenge, as most did not see any reason to change. Though many at NIMA were resistant, I found someone willing to give it a chance. Rikki Frintz, a former USAF HUMINT officer, was a seasoned, no-nonsense collection manager. She quickly became proficient in CVW. Realizing the capabilities of the tool and the power in the connection it provided to her counterparts at NSA, Rikki grew to be very supportive of this collaboration. She became one of the key players from NIMA in the upcoming Shadow Tracker exercise.

Michele's CVW icon (2000)

At the time, collaboration tools like CVW were not common. We had no live video, but everyone had an icon with their picture on it, so we got used to seeing people's faces in the virtual rooms. We learned the lingo of the other intelligence discipline and the players' names by conversing with them in this virtual environment. Those who embraced CVW learned the power of that virtual connection in building relationships, something self-evident today.

During downtime between training sessions, I got to know my training colleague at the SIGINT site, whom I had never met in person. His name was Myron, and I learned a lot about him, his family, and his career over many weeks of training sessions. Though we had never met in person, we became good friends.

Then the funniest thing happened months later when we were both at a big IC conference. I was sitting in the lobby waiting for someone, and he walked by. The thought crossed my mind for a split second: "Is that Myron?" I could not be sure because I had never seen him in person before—only the tiny icon of his face. A similar thought crossed his mind as he stopped dead in his tracks, looked back at me, and said, "Michele?" I said, "Myron?" We both laughed and said it was good to finally meet each other. Though we had never met in person before that time, we had built a relationship and felt like old friends by collaborating virtually for so long. I had similar experiences after meeting other CVW colleagues for the first time that day, but there was no one that I'd spent more hours with than Myron. It was like we were battle buddies.

A core group of us traveled to Yuma, Arizona, to be boots on the ground with the Marines doing the Shadow Tracker exercise. I love the Marines. My two uncles were Marines in the Vietnam war era, and my cousin Jerry Weslander was a Marine Corps sniper. The remark made by President Ronald Reagan is so appropriate: "Some people wonder all their lives if they've made a difference. The Marines don't have that problem."

The military breaks its traditional functions out by code. For example, Intel has code 2, Ops has code 3, and Comms has code 6. Each service has a different prefix. For the Marines, it was S, so the intel chief was the S2. That person was Major (Maj.) Dan Rodman. He welcomed and incorporated us into his operation so we could get to know his battle rhythm.

We had secured special permission to do collection over the United States and only for the footprint of the military installation as IC assets' intended use is for foreign intelligence gathering only. At the start of each day, Maj. Rodman would brief the Commander's Intent, which was the priorities for that day. Because of their connection through CVW, the collection managers for the national intelligence assets heard the commander's priorities. Then, without circumventing any established processes, they could effectively fast-track the necessary collection.

The Shadow Tracker exercise scenario was designed to address an issue we had faced in a previous conflict in Kosovo with what they call "short on-time emitters." In wartime, enemy radars shut down, move, change frequencies, and go into short on-time, electronically agile modes. SIGINT would get a hit on these emitters, meaning they would detect them, but by the time we got an image of the location where the emission had been detected, the mobile emitter was long gone.

We had to shorten the timeline of the tipping and queueing, i.e., SIGINT tipping IMINT to a target of interest and then queuing tasking for an IMINT asset to take a picture. By implementing new business processes using CVW—getting each participant to put their information in the virtual room where everyone could see it and enabling everyone to hear the commander's intent and talk with each other—we were able to shorten the timelines. This enabled national imagery collection to be relevant to a tactical fight.

Our team was thrilled with this success. We had proven the value of a new way of doing business using an enabling technology. This could give us the advantage to win battles and save lives. I appreciated the visionary leadership of Dan Rodman, who remains a friend to this day. He was willing to try something new, which set a precedent for what could be done to better support military operations and save lives.

The book *Black Hawk Down* was released the year prior, and I read it before the exercise. That was such a poignant story of a day gone horribly wrong. The tragic loss of life documented in this book could have been avoided with more timely and relevant intelligence. The story was a battle cry to effect necessary change within the IC, particularly in support of the warfighter. Migrating from siloed operations to collaborative operations shortened timelines, enabling us to provide more timely and relevant national intelligence. If we could make this SOP across the intelligence agencies, we could hopefully avoid another *Black Hawk Down* scenario.

The Director of Central Intelligence (DCI), George Tenet, ran the CIA and oversaw the entire IC. He recognized the success of our efforts through Shadow Tracker and awarded our team the Meritorious Unit Citation at CIA headquarters on 23 March 2001.

Based on our proven success and the DCI's recognition of the value, we thought the intelligence agencies would embrace this new collaborative way of doing business. We were wrong. Bureaucracies are loathe to change. Often it takes the pressure of an external force to cause the change, and we had no idea how soon that would come. It took the terrorist attacks of 11 September 2001, which occurred about six months after we received the Meritorious Unit Citation, to get the leadership in each of the agencies to be open to considering a new way of doing business.

Scitor executives took notice of the positive impact of my efforts and recognized my leadership in making it all happen. They promoted me to chief engineer, the company's highest technical position. I was the youngest to become a chief engineer in the company's history and only the second female to attain the rank.

A Vision for the Future

Despite the IC agencies' resistance to change, leaders like Col. Olsen and Col. Henley recognized there was great value in integrating IMINT and SIGINT operations. They discussed how we could take this grassroots collaboration to the next level.

Col. Henley had moved from California to be the commander at a SIGINT ops facility in Colorado, now known as Aerospace Data Facility Colorado (ADF-C). An imagery analyst named Mike was embedded there, and his work supporting SIGINT operations was already proving to be very valuable.

After the success of Shadow Tracker, these leaders saw the potential benefit of embedding someone from the imagery side who was also technical. The colonels told me that even though I was not a government employee, they believed I was the best person for the job. I had the necessary technical skills as a systems engineer and image scientist. More importantly, I was one of the leaders of the grassroots effort to further information sharing and collaboration between the two intelligence disciplines to benefit the national decision-makers and the warfighters.

When I discussed the opportunity with Lee, he was thoughtful. He said he would miss having me on his team in Virginia. However, he would support my moving to Colorado as he saw the potential value to the national security community and knew I wanted to pursue this opportunity. Lee got the Scitor corporate leadership to agree and remained my boss. Good bosses realize that to retain good people, you must let them grow. Lee demonstrated this characteristic when this opportunity arose for me in Colorado.

I was fortunate to have groups of friends in Virginia and Colorado who would invite me to join them in activities. After my divorce, I realized that because I didn't have a dad at home in my childhood and did not date much before I married, perhaps I could learn to be a better judge of character if I got to know more people. So when certain single male colleagues with whom I had a friendly relationship but did not know well asked me to go out with them, I agreed. None of these relationships became serious, but we had fun times together and remained friends. Even years later, when we crossed paths, there was always a friendly hello and often a hug.

It was good for me to socialize, and it was therapeutic to realize I wasn't perceived as "damaged goods" because I was a divorcée. A lot of people respected me, valued me, and enjoyed spending time with me. This was all part of my healing process.

The team of Multi-INT collaborators spanned the US operations facilities. I had become good friends with all of them through our shared experiences and also had the opportunity to meet some of their family members at social events. Most of them were married and seemed concerned that I was single. They would say, "How is a lady like you single? We have to fix this!" I told them I was happy being single until the right man entered my life, but that did not deter their matchmaking attempts. One couple set me up on a blind date, only to realize later that the only thing the guy and I had in common was we were both single. Some of you reading this can surely relate.

On the other end of the spectrum, I was taken aback by the remark a married colleague made to me one day while a group of us were on a business trip. We had all gathered together for a meal and were headed back to our hotel rooms when he asked if I would stay because he wanted to talk with me. I obliged but was in no way prepared for what he would say. He informed me he was very attracted to me and thought we could have a great physical relationship that could go on indefinitely. The way he propositioned me, it was clear he was confident this was an opportunity I would not want to pass up. He was wrong.

After I found my voice, I told him no and said I was shocked and horrified that he would ever suggest such a thing being a married man. To me, it was out of the question—impossible and unacceptable. Then I reminded him that he had an awesome wife who was beautiful and talented and could have an amazing career in her own right but had chosen to stay home and was a wonderful mother to their young children. It just so happened that I had become friends with her, so I knew her personally. I told him it was unconscionable to me that he would ever think of cheating on her, let alone with me.

Because of the heartache it would cause his wife to know he propositioned me, I never mentioned it to her. She deserved better than this, and he had demonstrated by his behavior that he was not worthy of her. I told him that because we had to work together and see each other socially, I would pretend we never had this conversation. Then I left.

Things were never the same between us after that. It was clear he had assumed I would jump at the opportunity to be his mistress and that my refusal bruised his ego. We had been a part of a group of friends for a few years, but it was always awkward being around him after that. Though I wanted nothing to do with him, I remained friendly with his wife because I considered her a personal friend. From then on, he became extremely competitive and progressively more adversarial toward me.

A note to the ladies—if a man propositions you like this, recognize he is motivated by lust, not love. His focus is on how you can serve his needs and desires and what you can do for him. You deserve better. Wait for the man who loves you and wants to marry you and spend his life with you. That's the basis for a healthy relationship with a future.

Another married male colleague who had kids in high school mentioned he and his wife had focused on their children for so long that they had neglected their relationship. He felt like they should date again and asked me for some ideas. I told him I thought it would be very romantic if he planned a memorable getaway and surprised her. They could stay at a nice hotel, have a special dinner, and enjoy being together. First, he should discuss possible dates to ensure they worked in her schedule before looking at options. Once he planned the getaway, he should let her know the scheduled departure date and time, the length of the trip, and how to pack her suitcase, but keep the exact details a surprise. He thought that was a great idea and got to work making plans.

As the big weekend approached, he was so excited. "Wish me luck!" he said as he left work that Friday. I did and told him I looked forward to hearing how it went.

He was a transformed man when he came back to work. It was like he was on cloud nine. He told me he had taken his wife away to the finest hotel in a nearby city, and they had a wonderful weekend together—like a second honeymoon. I was so happy for him. He asked me how I had come up with the idea, and I told him it was something I thought would be fun to do when I was married.

Sadly, when I was married and could make trips like that, my husband didn't want to do anything with me. It made him sad to hear me say that, but I told him I was happy to know the concept was a success and had proven valuable to him, his wife, and their relationship. He then told me his wife thought it was so wonderful that she was planning a surprise getaway for them. I thought that was awesome!

Rocky Mountain High

Having grown up on the West Coast—in California and Washington—I was excited to move back out west. During my travels to Colorado, I grew to love that area of the country with the mountains and over 300 days of sunshine.

By this time, I had made friendships with my colleagues in Colorado through our various collaborative initiatives. They were all married with families and thought I should move to what they called LoDo, which is a mixed-use historical district in lower downtown Denver. They imagined that was where a single person would want to be for all the social outlets—restaurants, galleries, shops, and nightlife.

However, I longed for something else. Growing up in apartments, or things called apartments, I wanted to have a single-family home—my own space with no shared wall, floor, or ceiling.

While house shopping, I found a new community being built in Parker, where many of my colleagues and their families lived. When I entered the sales office, the two ladies who greeted me were impressed that a young woman was looking to buy her first single-family home. After I signed the sales contract in the spring of 2001, they celebrated with me.

When my married friends questioned why I, a single woman aged thirty-one going on thirty-two, would choose to buy a single-family home in suburbia rather than live downtown, I told them I wanted my own space where I could play my music as loud as I pleased without disturbing the neighbors. I didn't expect them to understand that this was a significant milestone for me.

I've often jokingly referred to my time embedded in SIGINT ops as a foreign exchange program because I was in a new environment where the technical jargon and new acronyms made me feel like I was in a foreign country. Thankfully, I'd already learned some SIGINT lingo through my collaboration via CVW with the SIGINTers. Once immersed in the environment, I could better understand their language, along with the nuances of the SIGINT system and the unique authorities, so that I could converse fluently as an IMINTer with the SIGINTers.

In addition, by my mere presence on site, I became part of the SIGINT enterprise and came under the authority of the Director of NSA (DIRNSA), whom they called "dirn-sa." This enabled me to access datasets I previously did not have access to, which I realized could be very beneficial for IMINTers in performing their mission. However, the existing policies did not allow it. A couple of years later, I would be in a position to help fix that.

CHAPTER 13

Another Day That Will Live in Infamy

This takes me back to the story I told at the beginning of this book. On 11 September 2001, I was at CIA headquarters in McLean, Virginia, to give a presentation when terrorists hijacked four commercial airliners mid-flight. They ran two airplanes into the Twin Towers of the World Trade Center in New York City and one of them into the Pentagon in Arlington, Virginia. It is believed that the terrorists intended to fly the fourth airplane into the White House or the US Capitol building, but some brave passengers who learned other planes had been hijacked decided to stop them, and the aircraft crashed in a field in Somerset County, Pennsylvania.

That was a seminal moment for our country and our national security community. After this horrific event, leaders across the IC started being open to ideas about new ways of doing business, and things started changing for the better. There was a corporate realization that the intelligence apparatus had failed to connect the dots, i.e., failed to figure out this attack was coming and provide timely warning to the appropriate decision-makers.

Though I was scheduled to return home to Colorado at the conclusion of my business trip, I remained in the Washington, DC, area for two weeks following the terrorist attacks. After my hotel stay ended, I stayed with my mom, who was living in Alexandria, Virginia. It's times like that when you appreciate being with family.

My mom worked in information technology (IT) at the Red Cross, and they were busy planning for extended emergency response. She would eventually be sent to New York City for three weeks to help set up long-term operations there.

In early March 2002, I took the train to visit her in New York City, and we went to Ground Zero together. Our first opportunity was at night. As I walked up the ramp near St. Paul's Chapel and saw the gaping hole where the Twin Towers used to be and the devastation all around, I could not stop the tears streaming down my face. That is a scene I will never forget. The following day when we returned, I was more prepared, but it was still a horrific sight.

My mom and I were both fortunate because we had things to do in response to the terrorist attacks, which kept us busy. So many Americans just stared in horror at the TV and had no idea what to do.

Though I had completed the original purpose of my business trip to Washington, DC, in the wake of the tragedy, there was plenty of additional work to do in town. So I returned to ADF-E, where I once worked and helped in whatever way I could. The building had an atrium you had to walk through to get from the main building to an addition where the teams I was primarily working with were located.

In the atrium were photos of two colleagues who worked for Boeing Satellite Systems in El Segundo, CA. They had been on TDY and boarded American Airlines flight 77 out of Washington Dulles Airport, which the terrorists flew into the Pentagon. Chandler "Chad" Keller was a lead propulsion engineer and project manager, and Ruben Ornedo was a lead engineer in the systems engineering organization. They were both newlyweds and were returning home that morning to their brides in California. They never made it. Each time I passed by their photos, I was reminded that we were doing this work on their behalf and on behalf of all those who lost their lives that day.

Our grassroots team of multi-discipline intelligence (Multi-INT) collaborators went into high gear. Everyone was on CVW working to coordinate efforts, even if it wasn't SOP.

Myron started working fourteen-hour days seven days a week in what came to be known as The War Room at ADF-C. This relatively small room, which would become his office for months, was filled with six different workstations on classified networks at various security levels, plus various secure phone networks and a secure video teleconferencing (VTC) system.

Myron had been in the military and built relationships with the warfighters so that they came to trust him. He used an internet relay chat called mIRC, or "merk" chat, to connect to the warfighters downrange via SIPRNET, which was the DoD's Secret Collateral network used for mission planning. In time, the warfighters felt comfortable sharing high-level information with Myron regarding ops they were doing so they could get support from the broader SIGINT enterprise through him.

Eventually, that support extended to the IMINT enterprise, as well, via CVW collaboration. Myron would have to take the information he got on the SIPRNET workstation and then roll his chair over to a different workstation and type messages to people on the other networks. No universal network connected everyone at a single security level, let alone at all security levels. Furthermore, there was no internet access. The only "open-source intelligence" was on TV. We needed to fix this. Years later, I would be in the position to prototype a solution.

During my extended stay in Washington, DC, I worked to get buy-in and top cover for our efforts to collaborate across the IC. This included breaking through the policy barriers to enable better interconnectivity between the agencies, which would facilitate information sharing.

We found an advocate in the former DNRO, Jeff Harris. As you can imagine, he was very well connected. Jeff came to ADF-E to see what we were doing via CVW and thought it was great. We then brainstormed about who else he could invite to see what we were doing. Jeff knew we needed top cover, which was hard for him to give since he was no longer a government official. We also needed someone who could help enact necessary policy changes.

To that end, Jeff invited the IC Chief Information Officer (CIO) to visit. Upon learning what we were doing, the IC CIO endorsed our efforts. It was a big deal for me to meet these luminaries of the IC because it is not typical for an industry partner to get that chance. You may hear of them and revere them, but you rarely get the opportunity to interact with such senior officials.

Jeff and I hit it off. One thing that impressed me was how down-to-earth he was, particularly given his former position. Jeff was wicked smart but lighthearted and liked to make points with humor, which I like to do too.

He told me about a sailboat he was buying—a J/105. While I'd never sailed before, that sounded like fun. Years later, Jeff invited me to join his sailboat racing team. He knew I had not sailed before but was willing to learn the ropes. I gave myself the title of swabbie. We sailed from his house in Arnold, Maryland, and often found ourselves racing against the midshipmen from the US Naval Academy. We had great talks on those sails, and I enjoyed those days on the water.

After working in Washington, DC, for two weeks following the terrorist attacks, I finally flew home to Colorado. It was hard to remember where I had parked my car in the massive airport parking garage. Little did I know that in the coming year, when I would fly over 100,000 miles on United Airlines alone at a time when most Americans were not flying out of fear, this would become an issue as all my trips started blurring together. I made a point to write my parking space on the back of my parking garage ticket and put it in my wallet.

When I pulled into my driveway, a neighbor across the street came running over to me. She said that she was glad to see me. They were worried when they didn't see me for two weeks after the terrorist attacks, and she felt bad she had never said hello to me since I moved into the community six months prior. I thanked her for her concern and for saying hello. It was nice to meet her.

In a way, the days, weeks, and months after the terrorist attacks were a special time in America. People became aware of those around them that they may not have truly seen before. They set aside their differences and worked together toward a common cause, helping each other along the way.

There is no better example of this than how the people of New York City came together. It was beautiful to see. After the terrorist attacks, their number-one identity was something they shared in common—they were all New Yorkers.

We were reminded that, despite our differences, we were all Americans. Our enemies thought they could defeat us and bring us to our knees. Instead, we forgot our differences and came together to support one another and fight a common enemy. We stood united to rebuild our communities at home and combat terrorism overseas. The American people are resilient. We proved that the American spirit is strong.

We were reminded that, despite our differences, we were all Americans. We came together to support one another and fight a common enemy. We proved that the American spirit is strong.

My workdays following the attacks consisted of early mornings and late nights. I would have a cup of coffee while I got ready for work and then drive to my office on Buckley Air Force Base. During the day, I was so busy that all I would eat was a granola bar. When I got home late at night, I would have a bowl of soup and then go to bed exhausted. That was my life for many months. What kept me going was the mission and supporting those bringing the fight to the terrorists on their home turf so they would not come to ours.

Jeff Harris continued to network and socialize what we were doing to promote Multi-INT information sharing and collaboration. Before long, I was asked to return to Washington, DC, to give a presentation to the director of the Community Management Staff (CMS) and the deputy directors of the CIA, who all reported directly to DCI George Tenet.

Before that briefing, I wondered to Myron how I could effectively communicate what we were up against with the current systems and policies that did not support collaboration and information sharing. In the spirit of "a picture's worth a thousand words," Myron had a great idea—take a photo of The War Room. This idea had not immediately come to mind as cameras were not allowed in SCIFs. However, a person was authorized to take pictures on-site, and we got that photo. Then I used an image processing tool to blur all the computer screens, so there was nothing sensitive visible, thereby enabling us to share the picture at the unclassified level. It was funny that years later, that photo was in a briefing presented to me and somehow made its way onto Wikipedia.

As I entered CIA headquarters to give my presentation, I walked over the seal of the CIA on the marble floor. I also noted a Bible verse etched into the wall: "And ye shall know the truth, and the truth shall make you free" (John 8:32, KJV). Then I was escorted to the room where the meeting would take place. There I was introduced to the Director of CMS, Joan Dempsey, one of the first power women of the IC, and the Deputy Director for Collection, Charles "Charlie" Allen, a living legend. Both reported to

DCI Tenet. So much weighed on this briefing and their response. While I kept a poker face, my heart was racing inside.

We needed diversity of thought, experiences, and perspectives; without this, we risked failures of imagination.

In my presentation, I spoke about the challenges we faced concerning information sharing and collaboration due to the policies in place, or lack thereof. For one, IC components had been trained to work in isolation from each other, effectively in agency "silos," due to different classifications and program compartmentations and the philosophy of "need to know." The IC as a whole needed a change in mindset—they had to move from "need to know" to "need to share," or we would have no hope of ever connecting the dots. We needed diversity of thought, experiences, and perspectives; without this, we risked failures of imagination. DCI Tenet controlled the policy for the IC and could effect necessary change.

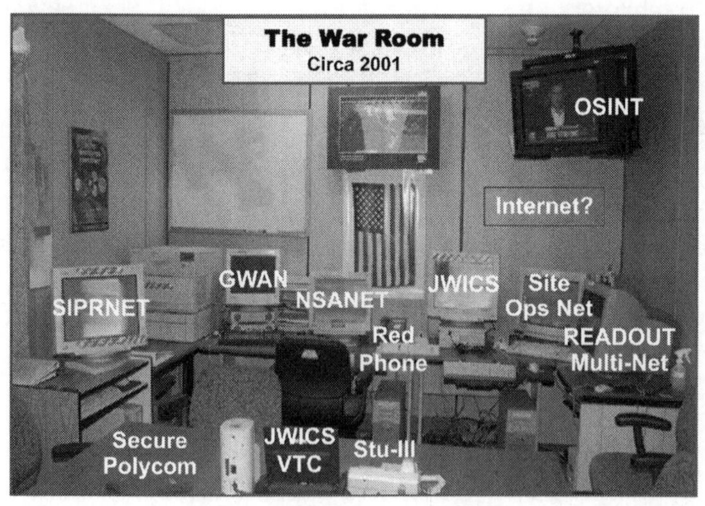

The War Room at ADF-C (2001)

The War Room photo proved to be a picture worth a thousand words. Once they saw that image, they understood the problem and wanted to help.

They told me there was no policy preventing this collaboration; the DCI had already written a policy stating it could be done.

Therein lies an issue. The DCI's policy made collaboration optional. Some people used the fact that collaboration was optional to collaborate because it needed to be done; others used the fact that collaboration was optional as an excuse not to collaborate and as a reason to prevent others from doing so. The DCI needed to write clarifying language in the form of a new directive to mandate information sharing and collaboration across the IC. They committed to doing what they could to help.

The response I received from these top CIA officials was encouraging. Afterward, one of the CIA officers who had helped set up the meeting said, "Great job! Aren't you excited?" I said, "Yes." Then she remarked, "It is hard to tell as you have kept a poker face the entire time." I told her that was intentional.

The poker face is something Lee taught me because when we first met, I had not yet mastered it—my facial expressions could tell all, even if I did not say a word. A couple of years prior, after a particular meeting with some IC colleagues, one of my coworkers came up to me and said, "You didn't believe a single thing that guy was saying, did you?" I told him that was true, but I had not said a word. He replied, "Oh, you didn't have to. I could tell from the expression on your face. Your eyebrow was over your head [like Mr. Spock from Star Trek]." Point taken. Years later, this experience proved I had finally mastered the poker face.

Then on 17 October 2001, I was part of a team briefing the new Director of NIMA (DNIMA), Lieutenant General (Lt. Gen.) James "Jim" Clapper, USAF (retired), at ADF-E. He had taken the helm of NIMA just two days after the terrorist attacks. Our mutual friend, Jeff Harris, arranged the meeting. Specifically, I was to brief DNIMA about the CVW collaboration capability and how we had used it to enable NTM assets to be more timely and relevant to the tactical fight. We proposed to leverage this tool to connect America's IMINT and SIGINT enterprises so they could better coordinate collection in response to the needs of the warfighters and national decision-makers.

This would require a change to the way business had been done for decades, and that change would need to be driven from the top. Given he had worked in SIGINT ops as part of his military career and was now the director of the premiere IMINT agency, we were hoping DNIMA Clapper would appreciate what we were proposing.

For whatever reason, some people at both NIMA and NSA did not want to see this change happen and fought it. Fortunately, Rikki, a seasoned IMINT collection manager, had seen firsthand through the Shadow Tracker exercise what a difference the collaboration via CVW had made. She had gone straight to CVW after the terrorist attacks to coordinate efforts with her SIGINT collection management counterparts. Rikki spoke up during the meeting, endorsing the value of collaboration via CVW. Unfortunately, her voice was drowned out by the naysayers and bureaucrats who insisted that was not how they did business.

As it turns out, DNIMA had heard of me and this initiative before that meeting. Specifically, he had been told I was an industry partner leading Multi-INT information sharing and collaboration efforts. DNIMA later told me he had advocated for that when he was still in uniform as a USAF general. During the meeting, he remarked to the people gathered that he had grown up in SIGINT, and now as DNIMA, he inherently understood the value of doing business in a more collaborative and integrated way. He was very open and receptive to what I shared in the briefing and supported Multi-INT information sharing and collaboration.

Given DNIMA's support of furthering information sharing and collaboration between NIMA and NSA and his interest and enthusiasm for what we proposed, my colleagues and I left the meeting upbeat. The opponents were not happy with that outcome, and I had no idea the lengths they'd go to stop it—including shooting the messenger.

Lee called me the next day and said we needed to meet with Col. Sparky Olsen. I was surprised to hear what Sparky had to share.

After the meeting with DNIMA, a man who was a senior executive member of the NIMA staff who worked at ADF-E went to a woman who was a senior executive at NRO. He intended to put a stop to all this talk of Multi-INT collaboration by taking me—the leader of the initiative—out.

This NIMA senior executive lied and told the NRO senior executive that I was a contractor trying to sell a tool developed by my company so I could make money for my company. In reality, MITRE, an FFRDC, developed

CVW; it was paid for and owned by the government. This man said other things that got her riled up. She then called Sparky.

He informed me her exact words to him about me were: "If she even breathes the word collaboration, I'll have her terminated from the contract and have her clearances pulled." Put another way, I would be fired from my job and no longer hold a national security clearance. I was in shock.

Sparky said it was clear this senior executive had been lied to and was now refusing to hear the truth. He looked at me and said, "You're right. She's wrong. But she won't listen to the truth. We cannot afford to lose you, so you need to lay low for a while."

Lee was dismayed about what had happened and agreed that I needed to stay below the radar for now. Sparky assured us he would work to ensure she heard the truth one way or another. He was confident this would eventually blow over, but he was unsure how long that would take.

Sparky defended me to his superior, and I am eternally grateful for that. When this powerful senior executive in his chain of command called and made that threat, it would have been politically expedient for Sparky to disown me then and there, but he didn't. He stuck up for me and protected me. Sparky saw the bigger picture and cared more about the mission than his future career. He knew we were in the right and what we were proposing had to be done, and he would not lose a leader of the movement.

In combat, Lee and Sparky are the people you would want in the foxhole with you. They are the type of leaders you would follow into a battle for a good cause—even if it looks like a suicide mission—because you know with certainty that they've "got your six," which means they've got your back.

Life of a Change Agent

The only thing constant is change.
~ Heraclitus, Greek philosopher

The life of a change agent is not easy but can be very rewarding. A challenge when trying to do something new is that people are often comfortable with the status quo and fear what they do not understand.

The new thing is seen as bad, as a threat, when in reality, it is good and a mission enabler.

At the time, I did not realize it, but through personal experience over the years, I've learned there are three stages of attack when people fear or are opposed to the change you are proposing. First, they attack what you are trying to do. Then, they attack you professionally. And if that doesn't work, they then attack you personally. At this point in my life, I've been at the receiving end of that attack cycle more times than I care to count, but I've lived to tell you about it. Despite people's attempts to intimidate and threaten me, my higher calling—the mission—always kept me going.

I've often said throughout my career, "It's all about trust and relationships." When you have trust in a relationship, you can do great things and accomplish what others might consider impossible. People may be willing to take a leap of faith and do something new that you are proposing if they know you are a person of integrity and can be depended on to do what you say you are going to do.

Reputation is also important. So, when I heard outrageous stories about myself, I was devastated and very concerned. Col. Henley told me not to worry and added, "All press is good press, Michele." I asked what he meant. He said that I was known only in some circles before all this happened. Due to the attention I was now getting—good or bad—I was known in a much broader arena. Col. Henley told me, "Regardless of what people have heard about you, they know you exist and respect the fact that you are a force to be reckoned with." In time, I realized he was right.

There was so much to do. Though I could not be so visible, I could still contribute behind the scenes. However, it seemed like forever that I had to stay below the radar. Eventually, after a couple of months, Sparky determined the coast was clear, and I could reengage as the leader of the Multi-INT information sharing and collaboration initiative. Col. Cope was now working at NRO headquarters, and he and I collaborated on meetings and presentations in the Washington, DC, area to further this objective.

Love to America

At the start of 2002, America was still dealing with the aftermath of the terrorist attacks, and New York City was still doing cleanup and rebuilding.

The Super Bowl halftime show that February is something I will never forget. The Irish rock band U2 headlined and played some of their popular songs. Then they started to sing "MLK," a eulogy to the late Rev. Dr. Martin Luther King, Jr., a leading civil rights activist assassinated on 4 April 1968.

As they sang, a massive banner with "September 11th, 2001," printed across the top came up behind them. As it was raised, you could see it listed the flight numbers of each of the planes that had crashed—American Airlines flight 11 and United Airlines flight 175 that had been flown into the World Trade Center towers, American Airlines flight 77 that hit the Pentagon, and United Airlines flight 93 that had crashed in Pennsylvania—and a list of the people who perished on those planes. They also had the names of those who had died at the Pentagon and World Trade Center, the police officers of the New York City Police Department (NYPD), and the firefighters of the Fire Department of the City of New York (FDNY) who perished trying to save people. That brought me to tears.

Then the music transitioned to the song "Where the Streets Have No Name," which starts with a guitar arpeggio. Bono, the lead singer, has traveled the world on humanitarian missions. The lyrics in the song reflect on a place where there are no divisions and you cannot tell the differences between people—their ethnicity, social class, or religion—based on where they live. It's about transcendence—a place where everyone comes together.

As the guitarist played, Bono shouted, "America!" He ran around the entire length of the stage and then rejoined the band and sang the song.

After the banner was fully extended to reveal all the names, it collapsed behind them. Bono made a heart out of his hands, held it in front of his chest, and sang "love" over and over. Then he finished the song and at the end sang, "I'll go there with you. It's all we can do." As he did so, he opened up his black jacket to reveal an American flag on the lining inside. Everyone cheered.

As the camera zoomed out to an aerial view, you could see that the stage was shaped like a heart. It was a moving tribute to all those who lost their lives in the tragic events—those who perished in the disaster and those who died trying to save those trapped in the wreckage. It was also a reminder that the USA has friends and is loved not only by Americans but by people around the world for whom America is a beacon of liberty.

The Land Down Under

The SIGINT community works closely with our Commonwealth partners in the UK, Canada, Australia, and New Zealand. In March 2002, I had my first opportunity to travel to Australia, also known as the Land Down Under. It is a very long trip from the United States East Coast. After twenty hours of travel from Washington Dulles to Sydney in New South Wales, I had to clear customs and then take a three-hour flight to Alice Springs in the Northern Territory.

Upon arrival in Alice Springs, I had to go straight to the ops site at Pine Gap to get my security briefing before I could check into my hotel and take the shower I desperately wanted. Waiting in the lobby, I looked around at the pictures on the wall and noticed a poster of all the poisonous native snakes and insects. I was thinking, "Welcome to Australia! Be careful you don't come across something that could kill you!"

I found the Aussies to be very friendly, and the team at the ops site was welcoming. We had very productive meetings discussing how we could better integrate our operations.

A US Army colonel named JP, who was stationed there, invited me to join him and some others for a morning run. He said we'd have to get up early, but it was worth it because you could see the Southern Cross in the night sky, only visible in the Southern Hemisphere, and then watch the sunrise. Given I was a runner and this was my first time in the Outback, I figured this was an invitation I could not pass up.

The next morning, I met JP and the group for our run. As JP led us through the dark, we were brushing up against things and stepping on things, and I hollered out, "JP, I sure hope you know where you are going! I probably don't want to know what we're running through right now!" He laughed and told me it would be fine, but I couldn't help recalling the creatures on the poster in the security office, and I said a prayer that we wouldn't come across any of them on the run.

The night sky was spectacular, and we had a great view of the Southern Cross. In time, we witnessed a beautiful sunrise, and when we returned to the site, it was daylight. I told JP, "That was quite an experience. Someday I can tell my grandkids that I went running in the dark in the Australian Outback!"

I would make trips Down Under again in 2003 and 2004 for work. In March 2003, I flew my mom out to meet me after my business trip, and we toured Sydney, Melbourne, Cairns, and the Great Barrier Reef. After seeing Sydney Harbor on TV, it was so special to be there in person. Sydney is one of my favorite places on earth, and I am confident more Americans would visit there if it weren't so far away. The sea life and colors we saw in the Great Barrier Reef were spectacular.

After my business trip in March 2004, I flew my mom to meet me in New Zealand, and we toured Auckland, Wellington, and Christchurch. The three Lord of the Rings movies were released in 2001, 2002, and 2003 to much acclaim. The Air New Zealand planes were painted with the slogan, "The Airline to Middle Earth," and the airport had massive gold Oscar statues. In Wellington, a giant dragon was perched on top of the theater. The Kiwis were a bit proud of the success of those movies, and rightly so. Someday I want to tour the areas where they filmed the movies—the scenery is spectacular!

CHAPTER 14

The Briefing

DNIMA Clapper was a man on a mission and wanted to affect positive change along the lines of what we had presented to him in October, but he needed his peer at NSA, Lt. Gen. Michael "Mike" Hayden, USAF, to join him in this endeavor. He continued to track the Multi-INT team's activities, including The War Room and other efforts.

In the spring of 2002, DNIMA said he would like me to present our Multi-INT efforts and lessons learned supporting the war on terrorism at the next NIMA-NSA quarterly meeting to be held at NSA headquarters in June. This was a tremendous opportunity to put the Multi-INT information sharing and collaboration efforts with all the associated barriers front and center in the hope that DNIMA and DIRNSA would jointly commit to effecting positive change. As word got out about DNIMA's desire for me to present at the next NIMA-NSA quarterly, so did the knives. There were severe antibodies to this effort.

The quarterly meeting was set for 11 June 2002, which seemed apropos as it was exactly nine months from the day of the terrorist attacks. When you are scheduled to give important presentations like this to directors of national agencies, many people want pre-briefs. This required me to fly out to Washington, DC, the week before to accommodate all the pre-brief requests.

I was preparing to head home for the weekend when I got a last-minute request. One of the NSA senior executives demanded I show up the following day at 0730 to give him a pre-brief. He said if I didn't do it, he would cancel the briefing from the directors' quarterly meeting agenda.

Col. Cope and I were at NRO headquarters in Chantilly, Virginia, about a fifty-five-mile drive down high-traffic corridors to NSA headquarters at Ft. Meade in Maryland. We decided we needed ninety minutes to make the drive and get through security at that time of day, so we planned to meet at NRO headquarters and depart by 0600 hours. Early starts were all the more difficult for me, given I tended to stay up late at night. Robin Williams's quip from the movie *Good Morning, Vietnam* crossed my mind. "It's 0600. What's the 'O' stand for? Oh, my God, it's early."

We made it to NSA, got through security, and were in the meeting room in time for the presentation at 0730. The NSA senior executive was not friendly. He told me to go ahead and do my briefing. Less than halfway through my presentation, he cut me off and told me, "There is no way that this is going forward to the directors." That was it. He dismissed me. The meeting was over.

Col. Cope and I were stunned. On the way back to NRO headquarters, we wondered, "What's going to happen now?" I flew home to Colorado for the weekend, wondering whether my briefing would still happen. DNIMA heard about what transpired during my pre-brief at NSA and assured me my presentation would remain on the quarterly meeting agenda.

The day of the NIMA-NSA quarterly at NSA headquarters arrived. Given what happened after the briefing to DNIMA Clapper in October, Col. Cope determined he would accompany me to be a government witness should I be falsely accused again.

When we arrived, we saw my presentation was last on the agenda. There were quite a few delays as the meeting ran on, and it seemed the staffers were intentionally stalling in hopes the meeting would run late and there would be no time for my presentation. Sure enough, the NSA senior executive who demanded that short-notice pre-brief announced we were out of time and they would not be able to hear my presentation.

DNIMA Clapper would not be so easily deterred. He was the one who had the long drive back to NIMA headquarters, and it was worth it to him to stay. He turned to DIRNSA Hayden and said he would like to see the briefing. DIRNSA concurred.

It was an honor for me to represent the efforts of so many to these two leaders, but it was also a considerable burden as so much weighed on the outcome. As I proceeded to give my presentation, it was clear from the looks on the faces of most of the audience that they were not happy their plan to foil my briefing had failed. This hostile audience was in no way supportive of what I was proposing.

The last slide in my presentation was a bold one. On behalf of a much larger team, I provided a list of tasks for these national agency directors to take on to tear down the barriers to Multi-INT information sharing and collaboration. I told them that if we were going to do this, they had to integrate their two agencies' teams and efforts and remove the policy barriers to doing so.

As I concluded the briefing, both directors were thoughtful. Then DNIMA Clapper turned to DIRNSA Hayden and said, "Mike, I think we should do this."

DIRNSA Hayden replied, "Jim, I agree."

Keeping a poker face, I gave a massive sigh of relief inside and thought, "Yes! We did it!"

Col. Cope and I were in a celebratory mood on the drive back to NRO headquarters. When I relayed the good news to the core team, they all cheered.

The past nine months had built up to that singular moment, and we had won a significant victory. Now I could finally get settled into my home in Colorado. Life got so crazy just months after my move, and I had been traveling worldwide. I had not found the time to unpack and get settled into my new house.

The Call

In mid-July 2002, four weeks after my presentation at the NIMA-NSA quarterly, I got a call from DNIMA Clapper. It was a Saturday afternoon, and I had recently returned home from Best Buy with the components of my brand-new surround sound system I was eager to set up. I had just opened all the boxes when I got the call.

He said, "Michele, I've been thinking about the challenge you gave DIRNSA and me, and I'm calling to ask if you would consider joining the government to help us lead that change."

Wow. This was an incredible opportunity to lead and make decisions to affect necessary change—not just advise government officials and hope they had the courage to do it. I knew this was my next calling and that I had to do this for my country.

After I told him, "Yes, I would be honored to do so," and we wrapped up the conversation, I looked at the boxes in my family room and thought, "I wonder if Best Buy will take this back."

After that call, I messaged Lee that I needed to talk with him, and we spoke via phone on Monday. He was thoughtful and said, "Michele, you know I hate to lose you, but I know you have to go do this. Our loss is the country's gain." Lee's words were brief and to the point, and he proved once again that he was a selfless leader. He wanted what was best for me and the country, even if it cost him and the company. I knew Lee would support me, and he did.

Scitor had just converted from private ownership to an Employee Stock Ownership Plan (ESOP). As a chief engineer and leader in the company, I made a considerable investment banking on our company's future success. The crazy thing is that as part of the preparation to enter government service, a lawyer in the NIMA General Council (GC) told me I had to divest all stock ownership. This seemed extreme, as though I would be a senior executive, I was not the head of an agency, and I would not oversee any Scitor contracts. Nonetheless, the GC told me this was a requirement for senior executives in the government.

When I called the Scitor ESOP plan administrators, the response I got was, "What? We just ESOP'd! We don't know how to help someone sell all their stock, as we just helped people buy in. We'll have to figure that out because you are the first one who has asked." They eventually figured it out, and I was fully divested of my interest in Scitor when I started government service.

My decision to bank on Scitor's success was good intuition. As I later learned from one of my former Scitor colleagues, everyone who bought into the ESOP made forty percent on their investment in the first year, and it only went up. It would have been nice to have some return on my ESOP investment, especially forty percent, but I didn't own shares long enough to earn any dividends.

Later, I would observe that men recruited out of industry into very high-ranking government positions—such as leading national agencies or even the Director of National Intelligence—were not required to divest stock. They even retained stock in the industry partner companies they came from and to which they often returned after government service. It appears that either I had an overzealous lawyer advising me from the NIMA GC, or the rules they applied to me didn't apply to those at the top. Regardless, I reminded myself that no one goes into government service to make money, and the things I would accomplish, including helping people in harm's way come home alive, were priceless.

CHAPTER 15

Oath of Office

DNIMA Clapper planned to make me the point person to lead the integration of NIMA and NSA and gave me the title of Chief Engineer for Multi-INT. During my first week in the government, I was in San Diego with Rob Zitz, a senior executive who reported directly to DNIMA. Rob was doing multiple site visits in the Southern California area with government and industry partners. He ran a group called InnoVision that DNIMA had established, focused on the agency's future. My work would tie into that, as Multi-INT was a new way of doing business.

It just so happened that DNIMA Clapper also recruited Col. Ted Cope to join NIMA. After years of making jokes about NIMA from one post or another within the NRO enterprise, highlighting all NIMA's issues and his frustrations in dealing with them, Ted was now a part of NIMA to help effect necessary change. He started just two weeks before me and was also on the trip. Ted and I went way back, but neither of us knew Rob very well. We all became fast friends during the weeklong trip. Rob was a kindred spirit.

We arrived in San Diego on the afternoon of Sunday, 25 August 2002. Meetings would begin early Monday morning, which was my thirty-third birthday. Rob informed me that before I could officially start work as a public servant, he had to swear me in. I asked if there were any particular requirements for this swearing-in. Aside from the official "repeat after me" script, he said the only other requirement was that I had to be facing an American flag. Having grown up about five minutes from the beach in Santa Barbara and being back home in Southern California, I told him,

"Okay, then this California girl wants to be barefoot on the beach facing the American flag at the Hotel Del Coronado."

So here's a bit of my personal trivia for you—I was officially sworn in to government service standing barefoot on a rock on a San Diego beach facing the American flag at the Hotel del Coronado. While Rob read from the official script, Ted took pictures. I'm sure it was curious for the passersby to see me with my right hand raised, swearing an oath on the beach. It certainly was memorable.

Michele's swearing in to government service, with oath of office read by Rob Zitz, facing the flag at Hotel del Coronado (2002)

During this trip, we had the privilege of visiting Skunk Works. The history of Skunk Works is fascinating. I had read a book about it and was excited about this opportunity.

Skunk Works was created in 1943 to design and build America's first jet fighter to combat the growing German jet threat during World War II. Lockheed's chief engineer, Clarence "Kelly" Johnson, led the group, which broke the rules and challenged the bureaucratic system that stifled innovation and hindered progress. This group worked on top-secret advanced programs of urgent importance. The team had a degree of autonomy, unhampered by bureaucracy, that enabled them to design and create cutting-edge aircraft in record time. They made legendary planes like the U-2, the world's first dedicated spy plane, and the SR-71 Blackbird, the world's fastest and highest-flying manned aircraft. During our visit, we saw the Joint Strike Fighter that was still in development.

We also visited the Navy and Marines stationed on Coronado Island. One of my past career highlights was working with the Marine Expeditionary Units in an exercise. This visit focused on their geospatial and imagery needs in support of operations worldwide.

By the end of the trip, Rob, Ted, and I were like the Three Amigos and practically completed each other's sentences. We had grand plans for the positive changes we would make at NIMA for the good of the agency, its customers, its partners, and the country.

The Bureaucracy

Rob and Ted headed back to Washington, DC, and I headed back to Colorado. I still had work to establish the first-ever NIMA imagery analyst cell in SIGINT ops. The work of Mike, the lone integrated imagery analyst funded by NRO, had proven to be very beneficial to the SIGINT mission, so it made sense to most everyone to expand that capability beyond one person and have NIMA run it. However, some people there did not want to see this happen.

Had Col. Henley still been the ADF-C commander, this would have been relatively easy. However, he had retired, and there was a new commander. For whatever reason, the new commander threw up all kinds of roadblocks to making this happen. One thing is for sure; he had a major issue with me being in a leadership position. He considered me to be too young and had a problem with the fact that I was female. His bias against me stemmed from two things I could not control—my age and my gender. However, someone's personal bias would not stand in the way of me doing what was right for the mission. The team and I got it done despite his attempts to thwart us.

Though I remained in Colorado for a few months to work on standing up the NIMA cell, I made frequent trips back to the Washington, DC, area, where I primarily worked out of NIMA headquarters in Bethesda, Maryland. Government officials serve in positions known as billets assigned to specific agencies or military services. Many national agencies that are dual-hatted, meaning they support both the DoD and the IC, have a director in a DoD billet and a deputy director in an IC billet or vice versa.

This was the case with NIMA, as DNIMA Clapper was in a DoD billet, and his deputy was from the CIA. DNIMA suggested I schedule a meeting with his deputy when I was in town so we could get a chance to establish a relationship, given he was the one who had recruited me. That sounded like a good idea, so I contacted her staff to arrange a meeting.

Frankly, our first meeting was like none I'd ever had before. She welcomed me into her office and then had me sit at the small conference table in front of and under the TV that hung in her office. However, she did not join me at the conference table. She remained at her desk.

She rarely looked at me as I shared about my projects. Instead, she looked past me and above me to watch the TV. Though I expected she might have inputs and ideas, she never shared any with me. In fact, she did not say much of anything. She appeared utterly uninterested and indifferent. That was awkward. Realizing that I didn't have more to share and she wasn't saying anything, I decided it was time to wrap up the meeting, so I thanked her for her time and left.

DNIMA asked me how the session went. I told him it was odd and like no meeting I'd ever had. When I explained what transpired to him, he said, "Hmm. Well, I encourage you to schedule another meeting with her on your next trip and see how that goes." So, I did, but it was just the same, and when I provided a similar report to DNIMA, he gave the same response.

After the third meeting with his deputy, I told him that the meetings were pointless and a waste of time. If this was supposed to be some "kiss the ring" (as in royalty) sort of meeting, I was not about that. I came into government service because I had a job to do, and I wasn't here to kiss up to anyone or play office politics in an attempt to further my government career. As a woman on a mission, I would choose to spend my time with those who wanted to help me accomplish it.

DNIMA asked me to host the next NIMA-NSA quarterly meeting in the fall of 2002. This situation was quite different compared to the previous quarterly meeting in June. Back then, I was an industry partner hoping the directors of NIMA and NSA would take charge to effect necessary change. Now I was a NIMA government official given the assignment to lead that change and sat as a peer to all those who would oppose me and what we were trying to do.

During the meeting, we discussed how beneficial the NIMA cell in SIGINT ops at ADF-C had been to the NSA mission. They talked about establishing a joint NIMA-NSA cell at NSA headquarters to do Multi-INT collaboration on high-priority targets. DIRNSA Hayden put none other than one of the staunchest opponents to Multi-INT information sharing and collaboration in charge of the GeoCell—the same NSA senior executive who had demanded the pre-brief on short notice, cut me off in the middle of my presentation, said he would not support what I was proposing and would block the presentation from being given. He was certainly an interesting choice for the role given his stance on Multi-INT operations, but I held out hope that perhaps, like the Apostle Paul, he could have a "road to Damascus" conversion.

They stood up the GeoCell just before Operation Iraqi Freedom (OIF), which started on 20 March 2003. We were not sure the Iraq war was warranted, but once troops were engaged, we were fully committed to supporting them. The real-time Multi-INT collaboration in the GeoCell proved valuable in our mission to provide timely, relevant, and actionable intelligence to the warfighters.

Back in the Beltway

After the successful stand-up of the NIMA cell at ADF-C, I moved back to northern Virginia in January 2003—twenty-one months after I bought my house in Colorado.

The housing prices had increased in Virginia. I purchased a townhouse in Fairfax to be close to Interstate 66 and the major freeways for my commutes in and around Washington, DC. By the way, Best Buy let me return the opened, but not yet unpacked, boxes with the surround-sound system components I had purchased for my house in Colorado. They were surprised, as they had not had anyone do that before, but they understood why I had to do it.

After moving back to the Washington, DC, area, DNIMA Clapper said it was time for me to have a formal Defense Intelligence Senior Leader (DISL) ceremony at NIMA headquarters. That was a memorable day for me. My family was present, including my mother, grandparents, aunt, and uncle. Close friends and colleagues gathered to witness this event, including Lee Akridge, Capt. Chris Quaid, Colonels Ted Cope, Sparky Olsen, and Kris Henley, and members of the Multi-INT collaboration team.

When it was my time to speak during the ceremony, I read excerpts from the book *America, Out of the Ashes: True Stories of Courage and Heroism*. One quote I read was, "A hero is born in one glorious moment, but he or she trains for a lifetime."

Glenn, Ruth, and Shirley Weslander with Michele following her formal DISL ceremony at NIMA HQ (2003)

Colonels Kris Henley and David "Sparky" Olsen (USAF, retired) with Michele following her formal DISL ceremony at NIMA HQ (2003)

A hero is born in one glorious moment, but he or she trains for a lifetime.

I also read the lyrics to the song "I Hope You Dance" because I felt the words fit my journey and my perspective on how to approach life and all its challenges. Don't sit it out—dance. Take chances, meet challenges head-on, risk loving someone, and be true to yourself.

After the ceremony, my friends and family joined me for a luncheon. It was a special time to reflect on all that had happened and the opportunities and challenges ahead. We also had a good time swapping stories.

I reflected on how God had carried me through every challenge I'd faced, used difficult and painful experiences to shape and mold me, and ultimately prepared me for a time such as this.

Ever since I moved from California, my grandparents and I had stayed in touch by speaking regularly via phone. This continued when I was out on my own, living across the country in New York. Before we said our goodbyes, they always asked me, "How can we pray for you?" Regardless of whatever else was going on in my life, I always asked for God's favor, wisdom, and discernment.

After I became a senior executive in the government, I continued this request and added, "Please pray that God would grant me wisdom and insight beyond my years, for I am serving at a very high level of responsibility at a relatively young age."

CHAPTER 16

Mission Impossible

As I started my work leading the charge to integrate operational components of NIMA and NSA, many people told me it was impossible. Some told me, "Hell will freeze over first."

I recalled a quote I first saw on a sporting goods ad while traveling in New Zealand, which I had written on the back of a receipt I had in my wallet. I decided to type it up, print it out, and put it on the wall in my office. Whenever discussions concerned the "impossibility" of the tasks my team and I had ahead of us, I would point to the quote. I've used it many times in presentations ever since. The quote is this:

Impossible is just a big word thrown around by small men who find it easier to live in the world they've been given than to explore the power they have to change it. Impossible is not a fact. It's an opinion. Impossible is not a declaration. It's a dare. Impossible is potential. Impossible is temporary. Impossible is nothing.

~ Muhammad Ali, heavyweight boxing champion

I hosted a multi-agency offsite at NRO headquarters to bring together key stakeholders in the Multi-INT integration effort. After the formal meetings concluded, we decided it would be a good bonding experience to go down the road to the Westfields Marriott and hang out in their lounge for a while. People ordered drinks and snacks, and we all shared ideas and stories. It's good to see people outside of a formal work environment because that's when you can get to know them.

After an hour or so, we wrapped up and started walking to our cars. A tall man about my age approached me and said, "You know, you're nothing like what I've heard about you."

I looked at him and asked, "Where are you from?"

He said, "Fort Meade (NSA)."

I said, "Oh, I can only imagine what you've heard. What, something along the lines of a six-foot tall Amazon warrior woman who takes no prisoners?"

He grinned and said, "Yeah, something like that." We both chuckled.

In that context, Col. Henley was right. Any press is good press because it gets your name out there. That's how legends are made. Love me or hate me, admire me or vilify me, you knew who I was and that I was a force to be reckoned with. Whether people agree with you or not, deep down, they have to respect you if you are courageous to take a stand for what you believe.

Whether people agree with you or not, deep down, they have to respect you if you are courageous to take a stand for what you believe.

As I write this, I am reminded of one of my favorite ads of all time, "Here's to the Crazy Ones" by Apple, Inc. Look it up on the internet and search for the video with Steve Jobs's voice track. Here's the quote:

Here's to the crazy ones. The misfits. The rebels. The troublemakers.
The round pegs in the square holes. The ones who see things differently.
They're not fond of rules. And they have no respect for the status quo.
You can quote them, disagree with them, glorify or vilify them.
About the only thing you can't do is ignore them.
Because they change things. They push the human race forward.
And while some may see them as the crazy ones, we see genius.
Because the people who are crazy enough to think they can
change the world are the ones who do.
~ Steve Jobs, American entrepreneur

The message is true to life. Those who think differently, challenge the status quo, have the courage of their convictions and the drive to make things better, are the ones who change the world. You need people who think differently on your team or you risk becoming irrelevant. If you are one of those unique individuals, recognize that though people may feel threatened by you, what you have is a gift. Use it for good.

Those who think differently, challenge the status quo, have the courage of their convictions and the drive to make things better, are the ones who change the world.

DNIMA recognized that it was imperative to have good leadership, and he started leadership programs for the government civilians. As part of this initiative, he considered offering senior leadership executive coaching. He asked if I would give that a try and give him feedback. This was my first experience with life coaching, which I have since become a big believer in; I am now a certified professional coach.

One of the first questions the executive coach asked me was about my personality type based on the Myers-Briggs Type Indicator. I told her it depended on my job role. She replied that it is supposed to be based on a personal preference. Out of curiosity, I went through the questionnaire solely from my personal perspective and then went through it again from my professional perspective.

There are four preference pairs based on the way you direct and receive energy (Extraversion E or Introversion I), take in information (Sensing S or Intuition N), decide and come to conclusions (Thinking T or Feeling F), and approach the outside world (Judging J or Perceiving P). My personal profile was Healer, coded as INFP—Introversion, Intuition, Feeling, Perceiving. My professional profile was Champion, coded as ENFP—Extraversion, Intuition, Feeling, Perceiving. Both were accurate.

We found it interesting that my personality type only shifted in one area. I went from slight introversion in my personal life to slight extraversion in my professional life. Many years later, I learned that there is a term for this—ambivert.

At the direction of DNIMA, Col. Cope recruited top-notch Air Force officers to his team, which DNIMA personally endorsed. These officers included USAF Captains Brian Beveridge, Chris Quaid, and Dan Ward. Brian worked at NIMA in St. Louis, Missouri, and Chris and Dan came to work at NIMA headquarters in Bethesda, Maryland.

DNIMA gave me a similar task. While I inherited some staff, I handpicked others; all were government civilians. One team member, Jim Long, was a former USAF officer I'd known from the start of my career.

During a visit to the Warning Center, where NIMA analysts do a first look at high-priority targets as the imagery comes in from the satellites, I met Sandra Simpson. She was proposing a radically new approach, which was to do first looks and then post the georeferenced results of the analysis on a web-based geographical interface. If a customer requested further information, only then would they do a more detailed analysis. This would enable them to work through targets of interest more rapidly and only do deep-dive analysis if necessary. That made sense to me, but she was fighting an uphill battle with her management, so I recruited her to join my team and help lead the necessary change.

Sandra was accustomed to a strict chain of command. When she first joined my team, she asked me for permission before she did anything not explicitly directed. Finally, I reminded her that I hired her because I believed in her and trusted her judgment. So she didn't need to ask me for permission before she did something she thought needed to be done for the mission. However, I would appreciate her giving me a heads up if something didn't go as planned—ideally before my boss found out or at least at the same time—so that I wouldn't be surprised and could be prepared to deal with the consequences. That newfound freedom and top cover helped Sandra to thrive.

In addition, I was fortunate to have Jennifer Johnson as my chief of staff. Though I hadn't known her previously, she was a competent, no-nonsense career government civilian who wouldn't take flak from anyone, even though she was younger than the rest of the staff. She had a good sense of humor, kept everyone in line with her sarcastic, good-natured zingers, and lightheartedly mimicked her boss.

At the time, the executives were issued Blackberry handheld devices for phone and email. Sometimes when I was talking with her about a message I had sent, she'd pretend she was typing on an invisible Blackberry device, and I would realize I was making those hand motions. Then we'd both laugh. It's always good to laugh at yourself, and Jen kept us laughing.

In the spring of 2003, NIMA started assembling a team for the Marine Corps Marathon, an iconic annual event in Washington, DC. The coordinators asked me to participate when they realized I was a runner. I told them that the furthest I had ever run was ten miles. A marathon is 26.2 miles. However, I realized that many people who are not runners and are not necessarily in great shape run marathons to say they did it. So, being a runner and in good shape, I determined to do it.

My work schedule during the week was crazy busy. On the weekends, I would go to one of the trails in the area, like the Washington and Old Dominion Trail, and run as far as I could.

Horizontal Integration

Shortly after the US invasion of Iraq and the OIF hot war, which lasted from 20 March 2003 to 1 May 2003, we had another NIMA-NSA quarterly meeting. The same NSA senior executive who had been such a vocal opponent of Multi-INT information sharing and collaboration, and had subsequently been put in charge of the GeoCell at NSA headquarters, reported on what the joint NIMA-NSA cell had done to support the war effort. It was impressive. After his remarks, he added, "We can never fight any other way."

Yes! That was the closest I would ever get to an apology from him. He had gone from a staunch opponent of Multi-INT operations to a firm believer and even an advocate, and that's what mattered. He had indeed experienced a "road to Damascus" conversion! It was a tremendous victory in winning hearts and minds for the Multi-INT collaboration and information-sharing cause.

Around that time, a buzzword started going around the DoD and IC—horizontal integration. The leadership corporately realized the organizations were too siloed. They needed to integrate their missions horizontally across their enterprises to successfully coordinate efforts to connect the dots, create a shared situational awareness, and defend the country. Shortly after that, DNIMA Clapper combined his military and civilian "special operations forces," as he called us, into one office with the moniker Horizontal Integration.

As a senior executive, I technically outranked Col. Ted Cope, so he became my deputy. That was just too funny to me—a colonel I had revered my entire career was now my deputy. Ted had no issues with this arrangement. We got to work brainstorming the good things our combined team would do together.

Ted and I had very similar philosophies about leadership and empowering people. Our combined staff was a dream team. As we saw it, we were to provide direction, top cover, and be the BS deflectors so our highly competent staff could do their jobs. We did not use titles or rank—we all worked as peers and on a first-name basis.

The way I ran meetings was similar—there were no titles, everyone was equal, and everyone was expected to speak up. If there was a decision to be made, once everyone had a chance to be heard, I would consider all the input and options and then make a decision. What I asked from my staff was their support for my decision. We could disagree and have a lively debate within the "family" that was our office. Still, we needed to have a unified front externally, as what we were trying to do was difficult, and the opposition would use any crack in our armor to weaken our defenses and try to use that to stop us. Because everyone had a chance to speak their mind and be heard, they supported whatever decision we made because they knew their perspective was considered. We were like-minded in our commitment to do what was right for the mission, regardless of the personal cost.

Ted and I decided to put Chris and Dan in the same office. That was a brilliant move, as they quickly became a dynamic duo. They made powerful presentations and wrote articles that challenged the status quo, particularly in the acquisition community. They came to me to get approval to submit their first article for *Defense Acquisition, Technology and Logistics* magazine, a publication of the Defense Acquisition University (DAU).

As you might imagine, their articles were not popular with the establishment contractors who had a vested interest in being what Ted called "purveyors of the status quo" because they made big bucks on their operations and maintenance (O&M) contracts for legacy systems. Ted humorously referred to people tied to the old ways of doing business and the legacy systems as Klingons (á la *Star Trek*).

However, almost everyone else resonated with what Chris and Dan said in their articles and could see the potential benefits if we changed the incredibly complex acquisition process as they proposed. They had a following that came to idolize them.

After returning from a class at DAU, one of Chris's former USAF bosses called him and was incredulous, saying, "People continually quoted your articles throughout the course!" Chris and Dan were prolific writers. Given the positive impact of their numerous articles, I considered it an honor that I signed the authorization for their first article to be published.

Some of my favorite quotes of theirs, which I've used in many presentations to this day, include the following excerpts from the "Rogue Program Manager Art of War" article published in the May-June 2005 edition of the *Defense AT&L* magazine. The first quote is, "The bureaucratic rules, processes, procedures… were not created for you, so don't expect them to work for you. Let your instinct be your guide, and do what you know needs to be done." Another is, "Assume significant risk must be taken to be successful. Weigh any potential risk against the value to the mission, and then move out, making vector checks as you go."

After quoting those in my presentations, I then add my insights, "Be prepared. Almost everyone is going to tell you no. But don't take no from someone who doesn't have the authority to give you a yes in the first place." Furthermore, "Don't accept things as they are today. Imagine how they could be and make it so. Recognize that if you are not leading the way and taking intelligent risks, you risk becoming irrelevant."

We provided a critical service for the country and realized that the people in harm's way every day were counting on us to do what was required to support their mission. We lived the motto: "If not us, then who? If not now, then when?" We took intelligent risks when others wouldn't, and we always had a sense of urgency and a bias for action.

To enable joint DoD-IC brainstorming and planning concerning Horizontal Integration, the DoD and IC leadership set up Saturday sessions for the key players, including the Joint Staff, Undersecretaries of Defense, and National Agency Directors. They alternated the location of the meetings between CIA headquarters and the Pentagon. DNIMA Clapper selected me, his Director of Horizontal Integration, as his "plus one" for these meetings. So, yours truly spent countless hours on many a Saturday morning meeting with the leadership of the DoD and the IC, deliberating matters of national consequence and making action plans.

One thing that amazed me was that these leaders would get enamored with a particular proposed project and not look at it in the context of the bigger picture. General James "Haas" Cartwright, USMC, the Joint Staff J8, and I constantly chimed in, saying, "First, we have to decide where we need to go. Then we can decide what will help us get there."

As we worked to better integrate efforts across the national security enterprise, I focused on how NIMA and NSA could better integrate, given that was my initial charge when I entered government service. While I was aware of NSA's authorities, i.e., what they could or could not do, I needed to gain more knowledge of the laws behind their authorities. In countless meetings, NSAers would tell me, "We can't do that. It's illegal." When I asked them, "Why?" or "Based on what law?" they would not answer me. Such conversations were frustrating and did not enable much forward progress.

So I decided to schedule a meeting with their General Counsel (GC). After spending a half day with the NSA lawyers—not only learning the laws but also discussing what we wanted to do and how that might be allowed or disallowed by law—I was truly dangerous because I could now combat the naysayers with facts.

In the next meeting with NSA, I refuted all their claims that the type of information sharing and collaboration we were proposing was illegal, quoting line and verse from the laws and their policies. This surprised them, but they eventually realized I would not be deterred by their efforts to resist the change that needed to happen for the good of the country and those in harm's way defending our freedom.

You may recall that when I moved to Colorado in 2001 to collaborate more closely with SIGINT ops, I had access to information unavailable to me before the move. By my mere presence at ADF-C, I fell under DIRNSA authority and gained access to data I recognized would be useful for imagery analysts.

Now, as a government official, I used that understanding and the insight I gained from my meetings with the NSA GC to draft a Memorandum of Understanding (MOU) for DNIMA and DIRNSA to sign. The MOU extended DIRNSA authorities to NIMA analysts appropriately trained regarding the nuances of the NSA mission and the legalities of data handling. That would be a game changer for Multi-INT information sharing and collaboration to support the mission.

CHAPTER 17

CAPSTONE

In the summer of 2003, I was honored to be selected to participate in the Chairman of the Joint Chiefs of Staff CAPSTONE program. This is the last formal training for the new one-stars—general and flag officers—in the military. Civilians in the senior executive ranks are sometimes invited to participate, and I felt fortunate to be afforded this opportunity. We were the fourth class of the fiscal year (FY) 2003 and were known as CAPSTONE 2003-4. The program was six weeks long, and classroom sessions were held at National Defense University (NDU) at Fort McNair in Washington, DC.

Everyone underwent a thorough health and fitness assessment as part of the program. I still have those records, which said I had seventeen percent body fat and effectively the body of an eighteen-year-old at age thirty-three. I chuckled to myself upon reading those results—that's what eating healthy and training for a marathon will do for you!

For two of the six weeks, the class was split into three groups for overseas travel—the Pacific, Europe, and the Southern Hemisphere. I was selected to go on the Europe Field Studies trip.

DNIMA Clapper received the details of my trip and reviewed them before passing them on to me. He said, "Michele, I see your trip starts in Azerbaijan."

My response was, "Azer-ba-what?" I had never heard of Azerbaijan but learned it was a country located on the boundary of eastern Europe and western Asia and had been a part of the former Soviet Union. We then reviewed the rest of the itinerary, which included Iraq, Turkey, Kosovo, Romania, Ireland, Belgium, and Germany. I was going to travel to eight countries in fourteen days via military aircraft, a.k.a. MILAIR. Based on my life experiences to date, this was going to be the trip of a lifetime.

We had to get all kinds of immunizations to prepare for overseas travel. My appointment was scheduled for o-dark-thirty at the Pentagon. They gave me two shots in one arm and three in the other. As I gathered my things to leave, they stopped me; they said they needed to keep me for observation and told me to take a seat. After thirty minutes or so, I asked if I could leave. They asked how I was feeling, and I said fine, so they said I could go.

I headed back to the office and my morning meetings. Sometime in the afternoon, I started feeling spacey. I stepped out of my office and told my assistant, Jen. The staff overheard me, and one of them chimed in and said, "Didn't you get immunizations this morning?"

"Yes," I replied.

"How many?" they asked.

"Five," I replied.

Then almost in unison, they said, "Well, no wonder you feel the way you do!" Good point.

On the first day of CAPSTONE, I arrived at NDU in a red business dress. As our class photo shows, I stood out in a sea of military tan, blue, and green.

Michele is pictured at the left end of the second row of the CAPSTONE 2003-4 class at NDU (2003)

That's not the only way I stood out. At thirty-three going on thirty-four, I was about fifteen years younger than my classmates. This was not lost on the lead trainer, a recently retired Navy captain who transitioned to a GS-15 position, an equivalent rank in civilian service. All day long, he kept weaving in the statement, "We're all rounding fifty, with one notable exception," into his remarks. He clearly could not get over the fact that I was there, and I got the feeling he did not think I belonged.

At the end of the day, we were all asked to stand and introduce ourselves to our classmates. We were in a tiered classroom where the seating was a squared U shape, and the seats were raised for each consecutively larger U. I was seated in the smallest U up in the front. They started in the back on the top tier, and I was the second to last person to introduce myself.

When I stood, my opening statement was, "In case you were wondering, I'm the 'one notable exception.'" Everyone laughed. That broke the ice. To my classmates' credit, everyone eventually looked past my age and accepted me as a part of the group. Unfortunately, the lead instructor never did, but that was my cross to bear. The saving grace was that most of my classmates saw this and told me they didn't think it was right, but we all realized this was his issue, not mine.

As part of the training, we heard from leaders across the government, including the Chairman of the Joint Chiefs of Staff, General Richard Meyers, USAF, and the Vice Chairman, General Peter Pace, USMC. We also visited the military commands in the continental US (CONUS), including Joint Forces Command (JFCOM), which no longer exists. At JFCOM we learned about war planning, which was very insightful.

One of my favorite visits was to Special Operations Command (SOCOM) and Joint Special Operations Command (JSOC). Throughout the day, they kept referring to Desert One. We couldn't have cell phones in the building, so I looked it up as soon as I had access to my phone again. It was then that I learned the tragic details.

Desert One was the staging area for Operation Eagle Claw. This hostage rescue mission failed and resulted in the deaths of eight American servicemen and the wounding of several others. I realized one reason I was unfamiliar with Desert One was that it happened in April 1980 when I was in fifth grade.

JSOC was created in the aftermath that same year. SOCOM was created in April 1987, the year I graduated from high school. That was all very sobering for me, and I realized most of my classmates were less than ten years into their military careers at that time, so it understandably had a significant impact on them.

For one of our flights to visit the commands, we flew on a KC-10 Extender. Some pilots wore Fat Boy patches on their flight suits; I learned that means that their first operational aircraft assignment was to fly the KC-10. An Air Mobility Command (AMC) advanced tanker and cargo aircraft, the KC-10 is a modified Boeing DC-10 and is one of a few different types of aerial refueling aircraft.

The ability to do aerial refueling has been a tactical advantage for the US military because we can increase the combat range of our aircraft, such as fighter jets and bombers. While the KC-10's primary mission is aerial refueling, it can also carry flight support personnel and equipment overseas.

Michele took this photo from the boom compartment of a KC-10 Extender tanker during refueling of a Tiger squadron B-2 Spirit stealth bomber; note the stuffed Tigger visible through the window (2003)

One of my classmates, Brigadier General (Brig. Gen.) Doug Raaberg, USAF, was Commander of the 509th Bomb Wing, Whiteman AFB, Missouri. The 509th led the way for America's first military response following the terrorist attacks on the USA in September 2001. It is one of only two units to operate the Northrop Grumman B-2 Spirit stealth bomber.

The B-2s were doing training missions near us, and our KC-10 did a refueling for one of them. Each of us got the opportunity to stand beside the refueling operator, look through the large window, and see the refueling of the B-2 close-up. The universal initial response was, "Wow!" The B-2 is one amazing aircraft, but seeing the massive bat-winged bomber up close in midair was truly extraordinary. They were the Tiger squadron and had a stuffed Tigger (from Winnie the Pooh) in the cockpit.

Part of the CAPSTONE program included visits to the intelligence agencies in the Washington, DC area—specifically, NIMA, NSA, NRO, and the Defense Intelligence Agency (DIA). When we were at the intel agencies, we were on my turf, and I was shocked at how little most of my military classmates knew about the IC and the intelligence capabilities we provided. The only one who had an accurate understanding had been a J2, the chief of intelligence for a Joint Command. There were no ops site visits either—everything was slideshows, and they were pretty weak.

One of the other IC civilians, Andre, who had commanded ADF-E, agreed. We both decided that the IC training for CAPSTONE needed revamping, and everyone should visit ADF-E to get a better feeling of what the IC did. So we worked to make that happen.

Every CAPSTONE class after ours would get the revised training and ops site visit, giving them a more accurate perspective regarding what intelligence could do for their mission. With the new training, they would better understand IC capabilities and have a more realistic expectation of what type of support the IC could provide. As they say, "An educated consumer is the best customer."

Then came our overseas trip. For the European field studies group, our first stop was Azerbaijan. It was striking how gray and drab the area was, having been under the control of the Soviet Union. Now that they were free of Marxist-Leninist communist oppression, they were abandoning socialism and adopting free-market capitalism to build their economy and catch up with the Western world. This entailed tapping their plentiful natural resources, and they had many oil and gas companies interested in working there.

One interpreter was a young woman with a perfect American accent. When I complimented her on her excellent American English and asked her how she mastered it so well, she told me it was by watching American shows on TV.

We traveled from there to Baghdad, Iraq, for a day. We were flown around the area in UH-60 Black Hawk helicopters, which afforded us a bird's eye view. The Black Hawks were manned with gunners keeping a close eye on threats.

Michele before boarding UH-60 Black Hawk helicopter at Baghdad International Airport, Iraq (2003)

While we were on the ground, we met with Lieutenant General (LTG) Sanchez, US Army, Commander of Combined Joint Task Force 7 (CJTF-7), and Ambassador (Amb.) Pat Kennedy, Department of State, Chief of Staff of the Coalition Provisional Authority (CPA). We got a firsthand account of how things were going from the leaders of the military and civilian efforts, which were a combination of combat and diplomacy. I made mental notes of things we could do back at NIMA to help them.

While visiting with groups stationed in one of the palaces, I slipped away to say a quick hello to the NIMA team. When I returned to our meeting place, I stood alone, waiting for my classmates.

Colonel (COL) Jeff Lieb, US Army, who was in charge of our security detail, approached me and said, "Ma'am, if you don't mind me saying so, you look a lot younger than the rest of your group."

I smiled and told him, "Indeed, I am."

We struck up a friendly conversation and swapped stories of how we came to be in Iraq. He had been in Iraq since March and was part of the hot war leading an offensive on Baghdad as the Battalion Commander of the 1st Battalion, 27th Field Artillery Regiment. Before we parted ways, we exchanged emails, and I told him to contact me if he and his team ever needed support.

1LT Brett Buchanan and COL Jeff Lieb, US Army, with Michele before she boards a C-17 Globemaster III at Baghdad International Airport, Iraq (2003)

In Turkey, we visited Ankara and Istanbul. Turkey is a part of Europe and Asia, and it was interesting to learn more about the culture.

Istanbul was formerly known as Constantinople after the Roman emperor Constantine I, who made it the capital of the new Roman empire in 330 AD. It was a trade hub because it was one destination on the path the Romans built to join Europe's and Asia's trade routes. The Ottoman Turks conquered the city in 1453. When the new Republic of Turkey was established in 1923, the name was changed to Istanbul.

A beautiful city, Istanbul is fascinating in many ways, including the fact that it connects Europe with the Middle East. It is home to so much history and sits on the banks of the Bosphorus River, which separates the European and Asian parts of Turkey. It was fascinating to tour the area, see the Hagia Sophia and the Blue Mosque and walk through the Basilica Cistern, also known as the Underground Palace, built in the sixth century. We also roamed through the marketplaces full of rugs, among other things.

We were fortunate to be able to stay at the Four Seasons Hotel Istanbul. The views from that property overlooking the Bosphorus River and the Mediterranean Sea were spectacular.

Our hosts treated us to a short cruise on the Mediterranean Sea. On the cruise, one of the security detail members assigned to us who spoke some English came to me and said, “You look like us.”

I smiled and said, “Yes, I do. My father is of Middle Eastern descent.” I did not elaborate on the fact that he was born in Persia to a Jewish father, that they moved to Israel when it became a nation, and that he was an Israeli citizen who fought in the Six-Day War. “Middle Eastern descent” was enough in this Muslim country.

He had a big smile and seemed proud to have me in his charge because, to him, I was one of them. It’s funny that most Americans don’t see Middle Eastern ancestry when they look at me, but most Europeans and Middle Easterners do.

We then made a stop in Pristina, Kosovo. Camp Bondsteel served as the North Atlantic Treaty Organization (NATO) headquarters for the Kosovo Force Multinational Battle Group East and was the main base for the US Army. We learned how the rebuilding efforts were going after the war there, which had lasted from 1998 to 1999 and had led to a humanitarian crisis.

Our next stop was in Bucharest, Romania. One thing I remember most was the elaborate promenade that led to the grand Palace of the Parliament, which holds the record as the world’s heaviest building and is very ornate. It was originally named the House of the Republic during the lengthy construction period under the communist dictator who wanted to turn Romania into a “multilaterally developed socialist society.”

But after the Romanian Revolution in December 1989, it became known as The People’s House. This is as it should be because it is reportedly the most expensive administration building in the world, and the citizen's labor built it, and their taxes paid for it. The tragedy is that the communist dictator constructed an elaborate building while his people suffered.

Our visit to Ireland was a diplomatic thank you for their support as our ally. Having visited Ireland nine years prior, it was fun to go back. The Irish people are amiable and hospitable. We not only share a common language, but we also share common values.

We then visited the NATO headquarters in Brussels, Belgium. NATO was a peacetime military alliance created in 1949 by the USA, Canada, and several western European nations to provide collective security against the Soviet Union.

The US led Operation Enduring Freedom (OEF) in Afghanistan with the support of NATO aircraft, and NATO supported the International Security Assistance Force (ISAF) after the Taliban was defeated. NATO was not officially a part of OIF but supported the US-led Multinational Stabilization Force in Iraq after the Saddam Hussein regime was ousted.

Our last stop was in Germany to visit European Command (EUCOM) headquarters at Patch Barracks in Stuttgart. The EUCOM leadership updated us on their activities in their area of responsibility (AOR), including their role in OEF and combating the Global War on Terrorism (GWOT). You may think that GWOT was contained to the Middle East, but there are terrorism networks worldwide, and you have to run the trap lines to see where terrorists are getting funding and support. I thought of my first overseas trip to visit Wolfram in Germany a decade prior and how I could have never imagined then that I would be back in Germany in this capacity.

I returned home to the USA very appreciative of this horizon-broadening experience—visiting new places and meeting new people. Upon reflection, I was keenly aware of the diplomatic aspect of the trip, as every location we visited was chosen for a purpose.

Meeting with each country's military and civilian leaders, I appreciated our need to reach a mutual understanding and find common ground to achieve shared goals. I also observed that the military leadership was friendly, even if there were political tensions between our two countries, as there were between the USA and Turkey at the time, as we had recently discovered that Turkish special operations troops were in northern Iraq. It seemed the military leaders knew they had to look past the politics and keep good relations because we were both members of NATO and fought wars together.

I took an international relations course in college and found it interesting. While there were fun aspects of almost every visit because our hosts were proud to show us their country and did a great job of making us feel welcome, I most enjoyed these diplomatic aspects and found them fascinating. It made me wonder if I had missed a calling—perhaps I was meant to pursue international relations and be an ambassador. Though I have never had "ambassador" as a title, I have served as an ambassador in many ways in different jobs. That ambassador-type role has come naturally to me because I enjoy meeting new people and finding common ground to work together toward shared goals.

Before CAPSTONE wrapped up, I was sure to gather all of my classmates' contact information. I became the class comms officer and sent periodic emails to everyone for years to come. These would become electronic roll calls where my classmates would "reply all" to the email and tell everyone where they were and what was going on in their lives. It was interesting to follow everyone's career path.

To this day, I've stayed in contact with some of my CAPSTONE classmates, who became personal friends.

General (GEN) Carter Ham, US Army, retired after serving as the Commander of US Africa Command (AFRICOM). GEN Ham went on to serve as the President and CEO of the Association of the US Army.

Vice Admiral (VADM) Tom "Killer" Kilcline, Jr., retired after serving as the Commander, Naval Air Forces, (CNAF), a.k.a. The Air Boss. Both the US Navy Strike Fighter Tactics Instructor program, popularly known as TOPGUN, and the Blue Angels flight demonstration squadron fall under the CNAF. Killer flew the F-14 as Iceman in the original *Top Gun* movie.

VADM Jeff Fowler retired after serving as superintendent of the US Naval Academy.

Major General (Maj. Gen.) Doug Raaberg, USAF, commanded the 509th B-2 stealth bomber wing. He did B-1 combat sorties for OEF and ISAF; he and his B-1 bomber squadron team hold the world speed record with refueling flying around the globe. Maj. Gen. Raaberg went on to serve as the Air Force Association's Executive Vice President.

As you can see, their careers have been impressive!

Jointness

Following my six-week CAPSTONE experience in the summer of 2003, I returned to NIMA with a greater appreciation and understanding of the military. One thing that stood out was that they had indeed implemented joint operations, whereas the components of the IC were not operating that way.

One of my military classmates remarked to the two other civilians from the IC and me, "We [the military] figured out joint operations over fifteen years ago, but you in the IC still haven't figured that out." That statement was so true.

The National Security Act of 1947 was a law enacting major reconstruction of the military and intelligence agencies following World War II. The Goldwater-Nichols Act of 1986 made the most sweeping changes the DoD had ever seen. Under Goldwater-Nichols, military advice was centralized in the Joint Chiefs of Staff rather than the military service chiefs, which increased the Joint Staff's power. Furthermore, it streamlined the military chain of command, from the President of the United States (POTUS) to the Secretary of Defense to the Combatant Commanders. It created SOCOM and strengthened the role of the Combatant Commanders. It reportedly was an attempt to fix problems caused by interservice rivalry, which had emerged during the Vietnam War and contributed to the catastrophic failure of the Iranian hostage rescue mission, the aforementioned Operation Eagle Claw and Desert One in 1980.

I understood what my military classmate was getting at—it seemed the IC needed something equivalent to Goldwater-Nichols to force a necessary change to create joint IC operations for the country's good. Furthermore, many of the policies that governed the IC in the present day had not been updated since 1947. A few things had changed since then, like the invention of the Internet.

CHAPTER 18

Rock Stars

Leaders realized the IC needed people who thought differently and that if you were born and raised in the IC, you likely had some blind spots. Shortly after I joined NIMA, DNIMA Clapper hired a consultant who was gaining notoriety in the national security community. He wasn't your traditional consultant.

In the early 1990s, Jeff "Skunk" Baxter, lead guitarist for Steely Dan and the Doobie Brothers, wrote a white paper that got a congressman friend's attention on the Armed Services Committee. Skunk was into acoustics, and the way he kept up on the latest technology was to read defense magazines. He had an insight along the way and wrote a whitepaper, an informational document, that a congressman read. Shortly after that, Skunk was hired by the Missile Defense Agency as a consultant.

After the terrorist attacks of 11 September 2001, Skunk was recruited to support the IC because they recognized we needed people who thought differently, and "rockstar" fit the bill. DNIMA had the two of us start working together on projects in 2003. Skunk would joke that we were DNIMA's stealth weapons. Who would take a rockstar and a young woman seriously?

It was to our advantage to be underrated. People would be very casual with us because they did not feel intimidated. Then one of us would ask a strategically placed insightful question, and people would be caught off guard, finally recognizing we knew and understood far more than they had anticipated.

Skunk and I hit it off right away. He used his musical talents for good, supporting fundraisers for various causes, and started inviting me to his gigs in town.

Oorah

The Marine Corps Marathon was held on Sunday, 23 October 2003. There were thousands gathered on the National Mall for the race. The camaraderie was palpable. We were going to do this together! Oorah!

Marathon participants were organized in tiers according to their expected finish times, and it took a few minutes before my tier started. Earlier in the year, I had run a ninety-minute ten-mile race without training, so my goal was to do the marathon in about four and a half hours. One of the keys to long-distance running is pacing yourself—not running too fast so that you run out of steam, but not running too slow so that you have a lot of energy left at the end.

Having never run a marathon before, I had to guess what pace I should take to make a strong finish over twenty-six miles later. It was hard to judge because the farthest I'd ever run before race day was sixteen miles.

It was great to have Marines along the way cheering for us. I kept thinking, "Yes, Drill Sergeant!"

Somewhere around mile 12, I came down on my right foot and felt shooting pain. That wasn't good, but I kept up a jog while looking for an aid tent. When I found one, I walked in and asked what they had for painkillers. All they had was Tylenol; Motrin (ibuprofen) would have been preferable. Given I was a part of the NIMA team, I was determined not to let the team down; I was going to finish the race. So, I took Tylenol and got back on the road.

As I was running along I-395 by the Pentagon, someone had a sign that made me laugh out loud. It was something to the effect of, "26.4 million people are sitting on their [butts] this morning, but you are running a marathon!" Oorah! That was the oomph we needed to continue to the final stretch—up the hill to the Iwo Jima memorial.

When I saw the 25-mile marker and realized I had about a mile left, I gave it my all. After I crossed the finish line, I felt like I could collapse, but I didn't dare stop. A race volunteer put a finisher medal around my neck, and I grabbed some water and looked for my mom, who had come to support me that day. We found each other, sat on the grass, and talked with others who had run the race. All runners were tired but energized after completing the Marine Corps Marathon.

Michele with her finisher medal after completion of the Marine Corps Marathon (2003)

The soreness hit me when I got up to head to the Washington Metro. You could tell the runners from the rest as we hobbled along and walked sideways down the stairs to the Metro train. Though tired and sore, I felt great. This sprinter had just run a marathon! Running a marathon is something I never thought I would do. Previously, I thought people were crazy to do it. Do you remember what happened to the guy who ran from Marathon to Athens? He collapsed and died!

My team at work congratulated me on Monday. They thought it was awesome that I ran a marathon—especially the Marine Corps Marathon. However, they showed me no mercy. They laughed at how slowly I lowered myself into a chair holding the armrests, raised myself out of a chair pushing up on the armrests, and walked slowly and sideways down the stairs.

The benefit of the pretraining was that I was able to recover in just a few days. By Wednesday, I was feeling pretty much back to normal, though my right foot still hurt. A few years later, following an x-ray, I learned that I had fractured it and someday would require surgery.

By the way, our NIMA team won a medal! My net time was 4:47:55, which was close to my goal of 4:30. That time was pretty good, considering I was running on an injured foot for over half the race.

GEOINT

On 24 November 2003, NIMA officially became the National Geospatial-Intelligence Agency (NGA) and was a three-letter agency like everyone else. The name change was part of the continued transformation of the organization. NIMA was a combined legacy of the Defense Mapping Agency (DMA) and NPIC—mapping and intelligence analysis, respectively. NGA further integrated these two disciplines into one called Geospatial-Intelligence (GEOINT).

While I remained the Director of Horizontal Integration in InnoVision, my other title transformed from Chief Engineer for Multi-INT to National Geospatial-Intelligence Officer for Multi-INT.

Capt. Chris Quaid, USAF, Michele, Col. Ted Cope, USAF, and Capt. Brian Beveridge, USAF, at an NGA formal event (2004)

I started receiving invitations to speak at conferences. On one of those first occasions, I participated in a panel discussion. I didn't know any of my fellow panelists but quickly became a big fan of one of them—Kathleen Reilly. She was former Navy and had been an analyst on the Navy EP-3E Aries II aircraft doing electronic signals reconnaissance. Kathleen was then a staffer with the House Permanent Select Committee on Intelligence (HPSCI) and is now a staffer on the Senate Select Committee on Intelligence (SSCI).We became great friends and worked from our respective positions in government to do good things for the warfighters.

CHAPTER 19

Boots on the Ground

While the hot war was over in Iraq, a battle was ongoing, and our military and allies needed support. Those of us with a pulse on what was going on had strong intuition regarding what we needed to do for those fighting the war on terrorism overseas; however, our words alone were not breaking through the bureaucratic barriers. Furthermore, the warfighters did not necessarily know what to ask for because they were limited in describing what they needed in the context of what they already had. As a technologist, I knew the art of the possible, so seeing what they were trying to accomplish firsthand would enable me to envision what capabilities would better empower them to achieve their mission.

Some of us realized we needed boots on the ground with the warfighters to observe their operations and capture what they needed in their own words. We would then use those requirements to lead the development of new capabilities. To that end, a trip was scheduled for me, Capt. Chris Quaid, and Army Chief Warrant Officer (CW2) Michael Campbell from the NRO Operational Support Office (OSO) to go to Iraq. We would take extensive notes and publish a detailed trip report with our findings when we returned.

We were to depart the USA on 13 December 2003. We would visit the Central Command (CENTCOM) group in Doha, Qatar, from 14-15 December, then travel to Baghdad, Iraq, to visit the teams on 16 December. I would spend one night in Iraq, have some meetings the next morning, and then depart Iraq for the USA on 17 December. Chris and Mike would stay in Iraq to visit other locations and return on 23 December. I had such a quick turnaround because I had to get back in time to give a briefing at the next NGA-NSA quarterly on 19 December 2003.

Upon our arrival in Doha, Qatar, we had to in-process, which means processing all the paperwork required for coming into the country. None of the men in Qatar would look at me or speak to me. The senior NGA rep, who was male, had to interface with them on my behalf. So, the interaction—all conducted in English—went something like this. The Qatari man at the counter would look at my male NGA counterpart and ask a question intended for me. I would look at the Qatari man and respond, but he would not acknowledge me or what I said. Then my male NGA colleague would repeat what I said, and the Qatari man would take action. This seemed very inefficient, but that was their culture. Considering how they treated women, and given the fine dust everywhere that made it look like we were on the moon, I was glad to have been born in the USA.

Our primary meeting in Doha was with Brigadier General (BG) John Custer, US Army, the CENTCOM J2. We quickly recognized he got it; he was energized and empowered to make changes. We became friends then and there. We got good intel from him regarding CENTCOM's top needs in the theater of operations, which included supporting the troops on bases like the one in Qatar.

Then we met with NGA and other IC staff stationed there. They were happy to see someone from headquarters come to visit who cared about what they were doing to support the war on terrorism. I provided my contact information and ensured they knew they could reach out to me anytime for support.

The next day we prepared to board the C-130 Hercules aircraft bound for Baghdad, Iraq. The military person preparing the paperwork for the flight came to me and said, "Ma'am, I need your signature." When I asked why, he informed me I was the most senior officer on the plane and therefore had to sign for the plane, all its contents, and the personnel. What a trip! The NGA staff in Qatar who overheard the conversation included that detail in their daily report to DNGA Clapper, and he got a real kick out of that.

If I thought that was a trip, so was the flight into Iraq! Mike, Chris, and I were in the aircraft's cargo bay, sitting on the red netting, which is not comfortable. The plane was packed with personnel facing each other, knees touching. There were no aisles to speak of, so when the crew had to get from one part of the plane to another, they just walked on top of people's legs.

After a while, a flight crew member came from the cockpit to speak with me. He said that given I was the senior officer on the plane, they wanted to invite me to sit in the cockpit with them. That afforded me a unique perspective.

As we approached Baghdad, they reminded everyone to strap in. We arrived in daylight, so they had to do evasive maneuvers as we came in for a landing. We zigged and zagged our way through the sky down to a safe landing at Baghdad International Airport, which the military called BIAP. It was previously known as Saddam International Airport, but since the US-led invasion in March of that year, the only flights in and out of that airport were via MILAIR because it was still a war zone.

When we disembarked the plane, the staff that greeted us told us they had just caught Saddam Hussein that very day. Chris joked, "He knew we were coming!"

The three of us were exhausted, having traveled over three days to get there with very little sleep. We met with special ops members shortly after getting off the plane, and I was fighting to keep my eyes open. When I looked back at my notes, my writing was hardly legible. I thought about how these military members are sleep deprived regularly and have to be on high alert in a combat zone. How do they do it? Then I understood why they all must master the art of the combat nap, something I had not achieved. It was a necessity!

We met with numerous NGA teams stationed at various locations, including CJTF-7; Camp Slayer, Iraq Survey Group; the SOF team that went after the high-value targets (HVTs); and the CPA.

I tried to meet with BG Barb Fast, US Army, CJTF-7 C2 (Chief of Intel), but our meeting kept being bumped due to operational needs that came up, which took precedence. So I told her staff I would take any opportunity to meet with her—even if it was riding between one location and another. They took me up on that.

My meeting with BG Fast was in a High Mobility Multipurpose Wheeled Vehicle (HMMWV) called a Humvee, driving eighty miles per hour between Camp Victory and the Green Zone. One of the statements she made that I used over and over again back home to beat down the walls of resistance was this: "I don't have time to wait for your fully analyzed and vetted intelligence products. I have deadlines to make decisions, and often your official products do not make it to me in time. I need what you have as you have it, and I will vet whatever you give me in the context of the other information I have."

In the IC, we used the phrase "timely and relevant intelligence." What she was getting at was though our products may be relevant, she often did not receive the products in time to use them in her decision-making process.

You have to make decisions in real-time when you're in combat. There can be no paralysis through analysis because people's lives are on the line, and you do not have the luxury of waiting until you have all the information you want. In a combat zone, you have to make a decision and then move forward but continue to take in data as you receive it and make vector checks as you go. Not making a decision is a decision in itself and has consequences.

Not making a decision is a decision in itself and has consequences.

That night while Chris and Mike had to sleep in the tent city, as a distinguished visitor (DV), I was privileged to sleep in a room in one of the palaces. COL Jeff Lieb, whom I had met during my visit to Baghdad with CAPSTONE in August, was still in the country. The Deputy Secretary of Defense (SecDef) had asked him to stay in Baghdad to lead the Joint Visitors Bureau (JVB), whose mission was to escort and provide security to all incoming VIPs in the Iraq theater, so he was my host. We had stayed in touch through occasional emails, and he greeted me at the palace.

Jeff noted I was wearing a flak vest with protective plates. Then he informed me that neither he nor his team had plates for their flak vests. What?! How could this be?! The plates make them bulletproof, so a flak vest serves no purpose without them. I told him to take my plates as he needed them more than I did; I was headed home the next day. He said thanks but wouldn't take them as he wouldn't wear the plates if his team didn't have them. That was one of the key insights I took back to my contacts who worked with Congress. How could they have the military members deploy into a combat zone without plates for their flak vests?! They needed to fix this!

He then escorted me to my room. It was huge and had sparse furnishings, which included a large bed bigger than a king-size in the US, a nightstand, a chair, and a dresser. There were huge floor-to-ceiling windows along one side of the room with sheer curtains.

There was also a rather large bathroom. I was looking forward to taking a shower after days of travel. The problem was, every time I turned on the faucet, it went from cold to scalding hot in seconds. So I could not take a very quick or efficient shower, having to turn the faucet on and off multiple times to catch the water at a reasonable temperature.

Once I had a shower, and after his duties for the day were over, Jeff and I could meet again to catch up. It was interesting to hear his firsthand account of what life had been like since we saw each other in August. Jeff told me he would return to work at the Pentagon on the Deputy SecDef's staff after his extended tour was complete. An extended tour is hard on anyone. It was clear how much he missed his wife and daughters; I could only imagine how much his family missed him. Our military members and their families sacrifice so much for our freedom.

When it was time to call it a night, I went back to my room and saw cots filling the open space. Jeff told me the cots were there because a group from the World Wrestling Federation (WWF) was coming to visit the next night as part of a United Services Organization (USO) tour. That group would be staying in the room, which goes to show you how big it was!

Then I noticed how bright the lights were outside and how little privacy there was through the sheer curtains. I remarked to Jeff about that and asked if other curtains could be pulled across the windows.

Jeff said no, but he had an idea. We could prop a bunch of the cots up against the windows to provide some semblance of privacy, at least at the ground level, so we set to work doing that. It was quite a sight when we were done. I thanked him and said good night, and he told me he'd meet me for breakfast in the morning. After a few days of sleep deprivation, I slept well that night.

When I walked out to the common area in the morning, Jeff had a breakfast tray for me. As a commanding officer, he had to get up much earlier and already had breakfast. We sat and talked about my scheduled meetings for the day. Then we discussed my trip back home, starting with my flight out of BIAP.

While we were talking, one of Jeff's staff members came and asked to speak with him. They talked off to the side, and he returned to the table with a big grin. The people who went to prep the room for the next guests were surprised to find all the cots up against the window and asked what to do. He explained the situation and told them they could set it up for the WWF crew coming in for the USO tour.

I wondered if the WWF guys would flip coins to see who got the big bed. It wasn't all that comfortable, but I'm sure it was better than sleeping in a cot. Regardless, I knew that any of us fortunate enough to stay in the palace had it much better than the troops who had to sleep in tents.

Chris confirmed this when he and the NGA senior officer came to pick me up and take me to our first meeting. He said it was not very comfortable and also quite noisy as they did not have solid walls to muffle the sound, and there was always some activity going on in the area.

Following my morning meetings, and after less than thirty-six hours on the ground in Iraq, Chris and the senior NGA military officer traveled with me to BIAP to see me off on the MILAIR flight to Doha, Qatar. From there, I would connect to my commercial airline flight back to the states via Europe. They asked travelers to arrive a few hours early for MILAIR flights, and we arrived right on time per the schedule they had given us for my return flight when we first arrived in the country.

When I checked in at the desk, the airman working the flight schedules told us the next flight to Camp Doha would be in a couple of hours. I asked for clarification, stating I was going to Doha, Qatar. He replied that the flight to Doha, Qatar, had already left, and I had been scheduled on the flight to Camp Doha, Kuwait. There had been a major mix-up.

I asked when the next flight to Doha, Qatar, would be, as that is where I had my connecting commercial flight. He said it would not be until the next day. I could not wait until then, or I would miss getting back in time for the NGA-NSA quarterly. I had to get on my way back to the USA that day.

The senior NGA military officer loaned me his cell phone, so I could call the NGA-contracted travel agency back in the US. When I got through, I spoke with Daisy, told her I was in Baghdad, Iraq, and then explained the situation. I told Daisy I needed her to cancel my flight out of Doha, Qatar, back to the USA and instead book me on a flight from Kuwait back to the USA.

Daisy said she could not do that and asked why I didn't just go down to the ticket counter at the airport and get the agent to change my tickets. I was incredulous that she would say that. Had she been living under a rock? I replied earnestly, "Daisy, have you seen the news lately? Baghdad, Iraq, is a war zone. The only airline flying in and out of here is MILAIR. There are no commercial airlines here."

She then asked why I didn't just handle this with the people at the ticket counter in Kuwait. I told her I couldn't chance that for a couple of reasons. For one, I would be arriving in Kuwait very late—just a few hours before catching the first flight out the following day, so I needed to ensure I was booked on that flight in advance. Secondly, and likely most important, was that I was a female, and Kuwait was a Muslim country. I knew, particularly after my experience in Qatar, that I could not risk trying to do a ticket transaction there, particularly with no male escort.

None of this compelled Daisy to do anything, and she continued to say that she could not help me. So I told her I had to speak with someone there who could and asked to speak with her supervisor. Daisy said that her supervisor was in a meeting. I told her that I would hold but reminded her that I was on an international mobile call, which was likely costing the American taxpayer a lot of money.

When her supervisor got on the line, and I explained the situation, she understood. She said it would be complicated, but she would handle this and ensure I had a confirmed seat on the commercial airline flight out of Kuwait connecting through Europe and onto Washington Dulles Airport. She did the research and gave me the flight numbers so I could write them down.

The MILAIR flight from Baghdad to Kuwait was filled with US Army Civil Affairs officers. Most were reservists and had been activated for quite a while as their career field was in high demand. They asked if I had ever been to Kuwait. When I told them I hadn't, a few said I should take the opportunity to go downtown and see the city. I told them I didn't think that was a good idea for several reasons. For one, I was a female in a Muslim country. Secondly, I had only a few hours to sleep and get a shower before catching my flight the following day. Regardless, I appreciated their suggestions.

When we arrived in Kuwait, they put us on a shuttle bus to the commercial part of the airport. They did a roll call. Everyone else was in the Army, and all responded with *HOOAH!*, the Army battle cry, except me. The person in charge looked at me and said, "Oh, yeah, you're the civilian. There is a ride for you." I was given a ride to the hotel on the airport property and told to be in the lobby the next morning at a specific time, where I would catch a shuttle to the airport terminal.

The room was small, and the accommodations were spartan for a hotel, but I did not care. I was so tired and had to be ready and back in the lobby in just a few hours. After trying to sleep for a couple of hours, I got up, showered and dressed, and headed to the lobby. A man in traditional Arab garb had my name on a sign, and I followed him to a shuttle.

He drove me to what looked like a back door to the airport. As I exited the shuttle, he told me to leave my bag with him and that he would take care of it. I was not sure I would ever see my suitcase again, but I obliged. When I got inside the airport, I realized I had indeed been taken through some back door as I never saw a formal entrance with security. I found a display with my flight listed and went to the gate.

As a woman in western clothing, I stood out. Looking around the gate area, I saw very few Westerners. Then I saw someone holding a DoD Common Access Card (CAC) and walked over to him and said, "Hi, I'm guessing you're DoD." He said he was and then asked about me. I told him my story and said I was glad to see another American.

He was amazed upon hearing my story and then asked to see my CAC. He flipped it over, looked at me, and said, "It is a good thing you did not leave the airport property. You don't have the endorsements to do that. A guy I worked with did that without the proper endorsements, and he's been under house arrest here for three months."

Inside I was thinking, "What?! Thank God that I declined the suggestion to tour downtown Kuwait. I could have been stranded here indefinitely!"

We stayed together and talked until it was time to board the plane.

Never in my life had I been so happy about a flight takeoff. As we taxied down the runway and took to the sky, I thanked God for keeping me safe through the trip and this ordeal. Then I closed my eyes and tried to sleep. Though I was tired, I had a lot on my mind, so I did not get much rest.

When I arrived for my connecting flight, I was informed that I had been upgraded to a business-class seat for my flight from Europe to the USA. I was very grateful for that! In 2002, I flew over 100,000 miles and earned United Airlines Premier 1K status. That was the top tier in their loyalty program, putting me somewhere at the top of the upgrade list for the flight.

Before we boarded, the agent called me to the ticket counter at the gate. She asked to see my boarding pass and then ripped it up. I thought, "Oh, no! I need that seat so that I can sleep!" My thoughts must have shown on my face because the agent looked at me and said with a smile, "Don't worry. I think you'll like the seat I'm giving you."

When she handed me the new boarding pass, I looked at it and noticed I was in row one. She had upgraded me to first class with sleeper seats! Never before and never since have I ever had that privilege, but there was never a time I needed it more. As soon as we were airborne, I reclined the seat to the fully flat position and fell asleep. I had no more worries. Soon I would be home.

Warrior Goddess

Against the odds, I made it safely home on 18 December 2003 and to the NGA-NSA quarterly the next day. My firsthand report from the battlefront was powerful, full of quotes from the military leadership conducting the war on terrorism. The directors agreed to take action on our initial findings.

In the end, Mike, Chris, and I compiled a twelve-page trip report of our findings and required actions, and the wartime imperatives helped us gain the momentum to effect necessary change. We were not popular with the bureaucrats, the Klingons, and the Purveyors of the Status Quo, but we didn't care. We were not there to serve them. We were there to serve those in harm's way, and they knew we were their champions.

Around this time, one of my special ops friends remarked in a group setting that now that I was a government official leading the charge for change on their behalf, my call sign needed to be upgraded from Warrior Princess to Warrior Goddess. The others present agreed.

To this day, I feel such a strong connection to and deep gratitude for those who serve our country in uniform. I've had a glimpse of their life and the sacrifices they make daily that most people cannot begin to comprehend. Having been to the combat zones and returning home after a short visit, I can only imagine what it is like to live that way for months. It must be surreal for military members to come home on leave from deployment only to return, for it's like living in two different worlds.

It has been my honor and privilege to collaborate with the military—especially SOF. Those experiences have been the highlight of my career. Their trust and faith in me and desire to give me a call sign like I was one of them meant so much.

CHAPTER 20

Ambassadors and Movie Stars

As the new year started, I had a fun event to attend—a gig Skunk had at the Hungarian ambassador's residence in January 2004. The Hungarian ambassador, Andras Simonyi, had a doctorate in political science and was an amateur musician. While serving as the Hungarian representative to NATO in Brussels, Belgium, he teamed up with his American counterpart to form the Combined Joint Task Force band. Then shortly after arriving in Washington, DC, as ambassador in 2002, he helped create a band called The Coalition of the Willing.

Hungarian Ambassador Andras Simonyi and legendary guitarist Jeffrey "Skunk" Baxter playing in the band Coalition of the Willing at the Hungarian Embassy in Washington, DC (2004)

Ambassador (Amb.) Simonyi was a lifelong lover of music, especially rock and roll. While growing up in communist Hungary, he listened to forbidden radio stations such as Radio Free Europe. During breaks between songs throughout the concert, Amb. Simonyi shared stories about life behind the Iron Curtain of the Union of Soviet Socialist Republics (USSR)—the bulwark of Marxist-Leninist communism.

The Iron Curtain was a political and ideological barrier erected by the Soviet Union after World War II to seal off itself and its dependent eastern and central European allies from open contact with the West and other noncommunist areas. The Berlin Wall was a physical barrier built by the communists to prevent people from fleeing East Berlin, which they controlled. As such, it was the perfect symbol of the Iron Curtain that separated the democratic western countries and the communist countries of eastern Europe, which included Hungary, throughout the Cold War.

It was fascinating to hear Amb. Simonyi's perspective about the role American rock and roll had played in the fall of the Iron Curtain. The music loosened the attitudes in communist societies. It emboldened people to seek freedom and start revolutions that led to the Berlin Wall coming down and the people becoming liberated from this oppressive regime. Hungary became a democracy in 1990 after forty years of communist rule.

As the Soviet dictator Vladimir Lenin famously said, "The goal of socialism is communism." People who lived through the Cold War, especially those subjected to Marxist communist regimes, know firsthand how such governments oppress their citizens.

Marxism destroys the middle class. Effectively, there are only two classes—the elite ruling class, who wields power and makes all the decisions and lives well, and the "workers" who have no freedom to live their lives as they choose and must live with the choices of the ruling class and take whatever the government gives them. The only people that benefit from a Marxist regime are those in the ruling class. Marxism has led to the deaths of over 100 million people.

The truth is free-market capitalism is the only form of government that has lifted the oppressed. Every country that has tried socialism has seen it fail and leave destruction in its wake. Those countries have eventually had to adopt at least some aspects of a free-market society to survive.

America remains the beacon of hope—the city of light on a hill—for all who suffer under tyrannical regimes. Because of America's Judeo-Christian founding values and moral belief that humans have inalienable rights that come from God, not the government, people have experienced liberty. They have had the opportunity to change their stars and achieve their full potential. I felt blessed to be born in the USA—land of the free because of the brave. So many sacrificed so much over the years to secure the liberty that I and millions of others enjoy today.

In March 2004, I was Skunk's guest for the Leukemia and Lymphoma Society's Seventeenth Annual Leukemia Ball at the Washington Convention Center. The main act was a Blues Brothers Revue based on the running *Saturday Night Live* skit immortalized in the *Blues Brothers* movie in 1980. John Belushi played Jake, and Dan Aykroyd played Elwood in the skit and the movie; unfortunately, John died two years after the film's release due to a drug overdose. His brother, Jim Belushi, stepped in to play the role of Jake, and Dan reprised his role as Elwood. Skunk was part of the band.

I thoroughly enjoyed seeing Skunk and his friend Dan play the classic Blues Brothers songs. Dan's wife Donna Dixon, DNGA Clapper, and I were seated at the same table. Donna was so funny and entertaining. She kept us laughing throughout the evening.

After the show, Donna invited me to their hotel across from Lafayette Square overlooking the White House to hang out with their family. So when the festivities concluded, we all went backstage, piled into a stretch limo, and headed for the hotel. It was a pleasure to spend time with Dan, Donna, and their family. You could not ask for more fun and down-to-earth people, and they're celebrities.

Dan later came to NGA for a special event. He has done good things for law enforcement and joint American-Canadian national security, but you may not know that because it's not advertised. Dan is very talented and has a big heart, donating his time to charitable efforts. It was fun to get to know Dan and Donna, who I consider friends.

Michele greets Dan Aykroyd at NGA headquarters as their mutual friend Jeffrey "Skunk" Baxter looks on (2004)

EXCOM

NGA underwent another reorganization in March 2004, and DNGA Clapper created the Technical Executive (TX) position on the Executive Committee (EXCOM). Rob, former Director of InnoVision, became the TX, and I became the Deputy TX. Rob was a political science major, so he told everyone I was the "T" in TX.

We were able to take a small staff with us, and so we handpicked people from the Horizontal Integration staff—Sandra, Rikki, Jim, and Chris. In addition, William "Buzz" Roberts, a former USAF Senior Master Sergeant who I knew by his outstanding reputation serving in NRO OSO, would join our staff when he started with NGA in June.

Kim Garner, a graduate of the highly competitive Defense Language Institute, joined our team as my executive assistant. She was competent, had excellent attention to detail, and got along well with the team.

DNGA called us his Spetsnaz, the Russian term for special operations forces. He had been the first American general to interface with a Russian counterpart after the fall of the Soviet Union and took a liking to that term. With DNGA's top cover, we got so much done. Top cover is golden, for when you have it, you can go further and faster than you could otherwise.

Though we had a team of five people, others assumed we had a staff of fifty. I would tell them, "No, we have five people who each do the work of at least ten regular staff officers." We had a great group, á la Warren Bennis's book *Great Groups*. Chris had corresponded with Warren Bennis and had given me that book to read.

Furthermore, like the Blues Brothers, we knew "we're on a mission from God." We worked hard and pulled long hours under immense pressure and with constant opposition, but we accomplished what others considered impossible because it had to be done. It was an intense time but also a highlight of my career.

Remembering D-Day

When you report to the director of a national agency, your schedule is not your own. There are a lot of regular meetings with the director or with the senior staff. Despite your best-laid plans, a task from POTUS or a Congressionally Directed Action (CDA) could trump everything, and you just had to go with it.

This is what I call Semper Gumby mode. The motto of the US Marine Corps is Semper Fidelis, which means "always faithful." Gumby is a flexible green character made for Claymation, reportedly inspired by the gingerbread man. Gumby was turned into a bendy green action figure and often paired with his faithful friend, the orange horse called Pokey. So, Semper Gumby means always flexible.

Furthermore, when you are an office director, your day is often spent with your team in meetings, project reviews, brainstorming sessions, etc. Sometimes, you only get to the work you planned to do once your staff goes home.

On one such day in May 2004, after most of the building was vacated and I was alone in my office working on my computer, the phone at my desk rang. It was DNGA Clapper. He often had special events in town and jokingly said he was dining for his country. I later picked up that phrase when I achieved a rank that warranted similar invitations.

When I picked up the phone, he said, "Michele, I am at the French Embassy, and you will never guess who I just met." This call was out of the blue and interrupted my train of thought, and I could not imagine who he had just met because the director met many different people at various events.

I cannot recall how I responded to his question, but I do remember how I felt when I heard the name, Tom Selleck. "What?" I replied. "I have been a big fan of his for years! I used to have a poster of him as Magnum P.I. in his red Ferrari on my wall in junior high!" I went on with something to the effect of, "Here I am at work, and you're out socializing with celebrities. I would love to meet Tom Selleck, and you probably don't care one way or another."

He was amused with my response and said, "Not to worry, I've sent my driver back to pick you up."

"Really?" I said.

He assured me it was true and advised me to wrap up whatever I was working on and meet his driver in front of the building.

His driver pulled into the NGA headquarters driveway and got out to open the door for me. He had a big grin when I told him that this surprise invitation made my day as I was a big fan of Tom Selleck!

The event at the French Embassy was the premiere of a movie in which Tom had starred. It was a made-for-TV historical war drama called *Countdown to D-Day,* scheduled to be aired on the A&E network. Tom played General Dwight D. Eisenhower, US Army. Ike, as he was known, had become a five-star general during World War II and served as the Supreme Commander of the Allied Expeditionary Force in Europe. I had a hard time picturing Tom as Ike because he was tall and had a thick head of brown hair and a mustache, whereas Ike was short, bald, and clean-shaven. Regardless, I would arrive just in time to catch the movie and hear the question-and-answer period with Tom and Ike's granddaughter.

The movie covers the ninety days leading up to Operation Overlord, the Allied invasion of Normandy, France, and how General Eisenhower brilliantly orchestrated the most important military maneuver in modern history against all odds. The story focuses on the senior-level preparations for the D-Day invasion on 6 June 1944, from the time of Ike's appointment as the Supreme Allied Commander in Europe to the establishment of the beachhead in Normandy.

The film recounts many of the challenges Ike had to face, which included dealing with some strong personalities in the leaders surrounding him and the need for tact and diplomacy to bring all sides together for what would be the largest amphibious assault ever attempted. Ike's D-Day speech to the troops was powerful, and those who survived the invasion likely never forgot it.

On 6 June 1944, more than 150,000 brave soldiers from the US, UK, and Canada stormed the beaches of Normandy in a bold strategy to force the Nazis out of western Europe and turn the tide of the war for good. It had to be done because of the fascist dictator Adolf Hitler's Holocaust, the state-sponsored mass murder of six million European Jews and millions of others by the German Nazis. So many risked their lives, and tens of thousands died that day to end Hitler's tyranny and liberate Europe.

Something like this had never been attempted before. Ike knew it could fail and drafted remarks he'd make in case the invasion was a failure. In those remarks, he said, "If any blame or fault attaches to the attempt, it is mine alone." Ike was a leader with integrity. He went on to serve as the thirty-fourth president of the United States. Ike said, "The supreme quality for leadership is unquestionably integrity. Without it, no real success is possible."

The supreme quality for leadership is unquestionably integrity.
Without it, no real success is possible.

Tom did a fantastic job portraying Ike during a trying time—for Ike personally, for America, and its allies as they strategized how to defeat Nazi Germany and the Axis powers during World War II. If you haven't seen the movie, I highly recommend it because this is a critical part of world history.

When the question-and-answer period wrapped up, Tom started walking up the theater aisle where DNGA Clapper and I were standing. I asked DNGA Clapper to introduce me, and he did. Tom stopped and looked at me with kind eyes as I said, "I've been a lifelong fan of yours. You did a great job portraying Ike." Then Tom gave me his characteristic smile and thanked me. Having been a fan of his for so long, that was a special moment for me.

CHAPTER 21

Sweden

In August 2004, I was part of an official NGA delegation to Sweden. The senior NGA representative was Tom Fergusson, who was great fun to work with, and it was clear the Swedes felt the same way about him that I did.

In the meetings, we were seated at a very long table, and each person had a nameplate along with a miniature flag that denoted the country they represented. During the first break, our host, a major general in Swedish intelligence, asked me about my name. He said that Weslander—just as I spelled it—was a common name in Sweden. I told him I hadn't heard that before, as Weslander was rare in America.

"Do you have any family ties to Sweden?" he asked.

"Yes," I replied. "My great grandfather, Gustaf Weslander, was from Kristianstad and immigrated from Sweden to America."

The major general stood tall and seemed very proud to welcome me to the homeland. This was my first visit to Sweden, and, given my heritage, it was meaningful for me to be there.

Tom and I toured Stockholm that evening before dinner. He knew it well and showed me all kinds of interesting old places.

Our hosts treated us to a lavish dinner on the waterfront. When they served dessert, the server asked if I would like coffee. As someone who cannot have caffeine past midday or I won't sleep, I asked, "Do you have decaf?"

There was a hush at my end of the table. The server and those around us seemed surprised at my question. Then, I learned the Swedes love their coffee—it is part of their lifestyle—but they don't do decaf. "If you're looking for decaf, you're in the wrong country." Regardless, they were gracious hosts.

Special Ops

As 2004 came to a close, we recognized that many challenges remained in supporting the troops who were a part of OIF and OEF. One of our former InnoVision compatriots, Ed, former Army special ops, offered to embed with SOF in Afghanistan to support them and provide us with reports from the battlefront.

Per feedback from SOF, sometimes operations had to be planned, but the most current imagery available was over twenty-four hours old. A lot can change in twenty-four hours, so it is crucial to have up-to-date information before sending troops into harm's way. National assets are in high demand but a limited resource; commercial imagery could fill the gap.

Over our careers, Chris and I worked closely with commercial satellite imagery providers, and we both had excellent relationships with those companies' leadership and team members. We determined it would be beneficial to make a trip to Afghanistan, similar to the trip we made to Iraq, to prove the value of this capability and get insights and feedback from the troops and their support teams downrange.

So in early 2005, with the support of DNGA, Chris and I made plans to spend some time boots on the ground with SOF in Afghanistan. However, some did not want to see a Weslander and Quaid battlefront reprise, complete with another twelve-page trip report from the combat zone that we would use to effect change as we did after our trip to Iraq. So they fought it.

New policies were implemented to prepare people for traveling downrange, including weapons training. Having never fired a gun before, aside from a BB gun at a day camp in my childhood, this was a new experience for me, whereas Chris was an expert marksman.

We did weapons training with the USAF at what is now known as Joint Base Anacostia-Bolling. Their weapons were in pristine condition. They trained us to clean and handle the 9mm guns and then took us to the range.

The military shows a lot of deference to general and flag officers; as a member of the senior executive civilian ranks, I was shown that same deference. They had an airman specifically assigned to help me with the 9mm. I had no idea what to expect, and my first shot was pretty accurate. However, after experiencing the recoil, I hesitated more on my next shot. We had to achieve a certain level of accuracy to pass the timed test, and the airman was not sure I would make it. Chris told him to wait, and I did it!

In February 2005, DNGA told me they were trying out a new executive version of CIA's "Crash and Bang" course in Richmond, Virginia, and suggested that Chris and I go through the training. Our instruction started with classroom training—both for driving and weapons—and then they took us to the driving course and the firing range.

I have not forgotten the story they told of two female CIA officers who had been through their program just weeks before deploying overseas. They had recently contacted the instructors to tell them that if it was not for their training, they would likely be dead; they had been ambushed but were able to get out due to the skills they had learned. That was sobering.

The firing range experience was different from that with the military. There was snow on the ground and dirt and gravel everywhere. The guns were dirty, and they jammed a lot. The instructors made an excellent point—in reality, especially downrange, the conditions are not pristine, and you need to learn how to deal with less-than-ideal situations. They put us at closer range to the targets than we were at the military base. They reasoned that, in reality, if an aggressor was any further than twenty feet away from you, the best option was run away from them. Good point. Their training was so much more practical. My grouping on these targets was much better. Let's just say that the enemy may not be dead, but he likely would not be able to talk or reproduce.

Then they took us to the driving course. They had old cars, and they told us they were so rough on them with this training that they had to replace the tires every three to five days. Some vehicles had anti-lock brakes while others had old-style brakes, and we needed to learn both because they had to be handled differently.

They gave us all helmets. The instructor was in the passenger seat next to the student driver, and other students were in the car's back seat. The instructor was clear that we were to drive as fast as we could while maintaining control of the vehicle. I would later joke that Chris only heard the first part of that instruction.

I drove first. Being told to floor it, I took off down the track. I had to maneuver in between and around pylons and other cars. After running through the course a few times, the instructor gave us a break before returning to the car.

When we got back in the car, I saw that the instructor had put cardboard in front of the windshield so that I could not see where I was going. He said that when he pulled the cardboard away, I would have to react to whatever was ahead of me. Then he said, "Floor it!"

After having run through the course a few times, I knew the layout. So, naturally, that was what I was expecting. However, when he pulled the cardboard away, I realized they had changed the course, and I had to react. Before the instructor said a word, I turned to him and said, "You made your point. We get comfortable with what we think we know and are unprepared when things change. We always have to be alert and on our guard."

"Yes, exactly," he replied with a smile.

This made me understand how statistics show that many people get in accidents just a few miles away from their houses. Why? Because they drive this way all the time, are comfortable with it, and can get lax and pay less attention than they should. Then something out of the ordinary happens or there is a change, and—boom—they have an accident.

It was Chris's turn to drive next, and, as I mentioned, I think he only heard "drive as fast as you can" but missed "while maintaining control of the car." I was sure glad I was wearing a helmet. Even then, I got banged up in the back seat. Chris, however, seemed to be having the time of his life.

The trainer remarked that I was a much better driver, while Chris was a much better marksman, so we may want to stick with our strengths downrange.

In the next phase of driver training, we learned how to drive three cars abreast in two lanes. Why? Because people operate that way in some overseas countries.

Then they had us drive down an alleyway created by a bunch of old beat-up cars. Suddenly, people jumped out from behind the cars and started shooting paintballs at us. Our instructor then told us to drive full speed in reverse using our rearview mirror, and then we had to spin around and get out of there. I felt like I was the driver on a movie set.

But wait, it gets better. Then we drove around in an open space, and the driver of an aggressor car started firing paintballs at us. The aggressor's car hit our car and sent us into a spin, and we had to get out of it. Not only did they teach us how to get out of the spin, but they also taught us how to put another car into a spin. This could be helpful if you need to buy some time to get away.

Michele and Chris Quaid with Crash and Bang instructors on the driving course (2005)

What can I say? This was a wild experience. After completing the course, I believed everyone getting a driver's license should undergo at least a subset of this training. While most people don't need to learn to drive full speed in reverse while people are shooting at them, everyone completing the training would have such a better appreciation of how to handle a car and how little you have to turn the steering wheel to cause the vehicle to move where you want it to go.

Driving back to Washington, DC, Chris and I talked about how exceptional the training was and how the drivers around us on the freeway had no idea what we were capable of doing.

When we returned to headquarters, the director's exec, an Army colonel, met us. He laughed and said, "I already got the report—she drives, and he shoots!"

When we returned to the office, Chris and I started making final plans for our trip to Afghanistan, feeling far better equipped than we had felt before our trip to Iraq.

Then, to our surprise, DNGA told us to stand down, citing pressure from naysayers, which included his deputy. We wondered how this could happen. NGA was a combat support agency—how could we not support the warfighters?

I pleaded with DNGA not to succumb to office politics and to let me make this trip for the good of the warfighters. As a technologist who knew the art of the possible, I could determine things we could do for the warfighter that they didn't know to ask for, and I had a proven track record of doing just that, including the trip to Iraq in December 2003.

DNGA finally agreed to let me go and told Rob he wanted him to accompany me as he did not want me to go alone. Rob was surprised and initially not too keen on the idea, but to his credit, he committed to going and joined in the planning for our trip. The timeline was key, as we wanted to get there before the start of the Spring Offensive, which happened every year as the weather in the area started to warm up.

GEN Stanley "Stan" McChrystal, US Army, was commanding JSOC at the time, and his chief of intelligence was Major General (MG) Michael "Mike" Flynn, US Army. Our NGA colleague, Ed, was friends with them, and we had a chance to meet and hear their mission imperatives firsthand. I knew GEN McChrystal by his reputation, and it was great to meet him in person. He was intelligent, humble, and down to earth, and it was clear that he got it. GEN McChrystal knew this was no conventional war—it was a war for hearts and minds.

MG Flynn realized we needed to approach intelligence differently. He also recognized that open-source (unclassified) intelligence was vital because we needed to be able to share with non-traditional partners, such as non-governmental organizations (NGOs), who did not have security clearances.

I was honored to travel with the SOF team to Afghanistan in April 2005. We flew in on a C-17 Globemaster III. As we approached in the darkness, they turned off all the regular lights on the plane and turned on the red lights. The song I was listening to on my iPod via my BOSE noise-canceling headphones was "Here Without You" by 3 Doors Down. To this day, I cannot hear that song without the image of that moment in my life coming to mind.

I observed all the SOF guys preparing for arrival—they were old pros, as they had done this many times before. I had, and always will have, a tremendous amount of respect for them. The SOF teams risk their lives for our freedom and rarely, if ever, get to talk about the amazing things they do because of the secret nature of their missions.

When we arrived in Bagram, Afghanistan, I was escorted to a women's "hooch," plywood living quarters with bunk beds. I picked an open bunk and ditched my stuff.

Then we headed to the Joint Inter-Agency Task Force (JIATF) building. It was a large room full of workstations on tables with a high, tented ceiling. The stairs in the back led up to a raised conference room. The US Navy Seabees were on base installing a more permanent structure, but it wasn't finished.

We would get into their battle rhythm while we were there, ignoring the local time and staying on the Zulu time, or "zero-offset time," a.k.a. Greenwich Mean Time (GMT) or Coordinated Universal Time (UTC). This meant we kept some odd hours, but it would be the same as those doing the mission planning and conducting the missions, which occurred in darkness.

Michele and Rob Zitz at Bagram Air Base, Afghanistan (2005)

Thus would start my week-long routine of working in the JIATF as the sun was low on the horizon and through the night. I would go to bed as the sun rose and try to get some sleep. Then I'd get up, shower, and brush my teeth in a double-decker trailer with water you could use to gargle with but not swallow. I would eat meals in the mess hall and occasionally some vegetarian MREs (meals ready to eat). You could tell who the SOF guys were in the mess hall as they had full heads of hair and beards, whereas everyone else had a crew cut and was clean-shaven.

We attended the regular ops-intel briefings each day. I remember sitting behind an officer wearing a double 9mm shoulder holster with barrels of the two guns facing me and thinking, "I hope he has the safeties on!"

Though Chris did not join us on the trip, he was still a part of the team working full-time to get a prototype set up that we would use in Afghanistan. DigitalGlobe was one of the first commercial satellite imaging companies. We both had excellent, long-standing relationships with Walter Scott, the founder, and Vic Leonard, the senior scientist, and we knew them to be especially forward-leaning. They were willing to take a shared risk with us to prove the value of new capabilities, including the one we would test in the JIATF.

For many years we had talked about the value of providing commercial satellite imagery to the troops downrange within minutes of the satellite's "time over target." Now was our chance to prove it.

In addition to the regular ops-intel briefings, every evening, there was a Rehearsal of Concept, a.k.a. ROC drill, in preparation for that night's mission. The ROC drill is an essential tool for planning and executing complex events and allows the participants to rehearse combat mission plans and implement contingency plans. It began with the US Army. They drew in the dirt for the first ROC drill and used rocks to represent soldiers and vehicles.

To date, the SOF teams had relied on analyzed and annotated classified imagery for their planning, but given it was classified, they could not share it with Coalition partners or take it with them on the mission. By providing the latest commercial imagery within minutes, the analysts would not only be able to review the most current image of the area of interest, but the troops conducting the mission would also be able to share the annotated product and take it with them.

To me and Chris, the inherent value of this capability was a blinding flash of the obvious, a saying we had picked up from Col. Cope. However, the bureaucracy needed some convincing. Hence, we decided to do this proof of concept in the theater of operations.

The JIATF imagery analyst was from NGA, and her name was Grainne. She was young and serving on her first deployment, but intelligent, competent at her job, and highly valued by the SOF teams. Grainne explained to me the process she went through every day in preparation for the ROC drills. Often she did not have current imagery. Ideally, they would have imagery just a few hours old but at most twenty-four hours. I shared that we would be working to get a commercial imagery collection as close as possible to the time she would be doing analysis to prepare products for the ROC drill, hoping that she could annotate a product that the SOF team could take with them on the mission.

That evening we got a commercial image of their area of interest. When Grainne saw the image on the computer screen, she pushed me aside and started doing the analysis and building the products for the ROC drill. Given that commercial image was not classified, the operators could take the annotated imagery products with them on the mission. This was a big deal.

Chris coordinated efforts back in the USA with the DigitalGlobe team, and we worked together to make this happen. The feedback we got from the SOF team was excellent.

It was no secret where the US base was in Bagram. We were told the local insurgents often fired mortar rounds at the base, but they generally had terrible aim. One evening, we were notified of an incoming mortar attack and told to get our flak vests and helmets and take cover. After retrieving my flak vest and helmet from the hooch, I wasn't sure where everyone else had gone to take cover, so I returned to the JIATF and continued working at the computer.

When they determined we were safe from further mortar attacks for the evening, Rob, who had been in a bunker, returned to the JIATF. When he saw me sitting alone at the computer wearing a helmet and flak vest, he laughed and said he wanted a picture because it was a funny sight.

Throughout our stay, we continued to work with the JIATF staff and the SOF teams doing the missions. Our commercial imagery proof of concept was a success, and the warfighters wanted this to be a permanent capability. It was not a program of record, meaning it was not an officially budgeted program, so we had to find the money to do it.

As I walked back to the hooch to catch a little sleep before starting the journey home to the USA, the sun rose over the beautiful snowcapped mountains. I thought, "If this country can ever get its act together, there could be ski resorts in those mountains someday."

Upon returning home, I started looking for funding sources to pay for this new capability that had proven valuable to the SOF teams. Given my position on the NGA EXCOM, I had access to information about the budgets of offices across the agency. In reviewing the line items, I found a few hundred thousand dollars set aside for "front office redecorating" and decided that was the money we would use to fund the commercial imagery server for the warfighters. When I proposed this to DNGA Clapper, he concurred.

When his deputy found out we had taken the funds from her redecorating budget, she was quite upset. When DNGA called me to share his deputy's displeasure, I responded, "You're running a combat support agency. The warfighters don't care what your front office looks like, but they need imagery. This is the right thing to do." He, of course, agreed, and we used the funds to procure the commercial imagery server for the warfighters.

Shortly after that, Chris moved to another office at NGA doing more direct warfighter support. This was an excellent fit for him.

When Grainne returned home, having won multiple awards from the military for her most excellent service, her NGA boss decided to grade her down on her performance appraisal. What was her boss's reasoning, you ask? Grainne wasn't at headquarters helping out their office. Well, no, she wasn't. Instead, she was in a combat zone doing far more for those conducting the war on terrorism than this staff officer back at headquarters.

When I told DNGA Clapper about this, he was furious. He called all the NGA leadership together for a meeting and said that something like this should never happen and that he better not hear about it happening again. We wanted people to deploy with the troops when needed, and we would not penalize them for doing so. After that, NGA started incentive and awards programs for people who deployed.

Don't worry about Grainne. Her personnel record got adjusted appropriately, and I recruited her onto my team. Then I took her on my next trip to Australia, the Land Down Under or Oz, to meet with our Commonwealth partners. As a vegetarian since high school, I was taken aback hearing Grainne's food orders. Wherever we went, she asked the waiter what local animal was on the menu she could eat. After that, I gave her a hard time about "eating her way through the exotic animals of Australia."

The Last of the Titans

In October 2005, I was thrilled to be invited to witness the last Titan launch at Vandenberg Air Force Base. The invitation was from Col. Regis Baldauff, launch commander. Regis had hosted Col. Henley and me at Kennedy Space Center when he was assigned there and treated us to quite the adventure of scaling their Titan launch complex.

This last Titan launch was the end of an era that began fifty years prior with the Titan I. An NRO payload would be launched on this Titan IV—the last of the Titans. For someone who had spent many a holiday initializing NRO imaging payloads after launch, it was fun to experience the launch firsthand instead of on TV. In addition, I had long heard about all the festivities that go with a launch, such as the Santa Maria barbeques, and it was fun to be a part of that.

The launch occurred on 19 October 2005. It was a beautiful clear day, so we were able to watch the Titan IV for a long time until it disappeared on its trip into space. The cameras set up around the launch site were able to get some excellent shots. Each successful launch must be an amazing thrill and relief for the squadron and team that pulled it off.

Launches are moving experiences for me. I don't think that will ever change.

Michele with USAF officers Maj. Chris Quaid [back left], Maj. Brian Beveridge [back right] and Lt. Col. Leslie Howell at Vandenberg AFB for the last Titan launch (2005)

The NRO launch squadron sold black T-shirts with the launch squadron logo on the front and NRO across the back in white text. I bought one and decided to wear it on the plane back to Washington, DC.

As I was walking on the jetway after disembarking the plane, two men approached quickly behind me. Sheepishly one asked, "Can we wear such shirts in public?"

"Yes," I replied. "The NRO launch squadron was selling them at the Titan launch!"

We exchanged knowing glances. Though the NRO's existence was declassified a decade prior, it was still weird for those of us who had worked in this business during the era of high secrecy to be able to talk about the NRO in public.

CHAPTER 22

ODNI

The idea of a Director of National Intelligence dates back to 1955 when a blue-ribbon study commissioned by Congress recommended that the director of the CIA have a deputy who ran the CIA so that the director could focus on coordinating the overall intelligence effort across the IC. This idea continued to emerge as a consistent theme in subsequent studies of the IC commissioned by the US government's executive and legislative branches.

After the terrorist attacks on 11 September 2001, there was a call for intelligence reform, including significant changes to the IC and a drive to create a Director of National Intelligence (DNI). The US Congress passed the Intelligence Reform and Terrorism Prevention Act in 2004. It was signed into law by President George W. Bush on 17 December 2004.

In February 2005, President Bush nominated John Negroponte, ambassador to Iraq, as the first DNI, and Lt. Gen. Mike Hayden, USAF, as the first Principal Deputy DNI (PDDNI), promoting him to four-star general. They were sworn in on 21 April 2005, and the Office of the DNI (ODNI) began operations the next day.

As the ODNI was being established, key leadership positions needed to be filled. DNGA Clapper and PDDNI Hayden, former DIRNSA, recommended that I become the IC Deputy Chief Information Officer (DCIO). They thought I was uniquely qualified because I had the technical expertise and operational experience and had run headlong into the policies preventing Multi-INT collaboration and information sharing across the IC. They told me that this was my opportunity to fix those policies.

In this role, I would update the IC's rules from the IT perspective, enabling the use of modern technology to facilitate information sharing and collaboration. This would create a better shared situational awareness across the IC so that we could connect the dots.

The timing of my appointment as DCIO was dependent on the CIO's Senate confirmation. The person who had been nominated to be the CIO was a former two-star general in the USAF who had done staff and comm jobs but had no career experience in the IC. By that point, I had about fifteen years of experience in the IC. He made a point of telling me he had never had a female deputy before. Regardless, he knew my credentials and recognized that my career experience in the IC was key to helping the new office of the CIO hit the ground running.

With my impending job change in mind, I worked discreetly to find the TX staff other positions within NGA. When I encouraged Sandra to take a job in the same group as Chris, she said, "You're pushing me out of the nest." She had done excellent work as part of my team, and now it was her chance to fly and shine in other areas. She joined Chris in his efforts, and they did great things for the warfighters together.

They worked for Bruce, a different CIA operative than the one I knew in PEB. He had mysterious pictures on his wall that he would not tell you anything about, but we knew there had to be a good story that went with them. When we asked, he said with a sly grin, "I could tell you, but then I'd have to kill you."

Chris was promoted to the rank of major in 2004, and in 2005 the USAF assigned him to serve on Air Staff at the Pentagon. Most airmen would consider that an honor because the USAF picks top-notch officers for this job, but Chris was not thrilled with the idea. He loved ops; he was not interested in being a paper-pushing staff officer creating PowerPoint briefings for the generals. However, once he was on Air Staff, they put him in charge of future planning for a next-generation radar imaging system, a great fit given his career experience.

In the summer of 2005, I was selected to participate in the Senior Managers in Government course at Harvard University's Kennedy School of Government (KSG). So, I moved to Boston, Massachusetts, for three weeks and lived out of the Harvard dorms that were within walking distance of KSG.

Shirley Weslander, Lee Akridge, Col. Ted Cope, USAF, and Michele at Major Chris Quaid's promotion party (2005)

Boston can be hot and muggy in the summers, but the weather was warm and pleasant that August. There is so much American history and culture in Boston. On our one weekend off, I enjoyed walking the famous Freedom Trail.

Being a part of the KSG program was a tremendous experience—meeting senior government leaders from all over the world and learning more about how the government works in America and how that differs from other countries. Many of our professors and guest speakers had worked in senior-level positions in past administrations, including with President Reagan, and they offered valuable insights. This was another excellent networking opportunity. I kept in contact with some of my KSG classmates for many years and had a chance to collaborate with some of them professionally.

The Senate confirmed the IC CIO in December 2005. Effective 1 January 2006, I assumed my role as the Deputy Chief Information Officer of the Intelligence Community, a.k.a. IC DCIO, at the age of thirty-five.

The IC DCIO position came with tremendous responsibility, and it was my great honor and privilege to serve in this capacity. After my official swearing-in that week, I was introduced to DNI Negroponte and the ODNI senior leadership at the morning staff meeting. I also started receiving a copy of the President's Daily Briefing.

The following excerpt from my Christmas 2005 holiday letter conveys my enthusiasm: "We have a huge responsibility but also an amazing opportunity to do good things for the national security community and the country. We share a common vision, a strong conviction that the community needs change, and a commitment to do whatever is within our authorities to enact policies that encourage information sharing and make information technology an enabler."

It was a unique time at the ODNI as we were creating something new with an eye on helping the IC successfully transition into the twenty-first century. Those in the top leadership positions were all new.

If it had been up to me, I would have created the ODNI entirely from scratch—establishing a lean staff and hiring people with the right qualifications and disposition for each position. To me, ODNI, in its oversight role, should be an enabler of those doing the mission.

In contrast, they took the former community management staff (CMS) that reported to the DCI and effectively put an ODNI wrapper on it. So, it started as a bureaucracy and grew to become more bloated. Furthermore, much of the CMS staff was not thrilled with being moved from the CIA to the ODNI, and they were not supportive of the new construct. Some former CMS staff did not support forward progress in the new direction, and some outright fought it and engaged in subversive behavior, which is unfortunate.

One of my colleagues on the ODNI senior staff was Dr. Eric Haseltine, who was recruited to lead ODNI Science and Technology (S&T). He was incredibly brilliant, easygoing and a pleasure to work with, and we were like-minded in our approach as ODNI officials. Eric's philosophy aligned with mine in that we both believed the best strategy was to have a lean ODNI team that worked to enable the various components across the IC to achieve success.

The CIO had a different philosophy, however. While we inherited personnel, the CIO continued to amass quite a staff totaling over 500, including civilian, military, and industry team members. Part of the CIO's staff included five highly paid industry partners whose primary job was to do research for him and write his speeches.

One of those individuals was Patrick O'Brien, who was highly competent, thoughtful, and thorough in his work. People like Patrick were not recognized often, but they made their bosses look good and were valuable members of the team.

The office of the CIO (OCIO) inherited some preexisting functions. One of the operations that came under the OCIO was INTELINK.

Created in 1994, this innovative IC startup had become an operationally critical capability. INTELINK was hosted at Ft. Meade with NSA. They utilized web-based capabilities to introduce efficiencies into the intelligence apparatus by providing a common platform for information sharing and collaboration across the national security enterprise—from analysts at headquarters facilities to warfighters downrange.

At the time, the INTELINK tools and capabilities were only available at two security levels—Secret (S) and Top Secret / Secret Compartmented Information (TS/SCI). During my tenure, we would make those capabilities available at the unclassified (U) level and accessible from anywhere.

Diplomatic Dining

CIO and I had a high distinguished visitor (DV) status. One of the perks of having a high DV status is that you get invited to various events, often formal affairs, around Washington, DC. We could bring a spouse or significant other to most events, but we attended only in our official capacities on one occasion—a benefit hosted at the embassies in Washington, DC.

Our invitation was to the Japanese ambassador's residence. During the advance coordination process, my executive assistant told them I was a vegetarian for meal planning purposes.

At the Japanese embassy, we were all seated at an enormous rectangular table. The CIO was the highest-ranking DV there, and he sat in the center on one side next to the Japanese ambassador's wife. I sat at the opposite side of the table next to the Japanese ambassador, who could not have been a more gracious host. It was a pleasure to talk with him, and I knew he loved American baseball, so we talked about that, among other things. The other side of the table was so far away that you had to raise your voice and look at someone to get their attention. The ambassador and I did a lot of talking one-on-one.

The waitstaff stood behind the guests against the wall and executed the service flawlessly. At one point, the server started to offer me a plate with seafood, and I told him no thanks because I was a vegetarian. I had no idea what would be on the menu or how many courses there would be because there was no printed menu, though there often is at formal events.

The ambassador took note and discussed with the server in Japanese, then assured me they would have vegetarian options prepared for me. I thanked him very much for his thoughtfulness and realized that the information my executive assistant had relayed did not make it to the right person. It didn't matter to me as I wasn't there for the food—I was there for the experience. However, I felt terrible because I knew how much honor meant for the Japanese, and there was an honest mix-up.

There were many courses served that evening. One was soup with seaweed. Next, I was given a plate with chunks of fried tofu and chopsticks.

At this point, I must tell you that I never grew up eating with chopsticks and only tried using them a few times with colleagues who liked to dine at Asian restaurants and used them quite proficiently. So, I drew upon my minimal experience and did my best.

I was pleased when I managed to use the chopsticks successfully with the first few relatively large cubes of tofu. The Japanese ambassador could likely tell that I was not adept at using chopsticks but appreciated I was making a concerted effort to use them.

Next came my "Pretty Woman" moment from the movie by that name with Julia Roberts and Richard Gere. In the film, Richard plays a wealthy businessman with expensive cars and tastes who regularly dines at fancy restaurants. Julia plays a young woman whom he picked up off the streets. He hires her for a week and invites her to a business dinner. She is excited to be dressed up and dining at a fancy restaurant. This is a French restaurant, and she tries very hard to fit in while the men discuss business matters. One of the courses brought to the table is escargot. She asks how to eat it and then does her best to crack the shell but ends up flinging one across the room. As luck would have it, one of the servers catches it. She looks up and says, "Slippery little suckers."

As the Japanese ambassador was sharing a story, I went to pick up another cube of tofu and felt I had a good grip—perhaps too tight a grip, in retrospect—and the chopsticks shifted in my hands as I lifted them to my mouth. The tofu went up in the air and landed under the table between the Japanese ambassador and me. I tried to be very nonchalant about it and keep a poker face, but inside I was mortified.

Then as adroitly as the server in *Pretty Woman* caught the escargot Julia's character sent flying, the server behind us swiftly bent down and snatched the tofu, and that little episode was over. The line going through my head was, "Slippery little suckers!"

The Japanese ambassador did not miss a beat and continued talking like he hadn't seen it. I hoped he hadn't, but who knows? It still makes me laugh as I write about it because it's one of those moments of my life that seems like it was out of a movie script, and the line went through my mind right on queue.

Tippy Top Secret

One of my roles at ODNI was serving on the Special Access Program (SAP) review board. That was an eye-opening experience. On the one hand, I learned about some exciting programs. On the other hand, it drove home the significant issue we faced with the amount of compartmentation in the IC.

Every SAP had its own security level, a separate compartment noted as a caveat to TS/SCI, and its own computer systems that operated in isolation from the primary network. Only a small number of people would be "read into" a SAP, i.e., briefed into that particular security level and caveat, and the numbers were intentionally restricted.

This was according to the long-standing philosophy that the fewer people who knew about something, the less likely there would be a leak. My response was always the same, "If you only read three people in, and one happens to be committing espionage, then the numbers don't matter. This is a human resources problem, not a numbers problem. If you have a hundred trustworthy people read in, you'll be less likely to have a leak than if only three are read in, and one is a bad actor. The bigger issue is ensuring that you hire the right people and they continue to warrant the trust you have placed in them."

No SAP would share anything they were doing with anyone not read into that particular caveat. As someone in SAP oversight, I could see opportunities for collaboration between SAPs, but the isolation of SAPs from each other and mainstream operations precluded that. I believed we needed to slash the number of SAPs we had and, at the same time, raise the barrier to entry for someone to create a SAP in the future. SAPs should be the exception, not the rule.

The CIA had hundreds of compartments or SAPs, which seemed insane. When I shared this thought with a member of CIA S&T who was read into various SAPs, he agreed and added that he saw potential synergies across SAPs quite frequently, but the different SAP managers would not work with each other.

This SAP model was by no means efficient use of taxpayer dollars, either. As has been proven repeatedly, having a diverse team tackle a problem often leads to finding a better solution sooner. Furthermore, if everything is classified "tippy-top secret squirrel," a sarcastic saying we had, what are we actually trying to protect?

Having collaborated with senior intelligence officials across the USA and the Commonwealth countries, I know that I am not alone in this thinking. We need a radical overhaul of our classification system, but no DCI or DNI has been willing to take that on.

CHAPTER 23

Tackling Policy Barriers

As mentioned previously, the IC had this antiquated process of passing clearances. If you didn't have a badge for a particular facility, you had to pass your clearances in advance. Upon arrival at the facility, you would have to present your ID. Then the security officer would check to see if they received your clearances before determining whether to give you a visitor badge and admit you to the building.

Countless people have wasted an incalculable number of hours over the decades sitting in the security office of some building because their clearances were "passed," but the security officers couldn't "find" them. It made sense to me that we should have an IC badge recognized across the community to eliminate this problem.

When I proposed this to DNI Negroponte in an ODNI staff meeting, he and others were interested. I stated that an IC badge needed to be created for all members of the IC, whether they were military, government civilians, or industry partners. While there was consensus from those seated at the table that we should do this for the military and government employees, some were not supportive of doing this for industry partners.

It was then that I made the point that industry partners are critical to the success of the IC. They were on contract to support the mission, billing hours accordingly. So we (the government) would receive the bill for their time regardless. Wouldn't it make more sense to have them productively supporting the mission rather than being stranded in a security office, unable to do their jobs?

DNI Negroponte agreed. That set in motion the development and implementation of the IC badge—blue for military and government and green for industry partners.

Ironically, years later, when I surrendered my blue IC badge upon my resignation from the government, I was never given a green IC badge when I returned to the private sector while still retaining my clearances. So, I had to resort to passing clearances and sometimes ended up stranded in security offices again. Regardless, I am glad that many others have been able to use the IC badge; this ultimately benefits the mission and makes more efficient use of people's time and taxpayer dollars.

Another challenge the IC faced was that personnel needed access to various networks at different security levels, each requiring a dedicated network drop. Recalling The War Room in which Myron had to operate following the terrorist attacks, I was determined to utilize modern technology and tools to simplify access to networks at various security levels. The trick was finding a security officer who understood the vision and would work with me to implement it.

This is how I made the case. Security thought that making every network air-gapped made it more secure. In reality, data had to get from one system to another, so an operator had to switch between the different networks, often at different security levels, and manually type data in, which was timeconsuming and could lead to errors. Furthermore, there was no audit trail, and there were no tools to flag information that potentially should not be transferred from a higher security network to a lower security network. By providing one interface to all the networks, we could simplify access. In addition, we could implement tools that would scan any information an operator was getting ready to transfer from one security level to another and flag any words or information that could result in a security violation. This tool would also provide an audit trail.

Fortunately, I found a security person at ADF-C, home of The War Room, willing to work with me. He had worked with Myron and others at the forefront of supporting tactical operations, so he understood the need to provide a better solution.

I worked in collaboration with the DIA CIO, Grant Schneider. We called the project Desktop Optimization Pilot (DOP), and we created what I called a "policy bubble" where we could suspend the current policies and determine what value this new capability could provide to ops and the benefit to the security team. DOP enabled a single access point to multiple networks at various security levels rather than requiring unique workstations for each network. The DIA team provided the technology solution, and I provided the top cover.

The pilot was a great success—it benefited the operators and provided more insight for the security officers. So, we worked to implement the DOP workstations at other locations.

A parallel initiative I did not have direct control over but worked to influence was how the IC did reporting. Analysts wrote reports at the highest security level, usually TS/SCI, based on the sources and methods used. Those reports were to be downgraded to a lower security level via a mechanism they called tearlines.

Typically, there was a lot of information that could be shared at a lower security level while still protecting sources and methods if someone took the time to do the downgrade, but too often, that didn't happen. There was a saying often quoted about the IC being a self-licking ice cream cone; this is why it was warranted.

If we took a different approach focusing on intelligence customers, analysts would write the initial report at the lowest possible level and get that product out as soon as possible. Analysts could subsequently add information classified at higher levels and release those reports appropriately. This way, we would provide more timely and relevant intelligence to users—particularly those in harm's way who were conducting real-time operations and typically didn't have the luxury of accessing a SCIF.

I discussed this with DNGA Clapper when we were both at NGA, and he agreed it made sense. Ultimately, DNI Clapper signed an IC Directive (ICD 209) in 2012, emphasizing the importance of producing tearlines for the broadest possible readership, finally fulfilling the direction given in the Intelligence Reform and Terrorism Prevention Act of 2004.

While change came slowly in the government, there were pockets of innovation. One source of innovation was the Galileo Award, created to encourage employees across the IC to submit new ideas to improve information sharing. Calvin Andrus wrote a white paper entitled "The Wiki and the Blog: Toward a Complex Adaptive Intelligence Community" and entered it in the Galileo Award competition. This helped to inspire the development of Intellipedia, effectively Wikipedia for the IC.

Intellipedia was established as a pilot project late in 2005. The INTELINK team initially built it as a small internal wiki for documentation for their software systems. One of the chief software engineers for Intellipedia was Chris Musialek. After reading Cal Andrus's paper, Chris realized the wiki could be used more broadly. Recognizing the value of Intellipedia, we made it a part of INTELINK's core services and formally announced it as an ODNI-sponsored program in April 2006.

On 11 October 2006, after a small plane accidentally crashed into a residential building in New York City, analysts across the IC immediately went to Intellipedia to start sharing what they knew about the situation. We collectively wondered out loud, "Imagine if we had that capability five years prior during the terrorist attacks of 11 September 2001—we could have pieced together what we knew as we knew it to connect the dots much faster."

Despite the benefits of collaborative analysis, many inside the individual intelligence agencies did not support this way of doing business. They were all about their agency producing and getting credit for the products. This made me think of the quote reportedly on President Ronald Reagan's desk: "It's amazing what you can accomplish if you do not care who gets the credit." The IC hadn't quite figured that out yet.

It's amazing what you can accomplish if you do not care who gets the credit.

The two champions for Intellipedia inside the CIA were Don Burke and Sean Dennehy, and there were some severe antibodies to their efforts. Understanding that situation, I brainstormed with them about what we could do. We decided it would be beneficial to do an ODNI Intellipedia media blitz to get the good news out to the public and help provide top cover for this much-needed capability.

We hosted members of the media at ODNI on 31 October 2006 for this session. As the Reuters article stated, "The U.S. intelligence community on

Tuesday unveiled its own secretive version of Wikipedia, saying the popular online encyclopedia format known for its openness is key to the future of American espionage. The office of US intelligence czar John Negroponte announced Intellipedia, which allows intelligence analysts and other officials to collaboratively add and edit content on the government's classified Intelink Web much like its more famous namesake on the World Wide Web." That positive press provided the top cover that Don and Sean and others like them around the IC needed, and the use of Intellipedia continued to grow.

Many modern technologies would be critical enablers if we could implement them in the IC enterprise, but that was easier said than done. The biggest hurdle was Certification and Accreditation, or C&A. Certification is a process that a security team goes through to approve a certain technology implementation by verifying that the product meets specific requirements. Then a decision authority determines whether to accredit the technology implementation and use it in operations.

The IC had a C&A policy called DCI Directive 6-3 (DCID-6/3) that had been in place for some time. This was incredibly inefficient, and it was no secret that I saw rewriting this policy directive as one of the top priorities for the OCIO at ODNI. The IC CIO even made a joke in a town hall, handing me a printed copy of DCID-6/3 he had signed, saying he knew it was my "favorite" policy. That was the town hall where I later announced an initiative to revise that policy.

As I often said, C&A via the DCID-6/3 process "takes twice as long, costs twice as much, and you get half of the capability in the end." That was about right. If we were ever going to move the IC into the twenty-first century, that policy had to be rewritten to be an enabler of technology adoption, not a hindrance.

This was a priority initiative we kicked off in 2006. The senior executive who led the OCIO security office, Sheryl, took the lead. Per our initial status meetings, the process was moving along very slowly, particularly in light of how high a priority this was in the OCIO. In a subsequent meeting, I finally asked Sheryl, "Who in your office do you have leading the initiative to revise the policy?"

I immediately knew the issue when Sheryl told me the person's name. She had appointed the very person who had written DCID-6/3 to take the lead in revising the policy. It was clear that was a conflict of interest, for the writer of the original policy did not understand the need for a revision and was not motivated to help revise it. I told Sheryl, "This is not a bad person, but she is certainly a bad fit for this role. We need to find her another job within the OCIO and get someone else—who understands the need for change—to lead the charge."

We made the necessary personnel moves, and it is surprising how quickly things started to take shape after that. It was an example of the tenet in Jim Collins's book *Good to Great*, "Get the right people on the bus, get the wrong people off the bus, and get the right people in the right seats."

A critical component in establishing this new C&A process was to have a shift in mindset. Previously, the focus was primarily on protecting IT without considering the impact on the mission. There had to be a balance. The risk could not be eliminated entirely, so decision-makers had to weigh the operational and economic costs of any protective measure against the requirements to accomplish the mission. This shift to a more balanced perspective would support decisions that embraced intelligent risk-taking and enabled mission success.

I had some long-standing relationships with our counterparts in the DoD. Given the partnership between the IC and DoD, it made sense to do this transformation in collaboration with the DoD CIO so that we would develop one certification process across the IC and DoD for the intelligence agencies, the military services, and commands. There was a lot of overlap in our enterprises, especially when people were deployed in support of operations. So, the IC CIO and DoD CIO offices collaborated on this effort.

My outreach to DoD extended to the Joint Staff J6 whose job was to assist the Chairman of the Joint Chiefs of Staff (CJCS) and support the joint (multi-service) commands. The Joint Staff J6 is the top DoD military CIO who looks out for the needs of the joint warfighters regarding command, control, communications, and cyber. The J6 also provides IT services while ensuring joint interoperability. All the joint commands must be interoperable within the continental US and overseas.

The J6 invited me to the J6 DoD-wide CIO offsite in Garmisch, Germany. While it was a long way to travel from Washington, DC, for an offsite, the

J6s were stationed all over the world, and it was a lovely location to get away from the day-to-day demands and think strategically.

When I spoke to the group, I shared a summary of initiatives I was leading on behalf of the IC to enable better information sharing and collaboration across the IC and with the DoD. One topic that we needed to tackle together was the matter of C&A.

Historically, every IC agency, military service, and DoD component had its own C&A process. This was not efficient by any stretch of the imagination. For example, a technology vendor could spend months going through the entire C&A process with one IC agency and then have to completely repeat the process if another component of the IC or DoD wanted to use the same technology. It could take years to implement a particular technology across the enterprise this way.

My vision was that we should get all our experts—from across the IC and DoD—to collaborate and come up with a common certification process. Then, in the future, if someone followed the standard certification process with any component of the IC or DoD, they could use that same body of evidence as certification in any other component and not have to repeat the process. Each accrediting authority would still make a localized accreditation decision based on their needs and acceptable risk factors.

It was another blinding flash of the obvious that we needed to do this, but I had to convince my counterparts. I knew that despite all the benefits this would bring to operators and taxpayers, there would undoubtedly be resistance due to bureaucratic inertia. As a whole, the CIOs gathered there agreed it was a good idea. We ultimately did that IC-DoD collaboration, and, in September 2008, the DNI signed an IC Directive (ICD 503) to establish the new risk management and C&A process.

Additionally, I told the DoD J6 and CIOs about INTELINK—specifically, how it provided a set of web-based services, tools, and technologies hosted for the benefit of the entire IC, to better enable sharing of intelligence and related information across the national security enterprise. Then I highlighted the initiative we were leading to provide common services once for everyone across the IC enterprise, rather than every agency CIO providing a service independently. This was not only more cost-effective, but it also enabled information sharing and collaboration across the agencies.

One initiative I was personally leading was based on the premise that everyone should have one email for the life of their career in government—not multiple emails based on different roles and career changes. Frequently, people worked across various agencies or worked across the DoD and the IC and had multiple email addresses at the same time. When people deployed overseas, they would get yet another email address. So not only were there multiple licenses per individual at some untold cost to the taxpayer, individuals had to check numerous inboxes via different logins.

Getting to one IC email and one DoD email would help to simplify things, thereby saving time and money. In the IC, we started with a common email address at the unclassified level. We called it U-Gov, with the domain @ugov.gov, and INTELINK-U hosted it. We created INTELINK-U for not only sharing open source and unclassified intelligence within the IC, but also with vetted federal, state, and local officials, which was something new.

It was common sense to me, and the users loved the idea because that capability would make it easier to do their jobs. However, the CIOs at various agencies and components fought it—yet another turf battle. Regardless, we made the service available to anyone who wanted to sign up, and people from across the IC subscribed. It was truly the one email account someone could access from anywhere; it quickly became people's primary email address.

Similarly, one of the most practical things the DoD J6 and CIOs could do was set up one email address for a person to use for their career in the DoD. Based on my experience as the self-appointed comms officer for my CAPSTONE class, it was hard to keep in contact with people because their email addresses changed with every new assignment.

Only my Army classmates kept the same email address over the years because Army Knowledge Online issued an email username@us.army.mil to every soldier. Why didn't every military service do that? Better yet, why didn't the entire DoD issue a username@dod.mil email for every member of the DoD, whether military or civilian?

It made sense to me and others in the audience, though a few seemed hesitant to let go of their service-specific or command-specific implementations. This was a no-brainer to anyone who had felt the pain of remote operations, particularly downrange.

The DoD finally implemented this capability many years later. They recruited a former INTELINK team member, John Hale, to the Defense Information Systems Agency (DISA) in 2009 to design and lead the implementation. Then in 2011, they launched DoD Enterprise Email with the format username@mail.mil. Over twenty-four months, they migrated almost 1.8 million DoD users onto the system as their primary email solution. John is presently the Chief of Cloud Services at DISA.

While working to create a common C&A process for the IC and DoD, I discovered the source of the four-eyes/five-eyes problem. Sometime in the past, New Zealand wouldn't allow the USA to park its nuclear submarines in its waters. Someone in the USA believed we should "punish" New Zealand by not sharing imagery with them.

In reality, that policy hurt everyone—including the USA—especially when we were doing joint combat operations with our Commonwealth partners. The Kiwis, as the New Zealanders were called, were part of the five-eyes coalition and needed to see the imagery just like the Aussies, Canadians, and Brits did, so we needed to overrule this ill-conceived policy. Once I found out the source of the problem, I told DNGA Clapper, and with a stroke of his pen, we resolved the issue once and for all!

Another issue I encountered as IC DCIO was that then-President George W. Bush had signed an executive order to provide the Commonwealth with access to the Secret Internet Protocol Router Network known as SIPRNet. Years later, the IC had yet to implement that mandate. While the intelligence agencies worked on the Joint Worldwide Intelligence Communication System (JWICS) at the TS/SCI level, the warfighters worked on SIPRNet at the Secret Collateral level, where real-time operations were planned.

The USA fights wars with partners; our closest partners are the Commonwealth. They needed to be on SIPRNet to have a shared situational awareness and participate in the mission planning. If we didn't plan together, we risked dying together.

No one was sure why no action had been taken to put the Commonwealth on SIPRNet. So I held a cross-community meeting to discuss the matter. During the meeting, I was informed the CIA did not support putting the Commonwealth on SIPRNet. POTUS had asked this to happen due to operational needs, as real-time mission planning was conducted on SIPRNet.

The CIA had its own separate networks and didn't use community networks. So, the CIA's dissent was a non-issue; operational needs trumped their dissent.

I informed those gathered at the meeting that we would proceed with implementing POTUS's order. If the CIA wanted to be in on the mission planning, they could join SIPRNet; otherwise, they could continue business on their separate networks as usual. It continued to amaze me the paralysis the community faced any time the CIA disagreed with something. This was another benefit of the ODNI providing an equitable cross-community perspective and decision-making authority. Ultimately, we got the Commonwealth onto SIPRNET.

CHAPTER 24

Life Partners

At this time in our lives, Chris and I found ourselves single and in the Washington, DC, area, hanging out with all the same friends in our free time. Though we had been stationed in different parts of the country since we first met back in 1999, because of our shared projects over the years, we got to know each other through work collaboration and occasional work-related social interactions while in the same town at the same time.

After he moved to the Washington, DC, area in 2003, we worked together daily and went to Iraq's combat zone that December. We had pulled long hours together at work under high stress. You get to know someone pretty well in situations like that; they cannot pretend to be someone they are not because you know better.

Chris was as genuine as they came, and you'd be hard-pressed to find someone more loyal and honorable. He was so upbeat it seemed nothing could get him down. When the odds were stacked against him, and people said it could not be done, Chris was even more determined to prove them wrong.

A space operator, Chris was once called The Teflon Major of Low Earth Orbit because it seemed nothing would stick to him. He was fond of saying, "We are Ameri-cans, not Ameri-can'ts!"

Chris was a man of high moral character and integrity, his word was his bond, and when he made a commitment, he did his best to see it through. He focused on others—how to improve their lives and ensure they got credit for their work. When hosting people, Chris wanted to be sure everyone was taken care of and had a good time. He had a great sense of humor and a strong sense of purpose.

Given that we had the same network of friends, I now had a chance to see Chris in more social situations outside of work and get to know his personal and professional sides. There was never a dull moment with Chris around. I appreciated his eternal optimism and enjoyed his terrific, if not sometimes mischievous, sense of humor.

In the over six years we had collaborated on national security projects, we always supported and worked to build each other up. Both purpose-driven people, we thrived on sharing ideas and brainstorming together and could often complete each other's sentences.

As we had more time to talk one-on-one, we found we shared so much in common—our core values, Christian faith, optimistic outlook on life, commitment to the national security mission, dedication to serving our country, and preserving freedom for ourselves and future generations. We realized we had many of the same interests outside of work, including movies and music, and biking and hiking the great trails in the Washington, DC, area.

In the fall of 2005, Chris asked me out—to dinner, to movies, on hikes, and bike rides. Our conversations were always amazing, like we could talk forever and never run out of things to discuss. We were like-minded and kindred spirits on so many levels. There was no happier time than when we were together, and we looked forward to those opportunities. We were better together, and those closest to us saw the positive difference we made in each other's lives.

We had both experienced abusive relationships in the past. Chris's experience was worse than mine, and he had endured it much longer before he realized he had a life-and-death decision to make. Our relationship helped both of us heal. After each being abused by an ex, it was so edifying to be in a relationship where we both felt valued and appreciated by someone we implicitly trusted.

We were both givers who thought of others and how to bless them but had found ourselves in relationships with takers who were dishonest, selfish, self-centered, manipulative, and did not care how their behavior affected others. We had both been relatively naive and not wise to the ways of the world—particularly the fact that some people will lie and do whatever they can to get what they want without considering the collateral damage because they feel the ends justify the means. Having both nearly lost ourselves to destructive relationships, we found it wonderful to be in a relationship where we experienced unconditional, selfless love. We both recognized this was a priceless treasure.

Within a few months after we started dating, we realized that our long-time professional partnership doing good for the nation would make a great life partnership. Once we started showing up to public events together, our friends and family started calling us a power couple. We were kindred spirits. Sharing life together was truly a joy.

Chris was a big fan of the movie *Monty Python and the Holy Grail*. When the show *Spamalot*, based on the movie, came to the National Theater in July 2006, he organized a group of our friends to attend together. Before the show on 2 July, we all met for dinner at Zola, a restaurant connected to the International Spy Museum. This seemed apropos, given our national security careers.

After everyone sat down for dinner, Chris got up and said he had an announcement to make. Anyone who knew him had seen this stunt before. He would often do this and then jokingly tell everyone he had gathered them together to sell Amway or some such thing, and everyone would laugh. This time was different.

Like any good Air Force officer, Chris presented a PowerPoint briefing. The title was "The Adventure Ring Acquisition." Anyone who has heard the Mervis Diamond Importers ads on the radio in the Washington, DC, area would know the gist. In those ads, one of the Mervis brothers describes going to the diamond mines of South Africa to select the finest diamonds. It's like an Indiana Jones tale but with a South African accent.

As part of his presentation, Chris described encounters with "scary beasts" and such with photos he had put on the slides for everyone to see. With his characteristic grin, he had a fantastic ability to tell tall tales; everyone went along with it because Chris was telling the story.

We all gathered where he was going with this. When he proposed, I, of course, said, "Yes!" All our friends cheered and told us we were meant to be together and made a great team. They had seen firsthand what we could accomplish together for the good of the nation and knew we would make great partners in life.

Everyone was in a very celebratory mood for the rest of dinner, and as we walked to the National Theater to see *Monty Python's Spamalot*. I still have the ticket stubs. A year later, Chris brought me back to Zola for my birthday.

Michele and Chris following their engagement (6 July 2006) [left] and celebrating Michele's birthday (2007) [right] at Zola, the restaurant connected to the International Spy Museum, Washington, DC

When Chris and I were finally alone later that evening, we talked about how things in our lives had not worked out the way we had planned but ultimately led us here, and we felt so blessed to be together. He told me, "You cannot change your name—you must keep Weslander because of your grandfather and because everyone knows you as Michele Weslander." I told him I appreciated that because I was very proud of the Weslander name, and there were not a lot of people to carry on that name. I also wanted to take his name as we would be a family.

Most Americans in my situation hyphenated their last name, but I was not too fond of that. I learned that Spanish ladies do not change their surname when they marry but sometimes add their spouse's surname after theirs. That was how I would do it—I would keep my last name and add his last name; my new last name would be Weslander Quaid.

Friends and family were overjoyed when Chris and I shared the news of our engagement. The theme we heard from all of them was, "You two are meant to be together. You've been an awesome team doing great things for

America. You'll make an awesome couple doing great things for the world." That was affirming. What more could you ask than to marry the person who had become your best friend and champion and would ultimately become your life partner and soulmate?

Recognizing I had built a strong professional identity over fifteen years as Michele Weslander, many people asked what my married name would be. When I told them, they said, "Weslander Quaid is a very cool-sounding last name." I agreed and knew I would be proud to carry both names. After all, Weslander and Quaid were long known as the dynamic duo doing good things for America.

After considering some options for wedding dates, we decided to do a New Year's Eve wedding in my hometown of Santa Barbara on 31 December 2006. It was the holidays, so most people had time off. Furthermore, I wanted my grandfather, Rev. Glenn Weslander, to walk me down the aisle and marry us, but my grandmother could not travel due to health issues. So we needed to go where they were, and who wouldn't want to visit Santa Barbara?

When Chris and I met for dinner a couple of weeks later, he said he had something to share with me. The US Army was short on Electronic Warfare Officers (EWOs), so they turned to the Navy and Air Force to help. The Air Force decided to reach out to their space operators to offer them the opportunity, and he jumped at the chance with the endorsement of his boss at Air Staff, Col. Mo Khan. Chris said, "I'm tired of making PowerPoint slides for the two-star [general]. I want to make a difference. I want to be in the fight." I understood.

He told me that initially, the Air Force generals at the Pentagon were not supportive of him deploying with the Army as an EWO and said that this was the Army's problem, not the Air Force's problem. Somehow, they forgot that jointness was required in warfighting, and we were all part of Team America.

Then, once they agreed to support this, they insisted that Chris wear his Air Force uniform while deployed with the US Army. Logic would dictate that one should not want to stand out in a combat zone—one should blend in. Thankfully, Col. Khan brought sanity to the situation, handed Chris a credit card, and told him to buy some Army Combat Uniforms (ACUs) to take with him. He said, "Wear your Air Force uniform on the flight out of the US but change in route, and don't put your Air Force uniform on again until you get home." Thank God for Mo Khan!

This was a historic moment as an Air Force officer had never worn an Army Combat Uniform. To commemorate the occasion, the Air Force historian requested a photo. So, Chris had his picture taken in his ACUs at the Pentagon before he deployed.

Official US Air Force Historian photo of Maj. Christopher N. Quaid, USAF, in the US Army Combat Uniform (2006)

Chris told me he would be trained as an EWO by the Navy on Whidbey Island and then go through Army combat training. After that, he would deploy with the Army to Afghanistan. I asked him, "When?" He said, "Sometime in January," but he did not know the exact date.

We decided that while we could continue with our plans to wed on 31 December 2006, we should postpone the honeymoon until after he got back from his deployment in 2007. We had originally planned to drive from Santa Barbara up north to Napa and Sonoma and tour California wine country. I told him if we had to wait nine months, we would upgrade our honeymoon to Tuscany!

Joy and Sorrow

For my birthday that August, we decided to make a trip to one of our favorite places—Rocky Mountain National Park in Colorado—for a shared adventure before Chris started combat training. We had such a great time, and it was fun to hike trails with him that I had hiked when I lived in Colorado.

On one hike, rain started pouring, and we ran back down the mountain, laughing all the way and passing up hikers much younger than us. I've spent so many birthdays hiking in national parks, and this was no exception. We looked forward to many adventures like this together as a family in the future. We would bring our daughter to Rocky Mountain National Park seven years later, when she was four years old, for her first hiking experience. There she joined the Junior Ranger Program and earned her first badge, and continued to do so at each national park we visited.

Michele, Chris, and their daughter, Sophia, hiking on Angels Landing trail in Zion National Park (2015)

The next day while we were at Denver International Airport waiting for our flight home, Dave Radcliffe, one of Lee Akridge's work colleagues, called me. When I answered, he said, "I am calling because I know you and Lee were good friends. Lee died of a heart attack yesterday."

I was in shock and collapsed. Thankfully, Chris caught me. I don't ever recall collapsing like that before or since. Still in shock, I asked for more details and then thanked David profusely for reaching out to me to let me know. He said, "Of course. I know how close the two of you were."

It breaks my heart that on my birthday, 26 August 2006, Lee, who was athletic and in excellent shape, started having heart issues while on his weekend bike ride. Never wanting to be a bother to anyone, he didn't ask for help. Lee died alone of a heart attack that day. I was hiking in Rocky Mountain National Park with Chris when he died.

Lee's passing hit me so hard. It seemed that I could not stop crying. Grief would suddenly hit me without warning, and tears would start streaming down my face. Chris was very understanding and supportive. Lee was his friend, too, and he knew how much Lee's friendship had meant to me over the years.

We were not alone. There were over 300 people who packed into the church for Lee's funeral on 1 September 2006, and more people would have been present if they had not had to travel across the country on such short notice to be there. I kept thinking, "There were over 300 people, Lee, who would have been grateful to be 'bothered' by you that day. If you had only reached out, it could have saved your life."

Lee made such an incredibly positive impact on the national security community. However, to my knowledge, he had never been formally recognized. So, I worked with the DNI to award Lee the National Intelligence Distinguished Public Service Medal posthumously. His eldest son, Doug, accepted the award on his behalf.

Chris and I stayed in contact with Lee's sons, Doug and Steve, who were in high school then. Chris later arranged for each of Lee's sons to have internships in the IC working with his team. I hope that the experience of that award ceremony and their IC internships gave Lee's sons a glimpse into what their father did for our country.

After Lee died, I came across a sealed envelope he had given to me when I transitioned from Scitor into government service in 2002. It said, "Do Not Open until 26 August 2007." That gave me chills because the date would be exactly one year after his death. Per his wishes, I waited until 26 August 2007 to open it. Inside I found a card in which he wished me a happy birthday, wondered what I would have accomplished in my life by then, and wondered if we were still in touch. I thought, "You left us a year ago today, Lee, but you are in our thoughts and hearts forever." Good friends like Lee are a treasure; we are better for having them in our lives.

Wedding

In October 2006, Chris started training in preparation for his deployment with the Army. To me, the most amusing part was his electronic warfare training at Whidbey Island, Washington. Chris was a psychology major with a master's degree in business administration (MBA). He was calling me—the one with the engineering and science degrees—excited about all the cool things they were doing with technology.

On one such call, he shared, "You should see what we were able to do to all the garage door openers in the area." I had visions of the garage doors in the neighborhood going up and down, which I'm sure would be quite a sight, but it came with the territory if you were on a base where they did electronic warfare training.

Chris had the funniest stories from combat training. The cultural differences between the two services were stark. The hardened Army drill sergeant did not know what to do with the Air Force majors. A good-natured interservice rivalry ensued.

He reported that at one point, the Army drill sergeant started mocking them, saying, "You Air Force majors want to be everybody's friend. That's not how it is in the Army!" He was referring to the fact that the Air Force officers were very casual with the enlisted Army members, which was in stark contrast to the strict formality between Army officers and enlisted.

Chris also joked that when the drill sergeant told them to drop to the ground, they had responded, "But it's muddy. We'll get dirty!" At that point, they were just giving the Army drill sergeant a hard time.

Given that Chris was in Army combat training and preparing for deployment to Afghanistan the months before our wedding, I was on my own to do the planning. This was complicated because I had to do it from across the country, nearly 3,000 miles and three time zones away. Thankfully, my childhood friend, Joanna (Anderson) Reyes, who was also my matron of honor, still resided in Santa Barbara and handled some of the logistics for me in the local area.

Michele and Chris at Pentagon Air Staff XOS Christmas Party (2006)

As Christmas neared, there were work-related holiday parties around town. This was something we both enjoyed very much. It was fun to see coworkers in a festive environment outside the office. During this time, Chris's Pentagon colleagues did a nice sendoff for him at Sine Pub in Pentagon City.

We decided to spend Christmas with Chris's parents, John and Martha Quaid, in Humble, Texas. My mom came along so that we could all be together for Christmas. It was an opportunity to see Chris's brother, Doug; his wife, Diana; Chris's sister, Robin; her husband, Dave; and their kids. We had all previously gathered in January for Doug and Diana's wedding. In addition, I got to meet other members of Chris's family and his childhood best friend, Randy Bayless, who would be his best man.

This also afforded us a chance to spend some quality time with Chris's children from his prior marriage—two sons and a daughter who were each three years apart in age and lived with their mom in a city about an hour away from his hometown. I had met his three kids previously and was looking forward to spending more time with them. Their mom was engaged to be married in the new year, and they were excited about their dad and me getting married. Though they only spent time with their dad during school breaks in the summer and over the holidays, I looked forward to being their stepmom and could already envision all the fun adventures we would have together as a family.

Chris and I arrived in Santa Barbara a few days before the wedding and picked up our marriage license at the Santa Barbara courthouse. Then we did a walk-through of the venues at Fess Parker's DoubleTree Resort, now known as the Hilton Santa Barbara Beachfront Resort. While considering many lovely venues in the Santa Barbara area, we ultimately settled on this location for a few reasons, one of which was a bit of personal history.

Fess Parker, an American film actor best known for his portrayals of Davy Crockett and Daniel Boone in TV miniseries, wanted to develop that property just across from the beach, which used to include a railroad roundhouse. His vision was to build a beautiful sprawling hotel, but he had to convince the Santa Barbara Planning Department to let him do the development, which was a long and arduous process.

It has always perplexed me that Fess Parker would be given such a hard time about this development, as the hotel he built is lovely and has become a landmark in the area. My mom worked in the Planning Department at the time and got to know him and his secretary, whom she said were both very nice.

The railroad roundhouse was turned into a large, open-air plaza with a balcony called the Plaza del Sol. That's where our wedding ceremony would take place.

Our reception would be in a room named after Ronald Reagan, one of Fess Parker's friends. We had booked the suite just off Plaza del Sol balcony, where we would host an after-party to ring in the new year with our guests.

Chris and I spent the little downtime we had finishing the music playlist for our reception. This was back in the days of the original iPod with the click wheel. We were both big fans of classic jazz like Nat King Cole and Frank Sinatra and modern jazz like Harry Connick, Jr. and Nora Jones. For the dance music, we had a more upbeat mix that included rock and roll songs that we had enjoyed hearing cover bands play at events we had attended.

For our first dance as a married couple, we would deviate from these genres to our only country song—"Keeper of the Stars" by Tracy Byrd. We both agreed that the words were just right for us. God knew what he was doing when he joined our two hearts.

As we said goodnight to each other on 30 December 2006, we talked about how surreal it was that we would soon be husband and wife after over seven years of being friends and colleagues. God had worked through us as business partners to do great things for America, and we envisioned he would do even greater things through us as life partners.

I awoke on the morning of 31 December 2006 and started getting ready. In time, my mom and Joanna arrived to help with the finishing touches. Then my mom went to take her seat, and Joanna and I prepared to walk down the staircase from the balcony to the plaza level. There I would meet my grandfather, who would walk me down the aisle.

There is a photo so precious to me that our wedding photographer captured of my grandfather and me when I took his arm. My grandfather had come to know and love Chris and was so happy we were getting married. After Chris and I got engaged, he shared it touched him that Chris had asked for his blessing after expressing his intent to propose to me.

My grandpa Glenn was the closest I had to a father figure in my life, and we treasured our relationship. Through various health issues he had, I would always tell him, "Grandpa, you must stay healthy and well so you can walk me down the aisle!" This was the day.

As Pachelbel's "Canon in D" played, Grandpa and I walked over to the red carpet that had been rolled down the aisle and then turned and walked up the aisle to where Chris was waiting. Chris always had a big grin, but people later said they had never seen such a big smile on Chris's face as when he saw me then, except when we walked down the aisle after being pronounced husband and wife.

Rev. Glenn Weslander prepares to walk Michele down the aisle on her wedding day (31 December 2006)

My uncle Bob, a Vietnam veteran, then serving as a chaplain for the police and fire departments in the Seattle area, started the service, and then my grandfather took over. I am so grateful we got a video of the service to capture this special event. It means all the more today because some people who are very dear to me and who are captured in that video have passed on.

People who have watched that video say that looking at the two of us, you can see our bond—best friends who deeply loved each other. It means a lot to hear that feedback, as what I saw in Chris was the man I admired and loved and who loved me like no other.

My grandfather read from 1 Corinthians 13 during the service. Chris and I exchanged rings as we said our vows to each other. Then my grandfather pronounced us "Major and Mrs. Christopher Quaid." Everyone cheered. Beethoven's "Ode to Joy" played as we walked down the aisle as husband and wife. We had never been happier.

Michele and Chris with Rev. Glenn Weslander and Robert "Bob" Weslander who jointly officiated their wedding ceremony (31 December 2006)

After taking photos, we joined our guests at the reception, followed by a luncheon in the Reagan Room. Chris and I ate very little, as we spent most of the time walking around to talk with our guests seated at the tables. We greatly appreciated everyone being there to share this special moment with us. It was the first of many parties we would host together as a couple, and it was something we enjoyed doing. We had guests from across America, but the guests who had traveled the farthest were Wolfram and Claudia Ragg from Switzerland.

That evening, we celebrated and rang in the new year of 2007 with our guests. It was the second party we hosted on our first day as a married couple, and our guests had a good time.

After everyone left, we got a few hours of sleep before we had to pack up and head to the airport for our flight back to Virginia on 1 January 2007.

On 2 January 2007, Chris registered me as his wife at the Pentagon. On 4 January 2007, I saw him off at Baltimore-Washington Airport as he started his deployment with the Army in Afghanistan as part of Operation Enduring Freedom (OEF).

CHAPTER 25

Deployment

In January 2007, I returned to ODNI as a married woman with her husband deployed in Afghanistan. Given my position as the Deputy CIO for the US Intelligence Community, I had access to many forms of communication with people downrange. Chris would take the opportunity to call whenever he could. Those calls often came with requests about the mission and coordinating something for him within the IC on behalf of the Army Task Force he was supporting.

When Chris arrived in Afghanistan, the 10th Mountain Division's Task Force Spartan was completing their tour and getting ready to hand the mission off to the 82nd Airborne's Task Force Fury.

During one conversation, Chris explained he had been trying to call for a few days, but the line to use the phone had been out the door. Leadership at the Pentagon had recently decided to extend deployment tours.

This affected the 10th Mountain Division, which was already transitioning out of Afghanistan back to the USA. Some had already returned home, others were en route home, and those who were still in the country were in lines to call home to tell their family and friends, who were expecting them to be home any day, that they now would not be coming home for a few months. As you can imagine, this did not go over well with their families back home, which made for long, emotional calls.

Chris felt sorry for all of them, and so did I. We could not understand why the Pentagon leadership would make a decision like this, which impacted families with little to no notice, particularly enlisted members. They had not seen their loved ones for over half a year and surely had made plans for things to do upon their return, and now everything had changed. Furthermore, the replacement troops were already on their way. If the military was hoping to get people to reenlist, this did not seem to be a good strategy.

Chris shared that the 10th Mountain Division was thrilled when they received a DVD of the movie *300* staring Gerard Butler, directed by Zack Snyder (Warner Brothers), that had recently come out. They watched it every chance they could. This story of the Spartans who saved Greece and the Western world in the battle of Thermopylae inspired the members of Task Force Spartan.

The 82nd Airborne colonel running Task Force Fury was a character. He was amazed at all the national intelligence support Chris provided to the team, given his connections throughout the IC. Chris became quite a celebrity for working in unconventional ways to get them the support they needed. He was able to tap into archives of imagery that had been collected and get it to the warfighters for their situational awareness and mission planning. The Army team had not had access to NTM imagery in the past, which astounded Chris. What good was the data if it didn't get to all the people who needed it, especially those in harm's way?

Chris spent most of his time "outside the wire." He was there to fight and be where the action was on the front lines—not to sit at headquarters in Bagram. Chris was at forward operating bases (FOBs) and on convoys with the Army along the Afghanistan-Pakistan border with the troops conducting operations. When asked to take a post on base, he informed the superior officer that he was "not in Afghanistan to fold the general's underwear."

Another task Chris had was to teach the troops about the electronic warfare (EW) equipment they took with them in the convoys. Many of the enlisted troops were eighteen and nineteen, and keeping their attention was challenging.

Chris had an idea. He acquired a copy of the game trailer *HALO 3: Starry Night* and played it at the start of every briefing. That got their attention. In the trailer, the main character creates a shield around him to protect him from attack. Chris explained how their EW equipment was doing the same for them. This is how he got the callsign HALO, which remained with him for the rest of his military career.

One day, Chris called and made an unusual request. First, I must preface with the fact that Chris loved REI. My home, which became his home when we married, was within walking distance from the REI store in Fairfax, Virginia. We eventually got the REI MasterCard to earn points to fund his REI shopping habit. Before he deployed, we went to REI to look at what he might need for deployment, particularly in the camping section. There we saw a titanium spork, and he remarked, "Now that's just what everyone needs!" He was joking at the time.

Fast forward to this call from Afghanistan, during which he informed me that they often had to take shelter during dinner time, as that was when the enemy liked to fire mortars at them, and he often found himself in a bunker with no eating utensils. Furthermore, eating utensils seemed in short supply when he was outside the wire at FOBs and on the border. So, he asked if I could buy him one of those titanium sporks and send it to him. I bought him two, so he could keep one at the main base and take the other with him when he was at the FOBs along the border, where he most often was. He sent me a picture of him in a bunker with his spork as a thank you.

Maj. Chris Quaid, USAF, wielding his titanium spork in a bunker with his US Army colleagues [left] and establishing a security perimeter after an improvised explosive device struck the lead vehicle in their convoy [right], Afghanistan (2007)

One night, I woke up and could not sleep, so I prayed for Chris's safety. Later, Chris informed me that the lead vehicle in the convoy he had been in was blown up by an improvised explosive device (IED). Everyone in the first vehicle died, and those in the second vehicle died within hours.

He told me how one of the American soldiers pulled from a vehicle looked fine, but the medic told him that his brain was fried, and he would likely die soon, and he did. It was a very tragic and sobering event. I thanked God that Chris's life was spared.

Office Dynamics

When Chris deployed, I was starting my second year as the IC DCIO. We had previously made a move from various buildings in the area to a new headquarters facility on what is now known as Joint Base Anacostia-Bolling, co-located with DIA. Though the commute was much longer for me and required a drive from Virginia into Maryland over the Wilson Bridge spanning the Potomac River, the facility was new, and it was much better to have a good majority of the team in one place, aside from the INTELINK team that remained co-located with NSA at Ft. Meade.

My focus was to deliver on the promises we made as the ODNI OCIO to effect positive change for the good of the national security community and its customers. However, I soon realized the CIO did not intend to follow through on those promises. In reality, I had laid out the plans because he had no previous experience in the IC. However, he had indicated he wholeheartedly supported them and talked about them publicly. Those early discussions and his apparent philosophical alignment and commitment to effect positive change had been an important part of my decision to take the DCIO position.

The CIO continued to spend an inordinate amount of time in town hall meetings talking about how he was the first Senate-confirmed CIO in the IC and how he got an eagle on his American flagpole because he was a presidential appointee. I chalked that up to him being arrogant and self-absorbed.

From all appearances, his role as the CIO was about the title, power, and perks that came with his position and getting as much visibility as possible to land a cushy job in his subsequent career. It was not about doing the work the CIO needed to do to deliver on the promises for the good of the warfighters, decision-makers, and America. This was incomprehensible to me, especially being he had formerly served as a general officer in the Air Force.

What mattered most to me was that the CIO hadn't interfered with the good things we were doing. He also supported my idea of the OCIO hosting the first ever combined DoD-IC Information Sharing and Collaboration Conference, a.k.a. DISCO, in 2006. I planned and ran the event with my former NGA colleague, Elizabeth "Liz" Dann, who had come with me to ODNI. Liz was very talented and a trusted friend.

The turnout was fantastic, and the conference was a great success. People across the IC and DoD remarked that it was great to have a combined event, and this would be the conference to attend going forward.

Incomprehensibly, when it came time to plan DISCO for the next year, the CIO said the event was canceled and gave no explanation. Everyone involved was in shock.

The CIO and I had very different leadership styles. He frequently used fear and intimidation with the staff to get them to do what he wanted. I was horrified and did what I could to shield the staff from his abusive behavior.

When I tried to address this with him and suggest a different tactic that might encourage the staff, his response was, "It's better to be feared than to be loved."

I replied, "It's better to be respected and loved. Those two things are not mutually exclusive."

He was often inappropriate with female staff, particularly the young industry partners, which was disturbing. His behavior was borderline predatory. For example, he would stand far too close to a woman when talking with her and make inappropriate and suggestive remarks. When he did that to me, I would merely step away to afford more space between us, ignore whatever inappropriate thing he said, and keep talking business.

The CIO came to realize I was a woman on a mission and was not going to let his unprofessional behavior be a hindrance to me doing my job. In a way, this suited him because he could leave the running of the office to me while he went on boondoggles. He was known for scheduling trips supposedly to visit industry partners that just so happened to be located in areas where he wanted to golf, and he would extend his stay to do just that.

He abused his position and perks in other ways, and I would either hear about it from a member of the leadership, such as the Principal Deputy

Director of National Intelligence (PDDNI) during a senior staff meeting, or from the Deputy General Counsel (GC) whose office was next door to ours.

One day after being asked about something the CIO had done for the umpteenth time, I remarked to the Deputy GC that if the ODNI leadership had issues with the CIO, they needed to deal with him directly. The CIO knew I was focused on the mission and would have nothing to do with his misconduct. He hid most of what he did from me because he recognized that if I knew about it, I'd put a stop to it.

Days were always busy at the office, and any business trips I made were for a purpose. You may recall that members of SOF gave me the callsign Warrior Goddess, and those same friends in SOF reached out to me in my role as IC DCIO when they deployed again. Before becoming the IC DCIO, I had spent time with SOF in Iraq and Afghanistan. They asked me to make another trip to spend some time boots on the ground with them to see their current operations and determine what we could do at the ODNI to better enable them to do their jobs.

Technology seemed to always be a limiting factor, as was policy, which fit squarely within the OCIO. We worked on the details and logistics of the trip for a few weeks, and I provided the CIO with regular updates as the plans came together.

Then, just days before I was scheduled to depart overseas, the CIO told me he would not allow me to go and was canceling my trip. I couldn't believe it!

I reminded him that I had been invited by SOF based on the positive impact of my past visits with them in theaters of operation and given my new role at ODNI. Furthermore, he had been fully aware that this trip had been in the works and many people had been involved in coordinating the logistics, which was complicated given that it was a war zone. If he had concerns, he should have raised them earlier. It wasn't right for him to demand the trip be canceled in the eleventh hour, given the value of the insights that would be gained and after all the time and effort invested in planning.

I asked him his reason for saying I shouldn't go, and he had none. He just said I didn't need to go. It was like a parent telling a kid, "No, because I said so." I was incredulous. Would he treat a male deputy the same way?

When I asked him again to give me a good reason, he said, "The military is not your concern." It was inconceivable that a former general officer in the US military would say that.

I told him the military was part of the IC, and they were absolutely my concern because they were defending our freedom in harm's way. We needed to do everything we could to support them!

The next person in my chain of command was the PDDNI. General Hayden had moved on to become the Director of the CIA, and the man who occupied that role at the time was an Army general. He had been upset numerous times about the misconduct of the CIO, but I soon found out that the good old boy network trumped all that. When I told PDDNI what had transpired, he condescended and said that if the CIO said I could not go, that meant I could not go. All the facts of the situation and my track record of impactful combat zone visits didn't matter to this man in uniform.

I was stunned. The CIO could go on endless boondoggles, and they wouldn't put a stop to it, but when I had a legitimate business trip to support the troops in a war zone, all the CIO had to do was say no, and it was off? Incredible! I could not imagine the PDDNI would respond the same way if I were a man.

The PDDNI's executive officer, a female Army colonel, empathized with me. She knew the CIO's reputation and marveled how the good old boy network seemed to cover for each other even at the expense of the mission.

It is interesting to note that months later, the CIO arranged for himself and the other IC CIOs to have what one would call a "grip and grin" tour of the combat zone. No one said, "the military is not your concern." Nor was anyone concerned that all the special protocols these DVs would require while touring the combat zone would put an undue burden on the military members who were busy doing operations.

When I traveled to the combat zones, I waived my right to have a special security detail and the protocol that went with my position because I did not want to be a burden and didn't want to stand out. That had been my MO since my first visit to a combat zone in 2003, for I wanted the troops to speak freely with me and not be concerned about a DV being in the room. My age was an advantage because they never guessed that someone in their mid-thirties could be a DV. I only used my rank to gain access to the commanding generals and others in leadership.

In stark contrast, the CIO wanted all this "pomp and circumstance" when he visited, and he surely got it.

As you might imagine, given his behavior, the CIO had issues with honesty. Practically speaking, as his deputy, I had to take him at his word, or there was no possible way our office could function. One time, this completely blew up.

It is customary that when a director or deputy director leaves on a trip, they give the other a summary of things they are overseeing and working on in case something comes up while they are away. As the CIO headed off on another trip, he told me a story about something that was happening. He stated it matter-of-factly with no secrecy or caveats.

Later, in a senior staff meeting, the PDDNI asked me about that topic, so I answered according to what the CIO told me before leaving on his trip. The PDDNI became very upset and said it went against the direction he had given the CIO. Once again, I found myself in the awkward position of not knowing the full truth of what was happening, which concerned me. When the meeting ended, I went back to my office and called the CIO. When I told him what had transpired in the staff meeting, he was furious and hung up.

When the CIO returned to work on Monday, he called me into his office and shut the door. He told me in no uncertain terms that he wanted me to take the fall for him. Then he told me point blank, "If you don't, I will open up a personnel file on you and destroy your career." Stunned but keeping my poker face, I wondered how many subordinates he had said that to throughout his career.

In the military, there's no place to go—a superior can destroy your career if there is not someone who outranks them and will look out for you. As a civilian—particularly someone with a stellar reputation across the community—I had plenty of options. I didn't need to continue to allow myself to be in a situation with a boss who was corrupt, incompetent, and unethical.

When he realized I would not submit to his demands, the CIO's behavior towards me went from bad to worse.

I had recently visited a doctor to discuss my chronic pain and insomnia. The doctor was very concerned about what I shared with him and ran several tests. Around the time of this incident, the doctor had a follow-up visit with me to share the test results. The doctor looked at me seriously and said, "Michele, you are perfectly healthy, but stress is killing you. I suggest you do something about the source of your stress."

The fact that Chris was in a combat zone was something on my mind, and I was constantly praying for his safety, but I knew that was not the source of the stress that was killing me. It was my work environment, particularly my boss. This latest incident was the proverbial straw that broke the camel's back.

Under normal circumstances, I would want to discuss everything that was happening with Chris. However, given he was in a combat zone and when he could call, his time was limited, I wanted to avoid burdening him with what I was dealing with in the short time we had to talk. My priority was to hear how he was doing and be able to provide an update to his parents, who were understandably concerned about his well-being.

Given my mom lived in the area, I reached out to her and asked if I could come over to her house on Saturday, which happened to be St. Patrick's Day, to talk. I shared with her the situation at work. My boss had gone from bad to worse when he threatened to destroy my career if I didn't cover for him and take the fall for what he had done. In addition, I shared with her what my doctor had just told me.

This was all very concerning to her. My mom was convinced I needed to take action to get out of this unhealthy work environment. She said I had to look out for myself and agreed this job was costing me my health because I had an abusive boss.

My mom's advice affirmed my gut instinct. I shared with her that being the IC DCIO was a tremendous opportunity to do good and effect positive change, mainly due to the influence and access the position afforded. Unfortunately, as the deputy to a man who was not interested in doing his job and was instead doing unethical things out of self-interest, my ability to do good and effect positive change was limited. My reputation meant a lot to me, and I was not willing to have it tarnished because of my professional association with him.

Furthermore, I learned that he had a history of inspector general (IG) and equal employment opportunity (EEO) complaints filed against him in his past positions. How he got promoted to the rank of general officer in the military was beyond me. I could not fathom how he had been nominated to a Senate-confirmed position, for which he would carry the honorific title "The Honorable" before his name for the rest of his life. He was anything but honorable.

I was conflicted because I was so honored to be the first IC Deputy CIO for the ODNI. Furthermore, I had a broad vision and executable plans for what we could achieve to enable all the components of the IC to do their jobs more efficiently and effectively. However, I realized I was risking my health and reputation by continuing to work with the CIO.

So, I spent the rest of that Saturday writing a resignation letter. It was very polite, and I stated that I needed to move on due to our differences in leadership styles. I had no idea what I would do next, but trusted opportunities would arise once the word got out I had resigned.

Sundays were sacred to me. However, in this instance, I felt a great concern and sense of urgency to go through my office and make sure that critical files were protected and that any personal effects, such as pictures and mementos from my career, were removed from my office and brought safely home. There was no telling what the CIO would do on Monday. He was prone to violent outbursts.

So, I spent all day until late into the night in my office and ensured that important documents were organized and locked in my safe. It was a good housecleaning exercise in preparation for an eventual job move, and I was able to get rid of outdated papers in the process.

Before I left the building, I made numerous copies of my resignation letter. Then I went to the ops center and asked the team to put a copy in the folders of members of the leadership team, including the DNI and his direct reports, to be delivered to their offices on Monday morning.

At about 2300 hours, I walked out of the building with my personal effects and headed to my car. I experienced many different emotions at that point. Some, frankly, were like those I had with my divorce—facing the fact that my hopes and dreams were never going to be realized and that this chapter was coming to an end.

But I also had a great sense of relief. As I pulled out of the parking lot, I turned on George Michael's song "Freedom 90" and jammed to that as I drove off the base. Every time I hear that song, I think of this moment.

It hit the fan on Monday morning. The CIO was livid that I had resigned and provided copies of the letter to the ODNI senior leadership team, as noted on the CC list at the bottom of the letter. He went into overdrive, trying to intimidate and threaten me. His coercive tactics only reinforced the fact I had made the right decision to resign.

The ODNI front office was alarmed I had resigned. Members of the senior staff asked me to stay. They admitted they knew the CIO was a problem. I wondered why they hadn't dealt with him. They had no answer, and I sensed they were afraid I would file an EEO or IG complaint. I told them I wasn't looking to file a complaint. I wanted to move out of a very hostile and unhealthy working environment.

They pleaded with me to stay. I told them that I would only do so on the condition that they deal with the CIO and do so swiftly. They said they would need some time to do that. Ultimately, I agreed to give them two months before I made any move. Considering their track record thus far, I had no confidence they would deal with the CIO. I decided to explore any opportunities that might arise once the news got out of my resignation. This was the IC, after all—RUMINT gets around fast!

Trusted friends, and even those I didn't know very well, reached out. Through some of those conversations, I learned even more about the CIO's long military career history of EEO and IG complaints that were somehow swept under the rug. So this was just par for the course.

However, a few things were different in this case. First, we were not in the military; we were civilians. Second, though he was technically my boss, people who far outranked him knew, trusted, and respected me; that gave me options. Third, to paraphrase Twisted Sister, I wasn't going to take it anymore.

The next time Chris called and had some time to talk, I gave him a rundown of what I had been going through while he had been deployed and the decision I had made to resign. He was surprised, saddened, and also very angry. He wanted to give the CIO a piece of his mind big time.

After I submitted my resignation, the CIO's hostility and attempts to intimidate me increased. He was having many more closed-door meetings with people and engaging in activities to follow through on his threat to destroy my career. Thankfully, my reputation was well-established, and his attempts were futile.

While I met with some of the ODNI senior leadership to discuss opportunities within the ODNI to get me out of day-to-day interaction with the CIO while they worked to get him out, I kept my options open. Unfortunately, as expected, the ODNI leadership did nothing to deal with the CIO or put him in check.

CHAPTER 26

Integrated Ops

During this time, Don Kerr, Director of the National Reconnaissance Office (DNRO), reached out to me. He told me he recognized I was one of the people promoting the concept of an integrated ground architecture for the NRO for over a decade. DNRO Kerr then asked me to be one of four people to advise him on the most radical transformation the agency had seen in fifteen years.

At the time, there were unique information architectures for each intelligence discipline. This new approach, creating an integrated architecture, would enable better redundancy and backup capabilities across the enterprise and facilitate multi-discipline collaboration and integration.

During the first decade of my career, I had worked closely with the NRO and knew this was a tremendous opportunity to effect positive change. So I accepted DNRO Kerr's invitation and moved from the ODNI to the NRO but remained in an ODNI billet detailed to the NRO, meaning I was an ODNI officer but on loan to the NRO.

The four of us selected by the DNRO had not previously worked together. We got to know each other's areas of expertise and collaborated to create an action plan. Once we had our respective tasks, we worked diligently to meet with people across the NRO enterprise to acquire accurate ground truth regarding the state of affairs before mapping out where we needed to go.

One of the tasks I took on, having just served as the IC DCIO, was to write the Concept of Operations (CONOPS) for the new-and-improved NRO Office of the CIO. Previously, the NRO CIO had mainly been a figurehead who wrote policy but did not exercise much influence across the enterprise because other offices in the organization controlled the mission and business IT architectures and policies. If NRO was going to move to an integrated architecture, there needed to be a master orchestrator, and the CIO needed to take the lead.

The CONOPS I wrote gave the CIO the authority required to set policies and standards the implementing components of the organization would follow. This would lay the groundwork for better interoperability and integration across the NRO enterprise.

The NRO also needed someone to lead innovation. That was the natural role for a Chief Technology Officer (CTO), and I wrote that CONOPS. Recognizing that was a natural fit for me, the DNRO asked me to serve as the CTO, which I was very honored and excited to do.

Shortly after my transition from ODNI to the NRO in July 2007, a member of the ODNI IG reached out to me. Unbeknownst to me, they had been investigating the CIO since my resignation and had gathered a lot of information about his misconduct. The IG representative said, "Through interviews with the staff, we have four pages specific to the CIO's treatment of you alone. Why haven't you formally filed a complaint?"

I told him, "If I thought it would do any good, I would, but I don't think anything would come of it. The CIO has repeatedly abused his position and his staff. The ODNI leadership has known this and been upset about it but has done nothing definitive about it to date. I don't see how filing a formal complaint will change that. Instead, it would likely be seen as a mark against me in my government career if I filed a complaint against my boss. The ODNI already has plenty of data to use to take action against the CIO; they do not need me to add to that."

The IG representative understood my position.

In addition to the outreach from the ODNI IG, I heard from ODNI OCIO staff members who said they had no idea how much I buffered them from the CIO's abusive behavior until I left. The general remark was they did not know how I endured for as long as I did, and they completely understood why I left, though they were sad to see me go.

The ODNI eventually dealt with this matter in some way. The CIO resigned from his position and left government service over a year after I moved to the NRO.

Under the Tuscan Sun

Chris returned from Afghanistan in July 2007, and I met him at BWI airport. A group of his Air Staff colleagues from the Pentagon held welcome home signs.

Michele welcoming home Maj. Chris Quaid, USAF, as he returns from deployment with the US Army in Afghanistan (2007)

When we made eye contact, Chris flashed his big characteristic grin. He had a "high and tight" military haircut and looked fit and tan in his ACUs. Chris gave me a big embrace, and we held each other for a moment.

We'd been apart for over half a year and missed each other terribly. It was great to be reunited again.

I booked us a night at a hotel in Baltimore as a mini honeymoon. We enjoyed walking and dining by the waterfront and catching up.

We were looking forward to our belated honeymoon in the Tuscany region of Italy in September 2007.

The day before we departed for Italy, Chris worked in the garage to put together some shelves he bought at Home Depot. We were living in the three-story townhome I had purchased upon my return from Colorado to Virginia, and I was on the top floor when I heard him yelling for me.

After running down two flights of stairs, I opened the garage door and saw him spinning around in circles with blood spurting out of his wrist. I immediately ran back inside and grabbed a thin towel to tie around his arm as a tourniquet to stop the bleeding. Then we got into the car, and I drove him to the emergency room (ER).

When I checked him in at the ER, the person at the front desk asked me why we were there. I told her he had cut his wrist on the sharp edge of a shelf and needed treatment. She said, "Is he suicidal?"

Surprised, I replied, "No."

Shortly after that, they took us to a room. When the nurse walked in, she asked why we were there, and I told her. She looked very concerned and asked me, "Is he suicidal?"

Surprised again, I replied, "No, he is not suicidal."

The nurse left the room and returned with the doctor. He asked what had happened, and I told him. Then he asked, "Is he suicidal?"

I thought, "Good grief, how do I convince these people Chris is not suicidal?"

I replied, "No, he is not suicidal. He returned home safely from a combat mission in Afghanistan just two months ago. We will depart on our honeymoon tomorrow. He is a happy man! He just had an accident while putting together shelves in the garage."

That must have convinced everyone that Chris was not a danger to himself, and they proceeded to treat his wound. He got stitches and a bandage we would have to change daily for the next two weeks while we were in Italy.

Chris and I departed Virginia for two weeks in Tuscany on 4 September 2007. We arrived in Florence on 5 September and rented a little Peugeot, which Chris called a "pew-jot" just for fun. He drove, and I navigated, as he was not gifted with a good sense of direction—something he was incessantly teased about when we worked at NIMA/NGA, the geospatial and mapping agency.

Our itinerary was Florence, Chianti, Elba, Chianti, and Florence, and we spent four days and three nights in each location. That was just right, as it was enough time to get a feeling for a particular area before moving on to the next location.

On our drives, particularly through cities, we had some movie scene experiences where it appeared that our car and the car approaching us could not fit on the road. Nevertheless, we slowly passed each other through careful and often tense driving. We drove larger vehicles in America, but there was no way those cars could fit on the old European roads.

We stayed at unique places—hotels I had seen during my previous visit to Florence and at an agritourism vineyard. The fanciest place we stayed was on Elba island, where Napoleon Bonaparte was exiled. The room had high ceilings painted like the sky and a balcony overlooking the water.

Chris and Michele on their hotel room balcony,
Elba Island, Tuscany, Italy (2007)

The hotel had a reserved table for meals and reserved seats on the beach. We did not want to lounge around and sip drinks with colorful umbrellas all day. While sitting on the beach, we eyed the coastline and some neat-looking rock formations and headed for a hike. The hotel staff was concerned that we might hurt ourselves and were relieved when we returned unscathed. Adventurous types like us were different from their usual clientele.

The people of Italy were friendly, and we appreciated their passion for life. In addition to the beauty of the countryside and the delicious wine, what impressed us most was the fantastic flavor of the food. Even the simplest-sounding items on the menus were exquisite because they were made with fresh, heirloom ingredients picked from the farm or at the market that day.

One evening we dined at a restaurant overlooking the Arno River in Florence. We ordered gnocchi quattro formaggi with truffle and were transformed. That was Chris's new favorite dish.

After we returned to Virginia, he asked the owner of our local Italian restaurant, Ciro's, if he could recreate the dish. Ciro did and was delighted to see his customer's satisfaction. When we dined in the restaurant from then on, the staff would ask Chris if he was ordering his usual. Ciro later told us that he tried putting it on the menu, but Americans didn't seem to appreciate it—they wanted Alfredo. However, he still made quattro formaggi for Chris and later for our daughter when it became her favorite dish.

Wolfram and Claudia drove from Switzerland to spend part of two days with us in Italy. We were headed to see the Leaning Tower of Pisa but never made it, as we kept stopping for them to shop for "spirals," evergreen shrubs groomed and trimmed in a spiral shape, at nurseries along the way. Though Chris and I were disappointed that we missed the opportunity to see the famous leaning tower, it was fun to see our friends, and we enjoyed wining and dining together.

Chris and Michele enjoying Chianti wine with Wolfram and Claudia Ragg at their cottage in Tuscany, Italy (2007)

The two weeks Chris and I shared on our honeymoon were some of the happiest moments of my life. We had such a blast. It was one the first of many great adventures we would have together as husband and wife.

CHAPTER 27

Changes

Just three months into the NRO transformation effort, and as we laid out the plan and got ready to execute it, Don Kerr was nominated to be the next PDDNI. He had the vision and the commitment to lead this necessary change at the NRO and would have to relinquish control and hand it off to his deputy. DNRO Kerr continued directing the NRO and meeting with other national agency directors as he waited for the Senate to confirm him as PDDNI.

During this transition period, the new Undersecretary of Defense for Intelligence (USDI), Jim Clapper, called a meeting with the big defense intelligence agencies—NRO, NSA, NGA, and DIA. While DIA was purely a defense intelligence agency, as reflected in its name, the NRO, NSA, and NGA were dual-hatted, reporting to both the DoD and the IC. The CIA was purely a member of the IC and did not report to the DoD.

DNRO Kerr told me I would be his plus-one at the meeting, and with twenty-four hours' notice, asked me to make a list of all of the key things I thought the USDI and defense intelligence agencies could take on to better enable horizontal integration. After over fifteen years working in the IC and DoD, I had all kinds of ideas and quickly drafted a white paper for him to share with his peers.

Some items on that list were no-brainers and should have been done decades ago, as far as I was concerned. That included a universal date and time across the global enterprise to facilitate operations and correlation of data collection and analysis. The varying time zones and date-time formats, along with the fact that some locations followed daylight savings time and others did not, introduced all kinds of complications and potential for error. All defense and intelligence systems needed to move to a single system time—Zulu time, the time at the Zero Meridian, more commonly known as GMT.

Geolocation was imperative if we were to correlate data collected from different sources. All collected data must have the date and time tagged in the metadata per the defined format and universal date and time standard. It was unconscionable that we were paying billions for data collection and not doing metadata tagging at a minimum.

As I had long said, "Just because we've collected the data doesn't mean we are any smarter. We cannot do intelligence by osmosis. Something has to look at the data, and there is far too much data collected for humans to review. So, we must rely on machines to do the first look and then tip the humans as to what items may be of interest."

To do the required automation and machine learning, we had to have a universal standard across the defense and intelligence enterprises. All collected data needed this information in the metadata fields.

DNRO Kerr reviewed the white paper while we were en route to the Pentagon and was pleased.

The route from NRO headquarters to the Pentagon included a drive down I-66. When we were on I-66 inside the I-495 Beltway, the driver pulled to the side of the road. I was curious to know why. Then, all of a sudden a police escort showed up. We realized that because DNRO Kerr was the nominee to be PDDNI, he was receiving police escort the rest of the way to the Pentagon. That was a new experience for me.

We were escorted straight to the USDI's office upon arrival at the Pentagon. USDI Clapper welcomed the two of us, whom he considered old friends, with his typical jovial manner. Then we all joined him at his conference table.

Each of the agencies was represented by either the director or deputy director. As it turned out, I was the only plus-one in attendance. DNRO Kerr handed out my white paper, which everyone reviewed.

Chris Inglis, Deputy DIRNSA, looked up from the paper and remarked, "Michele, this is all very insightful. Concerning date/time format, we have at least twenty-six different standards at NSA." I wondered if he just said that number off the top of his head for effect or if that was indeed the case; regardless, he made his point, reinforcing my proposal's value.

There were so many common sense things to be done, but no one had taken charge to do them. Now was our chance.

Shortly after that meeting, DNRO Kerr became PDDNI Kerr and moved from NRO to ODNI.

The Deputy DNRO, Scott Large, became the DNRO. Scott and I had known each other for some time and had a good working relationship. He knew my background and expertise and supported what his predecessor had intended to do.

Unfortunately, the person he made his deputy had other ideas. What DNRO Kerr's team of four advisors had put together was left for the new Deputy DNRO to implement, and what he implemented was vastly different from what we had proposed.

Michele's official NRO photo (2008)

In the process, the good old boy network of CIA officers detailed to the NRO went into action to pick prime positions for themselves in the resultant shuffle caused by the reorganization.

From the start, the plan had always been that I would eventually become the NRO CTO once the transformation was underway. A creator-innovator by nature, I would now officially have the charge to lead and facilitate innovation initiatives across the NRO enterprise working in collaboration with the various directorates, including mission operations and science and technology. This excited me because it was a niche in which I could excel.

I had a great partnership with NRO Media Services, and we collaborated to do interviews and short spots that would help inform the workforce of our direction and the new capabilities we were working to provide. These service announcements helped get the word out and solicit innovative ideas from the broader NRO enterprise—think Ideas in Action from my NRO ops days. The feedback from the workforce was very positive.

CXO

One afternoon, DNRO Large called me and said he had a favor to ask. Always wanting to be of service, I asked what it was. He replied that he knew I was the CTO, but he wondered if I would be willing to also be the DCIO.

That caught me off guard. I replied that after being the DCIO for the entire IC, being the DCIO for the NRO was not exactly career progression. I told him I'd be happy to be the CIO, though, and it made sense, given my experience and the fact that I wrote the founding documents for the new office of the CIO.

He then admitted he had already agreed to give the job to a CIA colleague who had run the COMM directorate and said he would retire unless he got one of the CXO jobs. So, DNRO Large offered him the CIO position. However, he realized the man was not qualified to hold the job. DNRO Large knew full well that I could step in and do the job and was wondering if I would be willing to do it as DCIO since he had already given his CIA colleague the role of CIO.

Trust me; this is not a good arrangement—ever. This was the second time I was asked to be a deputy to what Chris would call "an old white guy" who was not qualified to hold the job. At that point, I asked, "Why didn't you just ask me to be the CIO?"

He replied, "It hadn't occurred to me."

Ugh. Though I was not thrilled with the idea, I said yes because the mission comes first.

The Associate CIO was Ellis Fiedtkou-Leonard, and he was awesome. Ellis was an NSA officer detailed to NRO and a Navy reservist. He got it and was my sanity in all the CIA madness within the OCIO at NRO; the CIA primarily staffed the civilian slots to include the administrative roles.

In time, it became painfully clear that the man who had been given the position of CIO merely wanted the title to increase his odds of getting a good job offer from a company when he retired. He spent his time visiting different industry partners and attending conferences with various companies, so he was frequently out of the office and on business trips. Because he was not interested in doing the job of the CIO, I did my best to run the office and accomplish the objectives. Still, he had signature authority and was not interested in supporting any new initiatives.

There is one particular example in which I found a workaround because ops depended on it. Chris served as a Mission Director (MD), previously known as a Director of Missions (DOM). In this role, he oversaw all the operators flying the national reconnaissance imaging satellites. They operated in a room called the Race Track, which was oval and had tiers of workstations in concentric ovals. The MD worked from a glass-enclosed space that afforded line of sight to all the operators working at the various stations, all of which had computers on networks at the TS/SCI level.

Since returning from Afghanistan, Chris had been lobbying the NRO ops leadership to let him set up what he called a Joint Collaboration Cell (JCC). The purpose of the JCC was to better facilitate national intelligence support of the warfighters in the tactical fight, just as he had done with boots on the ground in Afghanistan. Chris had seen firsthand how his knowledge of and ability to connect to the national intelligence enterprise had supported the troops in conducting their operations; he didn't want that to stop just because he had returned home.

Chris also noted that the warfighters used mIRC (chat) to communicate with each other on the various networks, particularly SIPRNet, which was at the Secret level. The issue was they only had TS/SCI network drops in the Race Track.

Given my role as NRO DCIO, Chris asked me to come to ADF-E to talk with the team about this matter. The IT support person told me he could get SIPRNet installed, but he needed approval to do it and hadn't had any success in getting it.

I told the team it was clear this needed to be done—the Site Commander had approved the JCC concept and received approval up the chain of command. All that remained was for someone in authority to sign the required paperwork to get SIPRNET to the Race Track. They could not proceed with the project until that occurred. It just so happened that the CIO was on vacation, so I had the authority to approve, and I did.

The IT guy, an industry partner, was still very nervous. So I handed him my business card with a note stating that I had given approval for the SIPRNet drop and also gave him my direct phone line and told him to call me if there was any issue and I would handle it. This was the assurance he needed that I would give him top cover.

That was such a proud moment for Chris. I was glad to have been of service to the operators and the warfighters he and his team would be supporting.

The CIO's lack of interest in actually doing his job was frustrating. I worked to do as much good as possible in my role as the CTO.

He had a couple of people loyal to him who had followed him from the COMM directorate to the OCIO. It appeared he had tasked them not to do actual work but to act as spies to figure out what I was trying to do as CTO and then work to undermine me. I was incredulous. He wasn't interested in exerting any effort to do his job as CIO and instead seemed to spend his time trying to prevent me from getting anything accomplished. He proved to be the proverbial worthless, self-interested government bureaucrat and, like the IC CIO, nefarious in his deeds.

Fortunately, there were a few people on the OCIO staff who could see what was going on. One was Ellis, and another was Tim Stewart, an IT and Information Systems and Services expert. They were loyal to the mission and knew that was my priority, so they looked out for me and worked with me to accomplish what we needed to do for the broader NRO enterprise.

Ellis and I would strategize and then double-team the CIO to try and convince him to support our efforts. Tim, an excellent technologist, laid out the plans we needed to execute. Together we implemented initiatives that provided value to operations despite the CIO's subversive behavior.

CHAPTER 28

Family

Chris and I celebrated our first wedding anniversary on 31 December 2007. That day I received a call informing me that my grandpa Glenn was having trouble breathing and had been taken to the hospital. He had experienced a similar issue on Christmas Day and was taken to the hospital, where they pumped fluid out of his lungs.

This time they informed him that he had been diagnosed with mesothelioma. This news was devastating to our family. The hospital staff said they could do nothing for him and recommended he go into hospice.

Mesothelioma is an aggressive and deadly form of cancer caused by asbestos exposure. My grandfather had worked with asbestos in construction.

My uncle Bob traveled from Seattle to Santa Barbara to be with my grandfather and to look after my grandmother. Aside from the difficulty breathing caused by mesothelioma, my grandfather was in good health and mentally sharp. He had been handling all the affairs of his household in addition to caring for his wife.

My mom then traveled to Santa Barbara for two weeks to relieve Bob. I explained to the CIO that my grandfather was like my father and that I needed to be with him; he approved my taking leave for three weeks. So, I made plans to relieve my mother, and Chris made plans to join me for the third week.

Just before I departed for California, Chris and I learned we were expecting a baby. This was exciting news! However, we were just in the first trimester, so we decided to keep the news to ourselves. We both read up on the latest information regarding having a healthy pregnancy. I stopped drinking my morning coffee the next morning, and the headaches that day and in the days that followed were brutal but eventually went away.

In addition, I started discovering some foods I liked to eat my baby didn't like, as I did not feel well afterward. I tease my daughter that because of her, I had to go on a bland English diet for nine months.

Upon arrival at the Santa Barbara airport, I went to see my grandfather at the hospice facility. He had just walked across the room, was nearly out of breath, and struggled to speak when he saw me. Once he got the oxygen reconnected to his nose, he was better, but it shocked and saddened me to see him so weak and struggling to breathe. It became clear it was better to talk with him for a short while and then give him a chance to rest. So, after a quick hello, I headed to their house to see my mom and grandmother.

It was clear that my grandmother's condition had deteriorated since the last time I saw her. I marveled at how my grandfather took care of her and everything else, given how hard it was for him to breathe and the resultant impact on his energy and strength. He was an amazing man, and this was one more way he was amazing.

After my mom headed home to Virginia, I got into a routine of caring for my grandmother and visiting with my grandfather for a while in the late morning and again in the afternoon and evening.

Some days, friends of theirs agreed to sit with my grandmother so I could run errands such as shopping trips and visit with my grandfather one-on-one. Other times, my grandmother came with me to see him. She was concerned about what would happen to her, which preoccupied her thoughts. Everyone assured my grandfather that my grandmother would be well cared for by the family. This gave him some peace of mind in this trying time.

Those three weeks with my grandfather were precious to me. It was so hard to realize we were losing him. I thought of things I wanted to ask him, memories I hoped he would recall, and stories he would tell.

My grandfather had been an ordained minister since his early twenties, and while he had also held other jobs as a carpenter, he was always studying the Bible and praying. I asked him what he thought heaven was like. He told me he didn't know but would find out soon.

We talked about all the trips he and my grandmother made to see me, whether to help me move into new places across the country or to visit and go on excursions wherever I lived. We also talked about our adventures on the many trips I made to see them over the years.

I was like their fifth kid. We stayed in close contact as I visited them often and called regularly. Ours was a special bond that I will always cherish.

During one of these conversations, I shared with my grandfather that I was expecting a baby. I told him he was the first to know, as we were waiting to share the news with others after we made it through the first trimester. It was a bittersweet moment, for it pained both of us to recognize he would likely go to be with Jesus before my baby was born. He was very happy for me, but I could tell he was sad at the same time. So was I.

My grandfather went into the hospital and never returned to his house exactly one year after he married Chris and me. I told my grandfather how much it meant that he walked me down the aisle and married us. It was the promise I had asked him to make to me when he had health scares in the past, and he honored it—God allowed him to do so before taking him home.

Each day I sent email updates to my mom and her siblings. They reported that they planned to visit my grandfather on Saturday, 1 March. I finally told them I sensed Grandpa would not last until 1 March; if they wanted to see him and spend some quality time with him, they needed to come the weekend before. When I talked with my mom, I told her I felt this strongly, and she shared that with their siblings.

Chris arrived for the third week, and we had special times with my grandfather. In the evenings, I would share my thoughts and feelings with Chris. It was painful to realize I was losing this man I loved so dearly. Chris was good at listening and holding me while the tears flowed. He loved my grandfather, and my grandfather loved him. The two of them were both exceptional in their own ways, and I felt so blessed to have these two men in my life and felt so much pain knowing my time with my grandfather was short and he was suffering.

It didn't seem right that a man who loved God and faithfully served him should suffer like this, but I also realized that we live in a fallen world, and God does not promise us an easy life. God promises us eternal life with him, where there will be no suffering or pain, if we confess our sins, repent, believe in Jesus Christ as our personal Lord and Savior, and accept the gift of salvation.

As much as I grieved over my grandfather's situation and the thought of losing him, I had the assurance that one day we would be reunited again in heaven. He had modeled what it was like to have unwavering faith in God and trust God in every aspect of your life, regardless of the circumstances.

Grandpa Glenn was a marvelous example of loving people to God. He was a friendly and gracious person who loved God and wanted people to know God as he did. Grandpa Glenn wanted others to have the assurance that no matter what happens in this life, we can have peace knowing if we surrender our lives to God, we will someday live eternally with God who created us and loves us like no other. I was so grateful to my grandfather for his example and the wisdom and insight he had shared with me in my thirty-eight years of life.

My grandfather was good at speaking edifying words to Chris. He told Chris he was happy that we had each other and celebrated with us that we were expecting a baby. Grandpa reminisced how Chris had asked for his permission to marry me and how he had granted it. He knew we were a great match and saw the joy we brought to each other and how being together enriched both of our lives. That is the way a marriage should be.

To this day, I have the image of the last time I saw my grandfather indelibly marked in my mind. Chris and I visited with him privately and shared our goodbyes. We did our best not to let our emotions overcome us.

When we had to leave to get to the airport to catch our flight, I hugged my grandfather; we held each other for a moment. Then he kissed me on the cheek.

As I stepped back and looked at him sitting in a chair with a light behind him, he gave me his warm smile as he always did, though the usual twinkle in his eyes faded. We both knew this was our last moment together in this life.

I held myself together until we got to the car; then the tears flowed. They flowed in waves off and on during our entire trip home to Virginia. Chris was so good at wrapping me in his arms and holding my hand. This part of my story still brings tears to my eyes; the grief of losing someone we love dearly never goes away.

My mother and her siblings heeded my suggestion and had a family reunion with my grandparents the last weekend in February. I continued to call my grandfather after I returned to Virginia, and I talked with him on the day they were all together. He was happy and said he only wished I was there too.

On 1 March 2008, my grandfather struggled to breathe. My cousin Mark, visiting him from the Los Angeles area, called me to let me know. He held the phone up to my grandfather's ear so I could speak to him and tell him I loved him one more time.

I was an emotional wreck when I got off the phone. It pained me to hear my grandfather gasping for air.

Chris was good at comforting me, as always. He took me out to dinner that evening, and while we were there, I got the call that my grandfather had passed on. I inexplicably felt God's "peace that passeth all understanding," knowing that Grandpa Glenn was no longer in pain and was with Jesus.

Ultrasound

When I returned to the office, I knew I would never regret taking three weeks of leave to be with my grandfather. I only wished it could have been longer and that I could have been with him through the end of his time here on earth. Perhaps God knew it was better for me to remember him as he was that day we said our goodbyes, for visual images stick with me, and my last one of him is a happy one with him smiling at me—not struggling for breath.

I was grateful for God leading me to tell my mom and her siblings that they needed to come sooner than they had planned so that they could spend quality time with him. As it was, the day they had initially planned to visit—1 March—was when he passed away. This was one clear instance of God speaking to me, and I am forever grateful.

Returning to business as usual after an experience like that puts things in perspective. We are made for relationships, and our relationships matter most in life. It's great to have a calling and work that you enjoy, but if it comes at the expense of the relationships in your life, it is not worth it. There must be a balance.

We are made for relationships, and our relationships matter most in life. It's great to have a calling and work that you enjoy, but if it comes at the expense of the relationships in your life, it is not worth it. There must be a balance.

My team said they missed me, and I was grateful that they had done a good job of keeping things moving forward in my absence while doing their best not to concern me with affairs at the office while I was spending those precious final days with my grandfather.

Pretty soon, there was no denying I was pregnant. I heard funny stories of people saying that, from the back, I didn't look any different, but once I turned sideways, it was very apparent.

One of the office directors, Donna Hansen, was sweet to me during this time. She was the mother of a young child, and she would ask me questions about my experience and tell me things to look for and expect.

One such thing was the baby kicking during meetings; my baby did not disappoint. The first time caught me by surprise, as did a bump moving across my belly that was a visible sign of the baby moving an arm or leg within the confines of my womb. There is nothing quite like the experience of being pregnant. While the water weight gain and nausea are unpleasant, there are fun moments like these that you'll never forget.

Chris and I decided to get a 3D ultrasound, during which time we could find out the sex of our baby. We both wrote our guesses regarding the baby's gender on little pieces of paper before we went in and then shared our guesses. Chris thought we would have a boy, and I thought we would have a girl. The ultrasound technician informed us it was a girl, and I thought how special it would be to have a daughter to raise. If I could only have one child, for Chris already had three, I was glad it was a daughter because we could share many fun mother-daughter things.

We watched our baby move around, and the ultrasound tech took pictures. In one, she got a picture of our baby that made it look like she was sticking her foot in her mouth. We got a good laugh out of that. We also got to listen to the baby's heartbeat.

This drove home the fact that this was a distinct little human growing in my womb and that I had the privilege to carry her until she was ready to come into the world. I considered that a sacred honor. A mother's womb should be the safest place for a baby, and I did my best to take care of her while she lived inside me.

Reality Check

Throughout my career, it was often a struggle to get people at headquarters to have a sense of urgency. They lived in "administrivia land" and did not understand the demands of operations. At some point, the head CIA secretary who supported the CIO remarked about headquarters being the center of the NRO universe and that all NRO elements supported headquarters.

I was taken aback and told her that we were merely an administrative unit supporting the broader enterprise; it was ops that mattered. No government member of the OCIO staff truly understood what that meant because no one had been in ops except Ellis and me. This was very concerning to me because if the staff at headquarters did not understand that they existed to serve operations, not the other way around, the OCIO would fail to do the job the NRO enterprise needed us to do.

To address this, I arranged a TDY for me, my direct reports who ran the various CIO offices, and the two head secretaries. It was officially an OCIO visit to NRO ops sites. Only Chris and Ellis knew what I called it—the Get a Clue Tour. Please don't misunderstand. My default is to give everyone the benefit of the doubt, so I assumed they were all well-intentioned; unfortunately, they had only done staff jobs at headquarters, so they didn't have a clue about ops. They lacked the context to give them an accurate perspective of the OCIO's role in this enterprise.

When I ran this past my doctor, I was informed that the timeline was on the border of when they would start to recommend that someone pregnant not travel. We arranged the trip before the cutoff date, but it wasn't easy for me to travel to multiple sites when I was that far along in my pregnancy.

People who were used to seeing the slender and fit me were shocked to see the pregnant me. While I was self-conscious about this, I maintained my focus on the fact that this trip served a higher purpose.

After we visited three ops sites—two IMINT and one SIGINT—these OCIO staff members had a much better perspective of where they fit in the big picture. Headquarters elements existed to support ops because that's where the real mission was happening.

That Sunday That Summer

On the morning of 13 September 2008, I started having contractions. They were far apart, so there was no need to rush to the hospital.

By the evening, they were closer together and starting to hurt. We called the hospital. The doctor on duty, part of a team I had been seeing and who had always been rather condescending, told me this was too early and that my baby wasn't due for another week. I was sure my baby was coming sooner, like in the next twenty-four hours, but the doctor told me to stay home.

So, Chris and I walked around our neighborhood and returned to the house. When a contraction was so painful it caused tears to shoot out of my eyes, Chris said he'd had enough. He was taking me to the hospital.

When we arrived, the doctor said it was too early for me to have the baby and directed me to walk around the ward. During that time, he observed the pain level I was experiencing during the contractions and finally ordered me to be put in a room. The doctor said the baby had likely rotated, so I had what was called back labor, where contractions caused the baby's head to push against my spine. He gave me an epidural, and soon my body started to relax a bit as the intense pain was gone.

By then, it was late at night, and the doctor said I should get some rest. He hooked me up to a device that monitored the baby's heartbeat. Chris stretched out on a reclining chair beside me and slept.

I could not sleep and kept watching the monitor. By doing so, I noticed that the baby's heartbeat dropped every time I had a contraction. Concerned, I rang the nurse. I pointed this out to her and said I wanted to speak with the doctor.

The doctor entered the room, and I asked him to watch the monitor because what I saw concerned me. He said it was likely that the umbilical cord was wrapped around the baby causing blood flow to decrease during contractions and the baby's heart rate to drop.

When I asked him what could be done about this, he said something I will never forget. "We could take the baby via C-section, but that would leave a scar on you, so you may want to discuss it with your husband first."

I was incredulous and replied, "I didn't work hard to have a perfectly healthy pregnancy for nine months only to have my daughter harmed during delivery. I don't care whether I will have a scar for the rest of my life. Get her out!"

The doctor realized I meant what I said and directed that the operating room be prepped. I woke Chris and told him what was happening. As Chris donned a gown, the anesthesiologist told me he would have to numb me from the neck down. I thought that would be a bizarre feeling—like being a quadriplegic.

On the morning of Sunday, 14 September 2008, our darling Sophia was delivered safely and handed to Chris, who held her up for me to see. It was such a special moment for both of us. Sadly, the anesthesiologist gave me way too much anesthesia for my body size, and it would be hours before I could move my arms, which made me sad because I longed to hold her. In the meantime, Chris laid her on my chest and held her there so we could be close.

We had prepared a mix of classic jazz to play in the hospital room and kept it on loop on the iPod. That may be why Sophia enjoys that same mix to this day. We told her one of the songs was made for her—"That Sunday, That Summer" by Nat King Cole—for she had joined us that Sunday that summer of 2008.

We were blessed to have so many friends and family members send their congratulations. They said they were looking forward to meeting Sophia.

One fun invitation we received when she was just two months old was from my CAPSTONE classmate, VADM Fowler, then superintendent of the US Naval Academy. He invited us to be his guests at the Army-Navy football game.

We met astronaut and Naval Academy alumnus Jim Lovell and his wife, Marylin. In 1970, Jim Lovell was on the perilous voyage of Apollo 13, documented in a movie by the same name. We took a picture with the Lovells who were proudly celebrating fifty-six years of marriage.

Shortly after I returned to work following Sophia's birth, some colleagues asked me to meet them for lunch. One was a former Air Force officer, while the other had always been in the private sector.

The former military officer said, "Michele, I'd always figured you were a career girl. How do you balance your career and being a mother?"

I told him that before Chris and I had Sophia, our lives were wrapped up in our careers. Having Sophia brought balance to our lives.

His colleague remarked, "He didn't figure that out in time." I realized he meant the former Air Force officer had been so caught up in his career that he hadn't invested time in building relationships with his family. Chris and I were going to ensure that we struck the right balance, and we did.

Looking forward to Sophia's first birthday, we made plans to take her to Walt Disney World's Magic Kingdom and invited our moms to join us. It was a special day.

While in Orlando, Chris suggested we check out Disney Vacation Club (DVC). Following the DVC tour, we decided to invest. Sophia has been treated to a birthday trip to the Disney theme parks every year since; we have so many fond memories from those trips.

CHAPTER 29

Federal Innovation

As CTO, I hosted an innovation conference at NRO headquarters in early 2009 and invited Vivek Kundra, the Federal CIO, and other luminaries to speak. Vivek and I first met when he was the CTO for Washington, DC, and I was the IC DCIO. We realized we were kindred spirits wanting to effect positive change and worked together to help the government adopt modern technology and streamline technology acquisition.

Later that year, Vivek convened a dozen innovators across the government to discuss opportunities to implement enabling technologies. Some of the people in this group had just entered government service a few months prior, and I noted with amusement that they were still in shock.

They had been like me, thinking they could come into government and effect positive change. They had no idea how genuinely resistant government bureaucracies were to change, mainly because of bureaucrats who had risen to power based on the old way of doing business. This forum allowed them to commiserate with like-minded individuals, gain insight, and be encouraged to hear how other innovators overcame similar barriers to effect positive change in the public sector.

Vivek asked me to speak about the capabilities we provided for the IC via INTELINK. He already recognized that if we could provide common services for the whole of government like INTELINK was doing for the IC, it would enable cross-government information sharing and better interagency collaboration. After I shared, the entire group acknowledged how hosting such capabilities for all the federal government would be a huge enabler for intragovernmental collaboration and far more cost-effective.

As a group, we also focused our attention on how to improve government-to-citizen collaboration. For the most part, everyone there had previously been in the private sector. We all recognized that the government did not have the corner on the market when it came to good ideas, especially when tackling challenging problems.

Together, we came up with Challenge.gov to enable the government to bring the innovative thinking of the private sector to help tackle the country's problems. The message on the website was, "Here, members of the public compete to help the US government solve problems big and small." Any citizen could browse through the challenges posted on the website and submit their ideas.

SecDef Task Force

In June 2009, Stan McChrystal assumed the rank of general and became the Commander of the International Security Assistance Force (ISAF) and Commander of US and NATO forces in Afghanistan. MG Mike Flynn assumed the duties of Chief, CJ2, ISAF, and the Director of Military Intelligence for US and NATO forces in Afghanistan.

Shortly thereafter, I received a call from USDI Clapper. He said, "Michele, we have blackened the skies of Afghanistan with sensors without giving any thought to what we would do with the data once it hit the ground. Would you please come and help?"

Duty called, so I left my post at NRO. Remaining in an ODNI billet, I became the DNI's senior rep to the Secretary of Defense's (SecDef) Intelligence, Surveillance, and Reconnaissance (ISR) Task Force in August 2009.

I was the most senior ranking member of the Task Force, second only to the director, an Air Force general who had received his third star upon taking the post. A high-caliber team had been assembled to focus on stability ops in Afghanistan, and I enjoyed working with my colleagues there.

As part of the regular ops tempo of the ISR Task Force, we gave periodic briefings to the leadership at the Pentagon, including the Joint Staff. The director insisted on presenting these briefings himself. Consequently, each of the subject matter experts (SMEs) and program managers (PMs) would spend countless hours coaching the three-star general through the briefing slides so that he could present them. Regardless of this significant investment of everyone's time to prepare him, he still wanted the SMEs and PMs to come to the briefings as "backbenchers" just in case his leadership asked questions he could not answer. Given that we were supporting real-time operations downrange, I could not see how this was a good use of everyone's time.

If I had been running the ISR Task Force, I would have taken a much different approach, similar to what I had done when I ran offices. As necessary, I would have received briefings from the SMEs and PMs to stay informed and keep up to speed. Then, when asked to provide a briefing on our activities to senior leadership, I would have brought the SMEs and PMs with me, introduced them, and let them present their material.

Not only is that a much more practical approach and better use of everyone's time, but it also gives credit where credit is due—to the people doing the daily work and leading the programs. Good leaders provide their team members opportunities to have face time with their leadership, but you have to be a servant leader who is secure in yourself to do it. Unfortunately, not everyone put in a leadership position fits the bill.

As the leader of information sharing and collaboration efforts on the Task Force, I found an innovative way to encourage information sharing. There was a coffee maker in the kitchenette where coffee was brewed for the office. The former Navy guys who ran it believed that by not washing the coffee pot or the coffee cups, it seasoned things and made for better-tasting coffee. The coffee they brewed was not for the faint of heart and, to me, tasted awful.

I decided to get a Keurig coffee machine for my office. I invited everyone to use it, requesting a small donation to cover the cost of the K-cups. When colleagues would stop by my office to get coffee, I'd ask how things were going and what they were working on. This was valuable and a way to strengthen relationships with my coworkers.

Most people in this community focused on classified data sharing, and plenty of issues needed to be resolved there. However, there was one glaring gap—we desperately needed non-classified information, meaning unclassified without the UNCLASSIFIED banner, to share with non-traditional partners. DoD gives the label "non-traditional partners" to entities they are unaccustomed to working with, such as civilian government agencies that don't do classified work, foreign governments, nonprofits, and charitable organizations.

I'd been to combat zones. Shared situational awareness of what was happening was vital to everyone's safety. I knew that if we did not share with each other, we risked dying together.

Someone who understood this was Dr. Linton Wells III, Director of the Center for Technology and National Security Policy at National Defense University (NDU). Lin led STAR-TIDES, which stood for Sharing To Accelerate Research—Transformative Innovation for Development and Emergency Support. He was previously the Principal Deputy Assistant SecDef for Networks and Information Integration and the DoD Transformation Chair.

Lin worked closely with various humanitarians, such as Dr. Dave Warner, who was a true "Dr. Dr." or "Dr.^{2}," as he had both a PhD and an MD. Dr. Dave, as we called him, didn't think outside the box because, to him, there was no box.

Dr. Dave founded what is known as the "beer for data" program in Afghanistan. He took over the "Taj Mahal" guest house in Jalalabad from some Aussies and housed his ops and his team there. Dave networked with the local Afghans in their villages and also with non-Afghans in the area, such as other NGOs and UN Security Forces.

He invited people to the Taj bar, where there was a sign which read, "If you supply data, you will get a beer." This was a great HUMINT model, but Dave was no spook. In time, he had a disk drive full of information. The trick was correlating it geospatially to gain context and insight. This was where I came in.

When OEF started, there were no current maps of Afghanistan; that was a problem. Dave and his team, which he called the Synergy Strike Force, worked with a group that had been contracted to create maps for the area. Unfortunately, they only shared the maps with a limited group. We needed to be able to share those maps with anyone and everyone.

Apple, Inc. had recently launched iTunes. Initially, you could purchase any song for 99 cents, shareable across five devices. That frustrated people to no end, so they devised a new plan to sell the songs for $1.29, and you could play them on unlimited devices.

I told the member of Dave's team working with this group, "Ask them, á la the iTunes model, how much more money they would require to let us share the maps they created with anyone." He understood what I was asking.

The answer he got was, "For $55,000 more, you can share the maps freely with anyone." In the context of the $12 billion budget we oversaw at the ISR TF, this was a minuscule amount, and the return on investment would be great. I said, "Done!" We then had maps we could share with anyone and everyone we wished. This was a game-changer.

While the maps were useful, commercial imagery would be even better. I knew this from my visit to Afghanistan a few years prior. My next initiative was to get commercial satellite imagery they could share in the same way.

While the Afghan locals were used to seeing maps, satellite imagery afforded a whole new perspective, and it was a view they were not accustomed to seeing. The NGOs, however, were used to this satellite view from things like Google Earth. That imagery provided an excellent perspective of the terrain, what was going on, and where. This enabled a better shared situational awareness for the benefit of the mission and the security of all involved.

Rolling Stone

In January 2010, MG Mike Flynn published *Fixing Intel: A Blueprint for Making Intelligence Relevant in Afghanistan* in partnership with the Center for a New American Security. In the paper, MG Flynn and his two coauthors—Capt. Matt Pottinger, USMC intel officer, and Paul Batchelor, DIA senior advisor for Civilian/Military Integration—made critical points, some of which I will highlight here.

"Because the United States has focused the overwhelming majority of collection efforts and analytical brain power on insurgent groups, our intelligence apparatus still finds itself unable to answer fundamental questions about the environment in which we operate and the people we are trying to protect and persuade. This problem or its consequences exist at every level of the US intelligence hierarchy, and pivotal information is not making it to those who need it."

They quoted GEN Stan McChrystal, Commander of ISAF. He said, "Our senior leaders—the Chairman of the Joint Chiefs of Staff, the Secretary of Defense, Congress, the President of the United States—are not getting the right information to make decisions with… The media is driving the issues. We need to build a process from the sensor to the political decision-makers."

They went on to say that this was a need that spanned the forty-four nations involved with ISAF. Their paper was a blueprint for that process. It described the problem, detailed the challenges, and illuminated examples of units that were getting it right. The target audience was combatant commanders and intelligence professionals in Afghanistan, the US, and Europe.

You may have noticed that the paper was not processed through an official DoD channel, likely because that would have required a lot of coordination and signatures before publication, and the message was time sensitive, as operations were ongoing.

A few senior officials in the DoD were not too happy about this. One of them was USDI Clapper, and it was yours truly who worked to screw him out of the ceiling that day.

My words to him were this: "While the method of publishing may not have been ideal, the content of the publication is valid. We do need to fix intelligence to make it more relevant, particularly for counterinsurgency operations and the war to win hearts and minds."

Fixing Intel was very validating to my colleagues and me. We referenced this paper often, demonstrating how our efforts supported the objectives outlined in that paper. I led the non-classified collaboration and information-sharing efforts in support of those with boots on the ground in Afghanistan.

UnityNet was an initiative I led from Washington, DC, collaborating with colleagues across the country and Afghanistan. The UnityNet purpose was to encourage a self-sustaining, open sharing environment and extend stability ops doctrine as a preemptive counterinsurgency (COIN) strategy. To do this, we would connect third-world populations with the global community via the internet and provide an open-source data-sharing repository and coordination platform for humanitarian efforts.

The underlying tenet was that open information empowers and informs populations to take action. We hypothesized that people supported by an informed international community would be more likely to make better choices for their local communities and socio-economic and governance challenges. If we shared with them first by providing connectivity and data, they would want to share back with us and each other. A fundamental enabler was providing imagery and maps for geospatial context.

Our goal was that Afghan nationals could sustain this open-source, node-centric infrastructure organically. To do this, we had to form partnerships with a sponsoring organization willing to house the hardware portion of the node and become a virtual watering hole for disparate groups within a particular region, like Dr. Dave's beer-for-data program.

To do this, we leveraged the success of people who had already been operating in the area, like Dr. Dave. In that vein, you could call it "bandwidth for data." Together, we would eliminate that barrier to the internet, a resource to empower the Afghans to better understand how to address their needs and ultimately enable them to take charge of their country's stability.

Two members of DIA embedded with ISAF—David Muench and Gary Thompson—led the UnityNet-Afghanistan program. They shared an office at ISAF headquarters with the coauthors of *Fixing Intel*, Matt and Paul, and their daily dialog afforded valuable insights.

Dave and Gary published the UnityNet white paper in May 2010. The intent was to enable open information-sharing environments that would encourage non-government entities to communicate and cooperate in support of stability, security, transition, and reconstruction activities. This network would be independent of any military or government organization and provide a neutral sharing environment to collaborate on grassroots population-centric, socio-economic, and governance matters, including crisis management and stability operations.

In the developed world, we take access to the internet for granted. It was hard to come by in the remote regions of Afghanistan. I partnered with Dr. Dave and others to fund internet connections in strategic areas to better enable information sharing. For example, they could use the internet to provide telemedicine support to the Afghans and help save people's lives. This unconventional strategy benefitted humanitarian efforts and official DoD operations around the country.

In June 2010, news broke about the *Rolling Stone* article "The Runaway General." The journalist accused GEN McChrystal and his staff of mocking civilian government officials, including Vice President Biden, the National Security Advisor, and other senior administration officials.

On 23 June, GEN McChrystal offered President Obama his resignation, and the president accepted it. The entire ISR Task Force watched the news live on TV.

Immediately following the news conference, I observed the division in the office. People started taking sides. Many who had previously aligned with GEN McChrystal promptly abandoned him. I was shocked but recognized it was just another example of fair-weather friends. As they say in Washington, DC, "If you want a friend, get a dog."

GEN McChrystal was someone I had known to exhibit personal honor and integrity. He was a strong leader with the courage of his convictions and was willing to take a stand when others would not. I admired these things about him, and I knew we needed leaders like him, especially at this time. GEN McChrystal was also highly regarded by his NATO colleagues. This was something Obama didn't seem to appreciate or value. But then again, Obama didn't seem interested in America leading or winning this war.

I returned to my office depressed. We had been able to do so much good in collaboration with GEN McChrystal and MG Flynn. Once they transitioned out of Afghanistan, I knew that the DoD would likely return to the conventional way of doing things. As I was considering the ramifications, I was surprised that a tear started quietly rolling down my face. I instinctively knew things would be different and perhaps not better.

Soon after that, things got political. Part of the DoD wanted to return to the old way of doing business, but I saw the value in the innovative things we were doing and was outspoken that we needed to continue them.

There is only one way to avoid criticism:
do nothing, say nothing, be nothing.

A colleague who had been in the Army then worked on my team as a civilian at NGA and had recently been promoted to the senior executive rank pulled me aside one day to share his concern. He said, "Michele, if you take a stand, you risk polarizing people."

I responded, "We are in leadership positions. What good are we if we don't take a stand to do what needs to be done?"

As the ancient Greek philosopher and scientist Aristotle said, "There is only one way to avoid criticism: do nothing, say nothing, be nothing."

In early September 2010, I gave a presentation at the Gov 2.0 Summit hosted by O'Reilly Media in Washington, DC. It was entitled "Stability out of Chaos from Information Sharing" and introduced this experiment called UnityNet to the public. The UnityNet slogan was "Networking people together in a unity of effort for a common cause."

Oppressive regimes seek to limit freedom of speech and access to the outside world. By eliminating the barrier to entry and getting the Afghans on the internet, they could connect with each other and the broader global community that wanted to help them. This would provide an open-source data-sharing repository and coordination platform for humanitarian efforts.

The US military was involved in many humanitarian efforts in the country as part of stability operations. We had seen crowdsourcing in support of crisis response efforts empower and inform populations to take action on their own behalf. O'Reilly Media found this intriguing, and one of their correspondents asked to interview me following my presentation.

While this may not be the conventional approach of the DoD, this was not a conventional war; it was a war for hearts and minds. One way to win people over is to show them that you genuinely care and can be trusted. This took time and effort, but the investment was well worth it. GEN McChrystal and MG Flynn understood this, whereas many of their peers in the DoD did not.

Someone who got this better than most people was Major (MAJ) Jim Gant, US Army. Dr. Dave introduced us via email in October 2010. MAJ Gant wrote *One Tribe at a Time* based on his experience in Afghanistan. He had worked for a long time to develop relationships with the tribal leaders based on mutual trust, and he understood their culture and way of life better than any military officer I knew. MAJ Gant truly cared about the Afghan people, and they knew it. Some Afghans had adopted him into their family, which was a huge honor given he was an American.

While this was an unconventional approach for someone in the military, MAJ Gant recognized that working to understand the Afghans and build trusting relationships with them was immensely valuable to the overall goal of bringing stability to the area. Unfortunately, after the US Army leadership was replaced in Afghanistan, the senior Army officers decided that MAJ Gant's methods were not the way the Army did business. He lost support for his efforts.

The Bible verse that came to mind was, "Where there is no vision, the people perish" (Proverbs 29:18, KJV). In my view, once we lost the strategic leadership of GEN McChrystal and MG Flynn in Afghanistan, we lost the vision necessary to achieve success and the top cover required for innovators like MAJ Gant.

GEN McChrystal retired. MG Flynn came to the Pentagon to take a position in the Army G2 office before moving to his next assignment.

During this transition time, Chris invited MG Flynn to give a briefing to ADF-E staff. I traveled to the site to greet him and hear his presentation. As I recall, MG Flynn was still dealing with blowback from the national security establishment for publishing *Fixing Intel*, but Chris and I admired our fellow maverick. We needed more people in leadership like him who had the strength of their convictions and the courage to speak truth to power.

Shortly after that, Mike Flynn assumed the rank of Lieutenant General (LTG) and became the Assistant Director of National Intelligence for Partner Engagement. In 2012, LTG Flynn became the Director of DIA.

The Last Straw

In time, DoD leadership determined it would be beneficial to take the task force model we had created to support COIN operations in Afghanistan and apply it globally. We drafted a new organizational structure that included an Information Sharing and Collaboration office, which was a natural fit for me; I had been known as a leader in this area across the national security community for the past decade. I decided to raise the subject with the ISR Task Force Director during my upcoming one-year performance review with him.

When we met, the director told me how pleased he was with my performance and contributions. He praised my work, remarking that he regularly communicated to the USDI what valuable contributions I made and how he was glad to have me on the team. Then he informed me that he had just asked to extend my tour on the Task Force by six months.

That was great feedback and seemed like a perfect entree for me to express my interest in leading the new Information Sharing and Collaboration office. I was unprepared for his response.

He looked me in the eye and said, "You are far too young and female to be put in a visible position of leadership."

I could not believe I had just heard him utter those words. How biased and clueless could he be? Didn't he know he could get in trouble for making such a remark because there were laws about discrimination?

Stunned, I thought to myself, "Wow. Neanderthals still exist."

At that moment, I decided that I would agree to extend my tour of duty only because I cared so much about the mission. But after that, I was going to move on—out of government and back into the private sector.

This was the third time I'd been asked to effectively serve as deputy to a senior civilian or military official who was not competent to perform the job they had been given. I was officially done doing that. Those three men had wanted me to use my talent, knowledge, and understanding to lead an office and critical programs. They needed my support to be successful; at the same time, they felt threatened by my intelligence and competence and ultimately tried to undermine my efforts to support the mission because of their insecurity.

As yet another example of insecure leaders undermining good initiatives, I had been working for months to create a contract through NDU, in collaboration with Dr. Lin Wells, that would significantly enhance the speed and efficiency with which we could acquire and deploy new capabilities. This would be a tremendous enabler for the mission, and the Task Force Director had consistently expressed support for this effort.

However, when we finally had the contract ready for his signature, he refused to sign it. Both Lin and I were incredulous.

That was the last straw. There was no need for me to wait any longer. I submitted my resignation.

As we close out the story of my US government career, it is interesting to note that the same man who recruited me into government as DNIMA received my resignation from government service as the DNI. That man was Jim Clapper.

When I met with him in his office to officially submit my letter of resignation as an ODNI employee, he was like the old friend I knew from our joint battles to effect positive change in the IC and DoD for the past decade. I told him that when I entered government, I had determined that I would stay as long as I felt I could effect positive change but would leave once I believed I could do more good outside of the government than remaining in it. That time had come.

I added that if ever called to serve in the government again, I would consider it, but I would not agree to be a deputy. It would have to be a director position where I had decision-making and signature authority.

My last day of government service was Friday, 1 April 2011. Yes, I picked April Fool's Day intentionally—no fooling!

That evening, Chris and I attended the 54th Annual Dr. Robert H. Goddard Memorial Dinner, colloquially known as Space Prom. The Goddard always included luminaries from the space community, like former US Senator and astronaut John Glenn, whom I had the honor of meeting at the 2006 event. This gala was always fun because we saw many friends from our respective careers in the national security space community. It was a great way to celebrate my transition from the public sector to the private sector.

Michele greets former US Senator and astronaut John Glenn at the 49th Annual Goddard Dinner (2006)

CHAPTER 30

G2G

A creator-innovator at heart, I had my eyes set on Google. I reached out to one of my contacts there, whom I had met through my interactions as a government official at industry days. He told me, "We know you by your stellar reputation and would be very interested in hiring you."

Chris threw me a G2G party for my transition from Government to Google. We gathered at our favorite Mexican restaurant, Uncle Julio's Rio Grande, at Fairfax Corner, walking distance from our townhouse.

It was wonderful to hang out with friends who had been with me throughout my national security career and reminisce over swirl margaritas and chips and salsa. They knew it would be refreshing for me to be surrounded by innovators at Google. The common theme I heard was, "The government needs people like you, but we understand why you're leaving."

The Google founders' 2004 initial public offering letter included this statement: "Google is not a conventional company. We do not intend to become one. Throughout Google's evolution as a privately held company, we have managed Google differently. We have also emphasized an atmosphere of creativity and challenge." The thought of working in an environment like that was exciting.

After Google hired me, people who only knew me as a senior executive in government would ask, "Was it a culture shock going into Google?"

My response was always, "No, I felt like I was at home because I was surrounded by creator-innovators like myself. What was a shock to me was going into government!"

Google's corporate philosophy was to hire people who are good at many things and have certain traits—passionate change agents with a bias for action. They figured that if you're competent at your job and have those traits, you'd be good for Google.

They believed in open, collaborative environments and that if you give people freedom, they will amaze you. Their goal was to attract top talent and create a culture of innovation. That becomes a virtuous cycle—top talent drives innovation, which attracts top talent. They provided an office environment and internal tools that fueled this virtuous cycle.

The founders' challenge to Googlers was, "Dare to be audacious and have a healthy disregard for the impossible." They realized that failure is an option and is to be expected. If you don't take intelligent risks, you risk becoming irrelevant. I liked that corporate philosophy as it was similar to my own philosophy. I knew that successful innovators embrace intelligent risk.

I would work directly with sales teams for the first time in my career. However, my role was not sales; it was strategic. Given my reputation, I had street cred and could gain access and talk to leadership across the government and build relationships with them. My objective was to understand their needs and then determine if there were ways Google could help, especially with technology enablers. If so, then I would make an introduction to the appropriate sales rep.

Sales teams were part of the Enterprise group. I worked closely with those who interfaced with the government—federal, state, and local.

Upon my arrival at Google in April 2011, my title became Chief Technology Officer (CTO) for Public Sector. In that role, I got to work with a great team of people—sales reps, sales engineers, security engineers, product development teams, etc.—some who remain friends today. While a few had formerly served in the military, others didn't have a day of government service. Regardless, most of them sincerely cared about helping the government succeed at its mission because it benefited all citizens. This role was an opportunity to assist from a different vantage point outside the government.

One brilliant person I worked with was the true father of the Internet, Dr. Vinton "Vint" Cerf. We worked out of the same office in Reston, Virginia, and my desk was very near where he and his executive assistant, Carla LaFever, worked.

Michele's official Google Inc. headshot (2011) |
Sophia with Michael T. Jones, cocreator of Google Earth (2015) |
Sophia with Dr. Vinton "Vint" Cerf, father of the Internet; she is holding his "I want you to use IPv6" card (2015)

Vint was always in high demand and seemed to be perpetually traveling all over the world. When he was in town, Vint was generous with his time meeting with me and supporting the government-facing efforts. I occasionally had the pleasure of collaborating with him for meetings with customers, which was very synergistic.

Another awesome person I had the pleasure of collaborating with was Michael T. Jones. He was one of the cocreators of Google Earth and was based at the Googleplex in Mountain View, California.

Vint, Michael, and I had similar roles in that we were the company's public-facing representatives and spoke worldwide. This gave us a unique perspective of life within Google and other people's perceptions of Google. We also had a better understanding than most employees regarding Google customers' needs; we provided that insight to the product developers, whether they were working on the everyday tools you are familiar with from Google or the "moonshot" products of Google X, Google's research and development innovation lab.

Speaking of moonshots, here is a great quote that highlights the Google X philosophy of dreaming big, taking on hard problems, and not being limited by conventional thinking:

When you do something radically hard, you approach the problem differently than when you try to make it incrementally better. If you try to do things 10X bigger, you have no hope of getting that done using traditional methods. You have to rely on bravery, creativity, and perspective-shifting—that's what produces the magic, and makes seemingly impossible problems, all of the sudden tractable.
~ Astro Teller, Captain of Moonshots

The Force

Chris and I were both *Star Wars* fans, so it was common for us to quote lines from the movie now and then. We were tracking each other when that happened, but that was not always the case when we spoke with others.

In the summer of 2011, following their respective internships with the IC, we invited Lee Akridge's sons, Doug and Steve, over to our house. Throughout our lively discussion, we referenced scenes from *Star Wars*, and I realized that these references didn't seem to register with them. So, I asked if they had seen the movie. They hadn't.

In unison, Chris and I responded, "What?! You haven't seen *Star Wars*?!" Then I put the *Star Wars* (Episode IV) DVD in the player and skipped to the various scenes we had been referencing.

Sometime after they left, our daughter, Sophia, who was not yet three years old and had been enjoying full-length Disney films to date, told us that she wanted to watch the movie. Chris and I exchanged glances, and I said to her, "Oh, no, baby. That's a scary movie. You'll watch it someday, but not now." She persisted. Finally, after a brief parental discussion, we decided to start the movie and have Sophia sit in my lap and watch with the lights on.

When Darth Vader boarded the spaceship that Princess Leia was on, I said, "Oh, there's the bad guy! Baby, is this too scary for you? We can turn it off."

Sophia replied, "No, Mommy. I want to watch it!"

Of course, I covered her eyes in some scenes, but I continued to ask throughout the movie, "Is this too scary for you?" and she would reply, "No, Mommy. I want to watch it!"

Before we knew it, we were at the final scene where our heroes—Luke Skywalker, Han Solo, and Chewbacca—received medals from Princess Leia. When the movie was over, she was cheering.

Chris and I exchanged glances. "Well," he said, "She *is* our daughter!"

The next evening, Sophia announced, "I want to watch the scary movie again!" We told her that the name of the movie was *Star Wars*. Then we watched it together.

When we put Sophia to bed that night, I told Chris, "Go get it."

Here I need to fill you in on the fact that Chris gave me a lightsaber as a gift after we were married. He told me he remembered my story about having one as a kid and that it got lost during one of our moves. Of course, this new one was fancy—it extended, retracted, and made noise—a far cry from the white tube with a handle and a light switch I had in the late 1970s.

As soon as Sophia saw it, her eyes got big, and she got very excited. That lightsaber Chris gave me has been hers ever since.

On our trip to Walt Disney World for Sophia's fifth birthday in 2013, we signed her up for Jedi training at Hollywood Studios. She was the second-smallest child in the group. The Jedi Master took all the Youngling Padawan hopefuls through lightsaber training in preparation for fighting Sith Lord Darth Vader. There were fourteen kids, and each one got their chance to fight Darth Vader.

At the conclusion, the Jedi Master gathered all the Younglings to one side and said to the audience, "Wasn't this class magnificent?!" Everyone cheered. Then the Jedi Master turned to Darth Vader and said, "I told you that you were wasting your time. These Younglings will never turn to the Dark Side as you did."

Darth Vader fumed and then said to the Younglings, "Your power is weak. Come with me to the Dark Side, and with our combined strength, we can rule the galaxy!"

Then we heard the voice of Yoda. "Wrong you are. Skilled they are indeed, and when together they stand, very strong in The Force they are."

The Jedi Master said this was true and turned to the students and told them to activate their lightsabers. He then turned to Darth Vader and said, "We suggest you leave."

Darth Vader came at them with his lightsaber, and the Jedi Master yelled, "Use The Force to push him back!"

At that moment, our sweet little Sophia, with her lightsaber raised, pushed through to the front of the group to take on Darth Vader. It was a very proud moment for her parents.

Sophia's first Jedi training [left], and Chris, Michele, and Sophia [right] at Hollywood Studios, Walt Disney World (2013)

Our House

Shortly after I joined Google, they had an office picnic that we attended. Chris and I enjoyed interacting with my new coworkers, while Sophia enjoyed the "pony rides" on a full-size horse. That was the first indication she was a natural for horseback riding.

Following the picnic, we checked out some new home communities. Our townhouse was in Fairfax, and to find reasonably priced land, we had to look west of Washington Dulles Airport.

We found a community in Ashburn with standard estate lots at approximately one acre and conservancy lots starting at five acres and ranging up to fifteen acres. We loved how wooded the community was, and we found an available lot with woods on two sides. We decided to buy it and build our home.

The builder offered various floor plans, and we chose what ended up being the second smallest house because we liked the open floor plan. Even then, it was 7,000 square feet and would have two levels plus a walk-out basement, as the lot sloped down from the street to the woods. Neither Chris nor I had ever imagined we would live in such a house. We were excited that this would be the home where Sophia would grow up.

We started the project in the fall of 2011, and the house was ready in the spring of 2012. We visited the building site regularly to see the progress and walked Sophia through what would be her room, connected to a bonus room over the three-car garage that would make a great playroom. It was so fun to see the house come together and imagine how it would be to live there.

The day we closed on the house, we asked my mom to pick Sophia up from preschool. After the closing, we went to our new home, and Chris carried me over the threshold and kissed me. That was the little ceremony we had to say, "We did it! We built our house!"

We returned to our townhouse, packed up Sophia's toys and stuffed animals, and drove them to our new house, where we placed them in her playroom. Then we had my mom bring her over.

It was priceless to see the look on Sophia's face when she walked into her room and saw her things. She knew the place was now hers. To commemorate the occasion, Chris and Sophia gave me a house charm for my birthday to add to the Pandora bracelet they had bought me.

The day the movers came to pick up our household goods to move them to our new house, Chris and Sophia met them at our townhouse. That was a new experience for Sophia, and Chris assured her that though her belongings were boxed up and loaded on a truck, they would show up at our new house.

Later that evening, Chris was helping to move things into Sophia's new bathroom. Chris seemed to always be joking, and when she walked in, he asked, "Sophi, what do you think would happen if you were flushed down the toilet?"

Sophia replied matter-of-factly, "I would go through the pipes to our old house." That struck him so funny he had to come to tell me, and I laughed out loud. We guessed that in the mind of a three-and-a-half-year-old, that's how things worked!

We loved to host friends and family at our house, and now we had the perfect place to do that because we had plenty of space inside and outside. Chris and I started making plans for a big deck off the main level and a patio off the walk-out basement with a grill, walk-up bar, and fireplace. This would be our oasis away from the hustle and bustle of Washington, DC.

Promotion

On 17 September 2011, the NRO hosted a 50th Anniversary gala at the Smithsonian National Air and Space Museum Udvar-Hazy center. Having spent much of our careers in the NRO, it was fun for us to see historical artifacts from the CORONA program and meet some living legends.

Michele and Chris at the NRO 50th Anniversary gala hosted at the Udvar-Hazy Center, with a Skunk Works SR-71 Blackbird in the background (2011)

A year later, on 27 September 2012, Chris pinned on his lieutenant colonel rank—a silver oak leaf on each shoulder. The JD Hill Conference Center at NRO headquarters was filled with family, friends, and colleagues gathered to celebrate this auspicious event.

It may be a little unconventional for a spouse to speak at a military promotion ceremony, but then again, I've never been accused of being conventional.

Back in May 2006, shortly after I officially became the IC DCIO, a friend of ours who was a retired marine and former congressman, James "Jim" Longley, Jr., had given me a book entitled *Boyd: The Fighter Pilot Who Changed the Art of War* by Robert Coram. Just months before Chris's ceremony, I finally got around to reading it and wished I had read it when he had given it to me six years prior. It was a fascinating read, and my experience on the ISR Task Force only solidified how strongly I resonated with what Boyd said about the bureaucrats versus the warriors. I understood why Jim had given it to me—it was serendipitous.

Col. John Boyd was the first US Air Force officer who was both an engineer and a fighter pilot, and he challenged conventional processes of designing and building aircraft. He also created the OODA-loop, the cycle observe-orient-decide-act that has become a standard for combat operations. Boyd was not popular with the Air Force. Still, the Marines loved him, and he did many great things for the warfighters and America.

At one point, he spoke to one of the junior officers who worked with him, sharing his perspective and offering some advice. At Chris's promotion ceremony, I quoted Boyd's statement, which is as follows:

> "Tiger, one day you will come to a fork in the road," he said. "And you're going to have to make a decision about which direction you want to go."
>
> He raised his hand and pointed.
>
> "If you go that way you can be somebody. You will have to make compromises and you will have to turn your back on your friends. But you will be a member of the club, and you will get promoted and you will get good assignments."
>
> Then Boyd raised his other hand and pointed in another direction.
>
> "Or you can go that way and you can do something—something for your country and for your Air Force and for yourself. If you decide you want to do something, you may not get promoted and you may not get the good assignments and you certainly will not be a favorite of your superiors. But you won't have to compromise yourself. You will be true to your friends and to yourself. And your work might make a difference."
>
> He paused and stared into Leopold's eyes and heart.
>
> "To be somebody or to do something. In life, there is often a roll call. That's when you will have to make a decision. To be or to do? Which way will you go?"

Col. Henely was in the audience, and as I read that quote, he reportedly leaned over to another friend of ours and said, shaking his head in mock disbelief, "I don't believe she is reading this." Then he stopped, smiled, and said, "But of course she is."

Yes, of course, I was. He knew me too well. And we both knew how well that quote fit Chris and his career.

When I finished reading that quote, I looked up at Chris and said, "You have always been a doer and have done so much for our country. I am so proud of you. Congratulations!"

After the ceremony, Jim Longely said he was glad I enjoyed Boyd. Then he gave Chris a book entitled *Mr. Lincoln's T-Mails: How Abraham Lincoln Used the Telegraph to Win the Civil War*. Given how much I enjoyed the other book Jim had given us, I was determined to read this one sooner rather than later.

CHAPTER 31

Keynotes

As soon as I joined Google, I was asked to keynote at various events. Some were Google-hosted events held for partners and customers in locations around the country and the world. Others were special events led by a particular partner or customer where I was invited to be a guest speaker.

In November 2011, I was the keynote speaker at the National Guard Bureau (NGB) annual awards banquet. Chris had just accepted an assignment with the Air National Guard (ANG). He had always been in the regular Air Force, so this was a unique assignment for him and the ANG. He would still be on full-time active duty with federal orders like someone in the regular Air Force but in an ANG billet.

Regular Air Force had decided they would rotate Chris out of the area for his next assignment just as the Joint Collaboration Cells (JCCs) were taking off and showing value across the national security community. Some ANG officers had used the JCCs extensively while deployed; when they learned the man who created them was going to get shipped off to a new assignment, they thought that was a bad idea and would be a detriment to the warfighters. They had billets at NRO and approached Chris and said they would like him to stay and continue his work, and he could do so in one of their billets.

Chris would be transitioning to the ANG in December, so it was meaningful to speak at this NGB event just one month prior. When I remarked that my husband would be joining the ANG, there were cheers from the audience. They gave me a lantern fashioned after the one used by Paul

Revere, which is part of their symbolism. I brought it home as a gift to Chris, which meant a lot to him.

In April 2012, I spoke on a panel with the Department of the Navy CIO and other senior officers at the Sea, Air, Space conference held at National Harbor, Maryland. The audience appreciated what I said, and the event organizers asked me to speak the following year. They also invited me to stay for the formal dinner that evening. There, I met Captain Dale "Kid" Lumme, a retired naval aviator, and member of the leadership of the Navy League.

Dale was connected to the National Flight Academy (NFA). It was fascinating to learn how the NFA came to be. A bunch of military personnel from the Navy thought about how they could make Science, Technology, Engineering, and Math (STEM) more real for students and came up with a very creative idea. They took a building at Pensacola Naval Air Station and turned it into an aircraft carrier to create an immersive STEM environment. The *ship* was called AMBITION (CVT-11).

At the start of each training week, they would ring students on board using the ship's bell. Once inside the building, it was like they were on a ship. There were bunks, an ops planning room, a mission control room, million-dollar flight simulators "on deck" where they could learn how to do carrier takeoffs and landings, and a mess hall. They were using Google Earth for mission planning.

Dale said they would like to invite me and Sergy Brin, cofounder of Google, to be present for the commissioning and opening ceremonies in May 2012.

Sergey did not make it to the NFA commissioning in May, but I was glad I did. They had a reception the night before the big event and gave us a tour of the Naval Aviation Museum, which is very impressive.

During the social, I met some great people, including Neil Armstrong, the first man on the moon, and Eugene "Gene" Cernan, the last man on the moon. That was such a pleasant surprise, as I never imagined I would get the chance to meet them.

When that event was over, the director, a retired Navy vice admiral, asked if I would join them for a private dinner. When Dale and I entered the restaurant, the admiral invited us to sit at his table. His wife was seated to Neil Armstrong's left, and they placed me to Neil's right, and Dale was on my right.

I managed to send a quick text to Chris, "I'm seated at dinner next to Neil Armstrong!!!" He texted me back, "Get a picture!!!" So, I asked Dale to take our picture.

Michele with Neil Armstrong at dinner the evening before the National Flight Academy grand opening at Naval Air Station Pensacola (2012)

To start the conversation, the admiral's wife asked me, "Michele, what inspired your career path?"

I turned to Neil and said, "Never in my wildest dreams did I ever think I would be able to say this to you in person, but you did!"

He responded with a smile of pleasant surprise. I told him I was born in August 1969, a month after he walked on the moon. I'd wanted to go into space for as long as I could remember because he inspired me. I'm sure Neil never expected to hear this from the young woman he had just met that evening, but he took it gracefully in stride.

Neil was a gentleman with quiet humor. At one point in the evening, I said, "Neil, we look up at the moon and wonder what it must be like to be there. When you look at the moon, what do you think of?"

With a sheepish grin, he replied, "Girls." Later, when I saw the movie *First Man*, I had a much greater appreciation for what he likely meant when he said that, knowing about the tragic loss of his young daughter to a brain tumor.

Another thing we discussed that evening was trips to Mars. "You'd have to pack a lot of sandwiches," he quipped with his characteristic quiet humor and twinkle in his eyes.

When dinner was over and we prepared to leave, Neil turned to me and said, "Thank you for the honor of being my dinner companion."

Wow, I thought. Then I replied, "The honor is all mine, Neil."

The next day was the big event, the commissioning of the NFA. A huge crowd gathered, and as Neil walked out, everyone wanted to touch him. He handled it with grace. What struck me at that moment was that whoever decided Neil would be the first man to walk on the moon knew what they were doing. Neil was so gracious, so down to earth, without a hint of pride. Watching him, I thought, "That's my friend Neil. What an amazing man."

Sadly, we lost Neil a few months later, on 25 August 2012—the day before my birthday—due to surgery complications. He had just turned eighty-two earlier that month.

My family and I watched the memorial service video footage, and I read everything I could about the remarks his family shared. Neil Armstrong's family released a statement describing him:

> A reluctant American hero [who had] served his nation proudly, as a navy fighter pilot, test pilot, and astronaut… While we mourn the loss of a very good man, we also celebrate his remarkable life and hope that it serves as an example to young people around the world to work hard to make their dreams come true, to be willing to explore and push the limits, and to selflessly serve a cause greater than themselves. For those who may ask what they can do to honor Neil, we have a simple request. Honor his example of service, accomplishment, and modesty, and the next time you walk outside on a clear night and see the moon smiling down at you, think of Neil Armstrong and give him a wink.

Every time I think of Neil, I tell God how eternally grateful I am that he allowed me to meet Neil and get to know him. By the end of the dinner we shared, I felt we were friends, and I felt his loss that way too.

The Neil Armstrong memorial edition of *LIFE* magazine is displayed in our family room. To this day, I still wink at the moon in Neil's honor, and I will always cherish the photos we took together.

Outreach

During my four years with Google, I actively engaged in STEM outreach with schools and youth organizations and spoke at STEM events to inspire the next generation. One of the most memorable for me was when I presented at the 2015 X-STEM Symposium, part of the USA Science and Engineering Festival in Washington, DC. I shared with the students how I was inspired to pursue STEM and touched on the highlights of my career. After I sat down, Dean Kamen—inventor of the Segway and iBOT and founder of FIRST, which runs student robotics competitions—leaned over to me and said, "That was very inspiring."

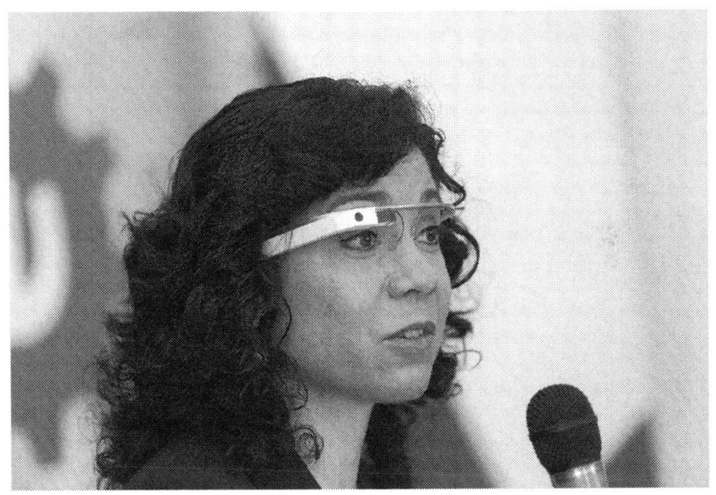

Michele speaking at the inaugural WashingtonExec K-12 STEM Symposium wearing Google Glass (2014)

In the local area, I supported the Fairfax County Public Schools (FCPS), with their Girls Excelling in Math and Science (GEMS) program. I hosted the GEMS students at our Google Reston office for presentations, interactive activities, and lunch in the cafe.

In addition, I worked closely with school administrators and teachers, helping them develop a new program called 21st Century Girls. We hosted a STEM event on a Saturday, and I led a track teaching the girls how to use Google Earth in a humanitarian assistance scenario. They were amazed by the tool and left the session with enthusiasm about what they had learned and a desire to explore the earth.

While with Google, I was able to sponsor some Advancement Via Individual Determination (AVID) students from FCPS to attend a week at the NFA. My purpose in asking that FCPS choose AVID students was to ensure young people who were in situations like I had been, i.e., they had the aptitude and desire but may not have the financial means, could participate. Using charitable funds set aside for the Google Reston office, we covered their roundtrip flights to Pensacola, Florida, and tuition for the NFA.

I saw the first group off at Washington National Airport. There were flight issues due to the weather. Eventually, the airline informed us the students would have to return early the next morning to catch a flight. One parent could not make the trip to the airport the following day, so we arranged for me to pick up her daughter at o-dark-thirty and bring her to the airport. I accompanied the group on their trip to ensure they made their connections and got checked in to the program, which they would be starting late.

Before flying home that day, NFA asked me to be the graduation speaker. So I returned at the end of the week to speak, toured the facilities with the students, and heard about their experiences. They shared more stories with me on the flights home.

Suffice it to say, the students who boarded the plane in Washington, DC, for NFA were not the same students who came home to their parents. They were changed—inspired by what they could accomplish—and it was gratifying to see. Some who were not that excited when they left were beyond excited to share their experiences. Others who had never thought about the military were considering careers in the military. All were thrilled to have seen the Navy's Blue Angels and were excited about STEM.

As for me, it was so rewarding to see these young lives transformed—their dreams bigger, their horizons broadened. The students were inspired to change their stars and fulfill their dreams!

Google Ambassador

NDU had an Organizational Culture Leadership class. As part of the course, the military and civilian students traveled around the greater Washington, DC, area and spent time talking with people in the private sector.

In May 2012, they came to Google, and I was the speaker. Following the session, the professor, COL Nate Allen, US Army, asked me to be the speaker for future events. It was a perfect fit as I had been in government and spoke their language and was also a Googler, so I could easily translate between Google-speak and government-speak.

Speaking of translating, I have an amusing story to share. I was at the Googleplex for other meetings when the head of security, Eric Grose, told me Sergy Brin would be meeting with the Deputy Secretary of Homeland Security (DHS) and asked if I would attend. They had booked a conference room with a large, rectangular table. I sat to Eric's right; the seat to Eric's left was reserved for Sergy. The other Googlers in attendance filled out the table on either side of us.

When the deputy secretary of DHS showed up with her entourage, they sat down along the other side of the table. Inside I was chuckling to myself about the contrast—the suits with lapel pins on one side of the table and the T-shirts, jeans/shorts on the other. Casual dress was the typical attire of Googlers, except for the few of us who dressed business casual as a norm when not in formal meetings.

But the icing on this cake was what happened next. Sergey rollerbladed into the room wearing tech gear and took his seat in the center of the Google side of the table. I thought that had to blow the minds of the visitors from DC—they had surely never seen anything like that before. They would be accustomed to people dressing up to meet with them. But this was the Googleplex, Sergey's territory, and he did not see the need to dress to impress. And I'm sure they had never seen anyone rollerblade into a meeting.

After about ninety minutes, Sergey decided we could carry on the rest of the meeting without him, and he got up and rollerbladed out. The discussion continued for some time after that. When we wrapped up, everyone shook hands, and the delegation from DC headed out.

We Googlers gathered together for a quick debrief. Then, the head legal counsel exclaimed, "Michele, you were amazing! You could translate what the government people said for the Googlers and what the Googlers said for the government, giving relevant examples to drive home the points. What an ambassador!"

Until then, I had not thought anything I had done was extraordinary. I did what came naturally to me. That's one way to know your job is a good fit.

Something Chris shared with me one day after work drove this home. A retired USAF colonel who worked for him approached him that day and said, "You know, I could never do what your wife does."

Chris asked, "What's that?"

He said, "She can see things that don't exist and create them. She can see how things could be and make them so. I can't do that, but once it's established, I can run it."

That was a seminal moment for me. Until then, I had not considered what I did as unique, special, or something others couldn't do. A creator-innovator by nature, I just did it. That insight gave me perspective. I realized I had a gift—something that was unique to me—that I could contribute to society for the greater good.

CHAPTER 32

Building Trust

The team I worked with most closely at Google was federal sales. Their customers included military services, joint commands, and national agencies. My role was strategic; it was about establishing relationships and building trust with potential government customers. My activities included speaking engagements and site visits.

Tom Wojszynski covered the USAF, NATO, AFRICOM, and EUCOM accounts at Google. He asked me to speak at the NATO Networked Enabled Capabilities Conference in Vienna, Austria, in March 2012. This event allowed me to share some innovative things we had done in the USA to support coalition efforts and opportunities to improve collaboration among NATO allies in the future with a multinational audience. I wondered again if I had missed a calling as a diplomat, as I have always enjoyed meeting new people and experiencing different cultures overseas; this was no exception.

From Austria, we traveled to Germany. There we met with personnel from EUCOM and then AFRICOM. We had the opportunity to meet with my friend and CAPSTONE classmate, GEN Carter Ham, the Commander of AFRICOM, a relatively new command established in 2008. They faced challenges because while there were a lot of civil wars and other issues in Africa, most of the resources and attention were going to CENTCOM's AOR.

While there, I spoke at the Women's Leadership Forum hosted by GEN Ham's wife, Christi. The participants included DoD personnel and spouses, and this event afforded insight into what these female military leaders and civilians were doing.

That evening, we enjoyed an informal dinner with Carter and Christi, accompanied by one of the AFRICOM deputies and his wife. It was great to catch up and hear more about what had transpired since Carter and I last saw each other.

Carter has a great sense of humor, and he is very humble. He made self-deprecating remarks about being lucky to get his fourth star and have this opportunity, but I knew his promotion to four-star general was well deserved. Carter is someone I hold in the highest regard, and I knew that America was fortunate to have a highly competent leader and person of integrity commanding AFRICOM.

Quentin Finney, who had previously been in the Marine Corps, covered the Navy and Marine Corps accounts. He wanted me to speak at a conference in South Carolina in October 2012.

He was an alum of the Citadel and asked if I would be willing to speak at the Citadel while we were there. It would be my first time at the Citadel, and I was looking forward to speaking with the cadets and seeing the campus.

First, I met with all the female engineering students at the Citadel. There were only a few, and it was nice to have an informal session where everyone had a seat at the table and felt comfortable asking any question that came to mind. We had a great discussion.

When that session wrapped up, the lone senior female engineering student walked me to the classroom, where I would speak to the senior class. On the way, she shared some personal struggles. She said that no one in her family understood her desire to be an engineer or become a military officer. In her family's culture, they did not see the value of a woman doing that. They told her she needed to get married before she was too old.

I understood what she was saying and shared that there was no one with a technical background in my family and that I was a first-generation college student. However, I never felt the pressure from my family that she did to get married so young.

The cadet was surprised when I told her that if she asked my young daughter what age she had to be to get married, she would say thirty. Based on our personal experiences, my husband and I believed that sometime around thirty was a good age to get married. By then, you are wiser about the ways of the world, settled in your career, and have a better idea of who you are, your priorities, where you want to go, and what you want to do in life. Then when you find someone you can't live without who shares your values and wants to share life with you—that's when it's the right time to get married.

We reached the large classroom where the seniors were seated, and she took her seat. The host, a professor with the rank of major, made an introduction. I then shared my life and leadership insights with the senior class.

During my remarks, I said I had recently read two good books and proceeded to share about the first one. Then I continued with my points on leadership.

During the question-and-answer period, the professor raised his hand. He said, "Michele, you mentioned that you had recently read two good books. While you gave us the title of one, you didn't give us the title of the other. What was that book?"

I replied, "Oh, that book was *Mr. Lincoln's T-Mails: How Abraham Lincoln Used the Telegraph to Win the Civil War*." Then I went on to the next question.

After the session ended and it was just the two of us waiting for the professor hosting us to wrap things up, good-natured Quentin looked at me with a big grin and started chuckling. I asked him what was so funny.

He put his hand on my shoulder and said, "My dear California-born friend. You are in the South. Here, Abraham Lincoln is not a hero." Then he added in a slow southern drawl, "The Civil War is known as 'The War of Northern Aggression.'"

"Oh," I replied, "but that was over 150 years ago."

"Yes," he said, "but they have not forgotten." It shows that old grudges die hard, especially when passed down from generation to generation.

The professor was generous with his time and gave us a tour of the Citadel campus. In building after building, there were plaques and memorials the professor described to us regarding "The War of Northern Aggression."

Quentin was not kidding. They were serious about this. The South still held a grudge against the North. More importantly, they held a grudge against Abraham Lincoln, who I had always considered a hero for ending slavery and keeping the United States together. This was an eye-opening experience for me regarding the culture of the South.

Later that evening, Chris and I had a chance to talk via phone. When I started to tell him about the professor asking me for the title of the second book and my response that it was *Mr. Lincoln's T-Mails*, he cut me off and said, "Oh no, you did not!"

Then he started to laugh, and he laughed hard because it was very humorous to him. Chris grew up in Texas and was well aware of the perspective of the South, and he would never have made the faux pas that his well-intentioned but naive California-born wife had just done—at the Citadel, no less. He had to call his parents. This story was just too good.

According to Chris, his call with his parents was similar to our call. When he got to the point where he told them the name of the book I shared, they both interjected, "Oh no, she did not!" Then they all had a good laugh at my expense. Today, I cannot remember the name of the first book I recommended to the class—it was likely the Boyd book—but there is no way I could ever forget the second one!

Scott Frohman covered the big intel agency accounts at Google. He had never spent a day in the government but was passionate about helping them. We frequently traveled to meet with his customers. We both enjoyed red wine, so we always got a bottle to share over dinner, even if it was just the two of us. While we had fun trying wines from different regions, we tended to both really like cabernet sauvignon.

Sales reps have a different compensation package than everyone else. They make less base pay; however, once they hit their quota, they can start making significant amounts of money with multipliers. Scott had been working on a deal for a couple of years, and I had assisted him a lot in building relationships with the government and understanding how Google could best help them. He landed the deal right before Christmas; it had taken a long time but was worth a lot of money. Scott blew way past his quota and got big multipliers as a result. His wife later told the story of him toasting to his great success and then driving around on his riding lawn mower whooping it up.

The next time we saw each other in the office, I congratulated Scott and asked him, "How good was the multiplier?" He indicated it was very good—like cash for two sports cars in the driveway. Though that was just an analogy, I got the picture. He told me he had something for me but wanted to bring it to my car after work because it was heavy. He had my curiosity up.

When we wrapped up the workday, Scott met me at my car with a case of cabernet sauvignon. No sales rep had ever done something for me like that, and his thoughtfulness in showing appreciation for my contribution to his success in making the deal meant a lot to me.

Medallion Award

SPU contacted me in the fall of 2013 and surprised me with the news that I was selected to receive the alumni Medallion Award. They would host an awards ceremony and luncheon at SPU in honor of the other award winners and me in February 2014.

When I told Chris, he was excited. I reached out to my mom and invited her to join us. We had family in the greater Seattle area and would have the opportunity to see them while we were there. I booked our airline tickets and a rental car and reserved a two-bedroom residence-style hotel room so we could all stay together. Then I got to work on my remarks.

In February 2014, we flew out to Seattle. While in town, we visited my grandma Ruth in the home-based care facility near my uncle Bob's house. My mother had not seen her in a long while, and I'm sure it was a shock to see how frail her mother was. Though my grandmother would smile at us, we could not be sure she knew who we were because she had dementia and did not acknowledge us by name.

My grandmother completely depended on others, just like a newborn baby. It was sad to see her in that state, but it was good to see that the staff was kind and gentle with her, and she was gracious and appreciated them. I was so grateful we had that time together with my grandmother, for she passed away peacefully in her sleep later that month.

While February is not the ideal time to be in Seattle, it was fun to be back at my alma mater and wonderful to see dear friends—professors, classmates, and recent graduates I had mentored. My sophomore-year roommate, Melani (Shoemaker) Plett, had earned her PhD and was now a professor. She had invited me to speak with the engineering students whenever I was in town.

Erica Christiansen was one of the recent graduates whose life I had the privilege to touch. Chris and I helped her get an internship in the IC. She was there with her brother, sister, and parents. They celebrated with me and paid tribute to my positive impact on Erica's life.

Her mother wrote me the sweetest letter that brought tears to my eyes. Their kind words meant so much to me—they were edifying to my soul. Erica later told me that her mom lives by the verse: "Do not withhold good from those to whom it is due, when it is in your power to act" (Proverbs 3:27, NIV). That is an excellent motto for life.

After receiving the award, I gave my remarks. I thanked Professor Peter and honored Professor Crichton, who had passed away. Then I spoke about how much the support of my family—grandparents, mother, aunts, uncles, cousins, husband, and daughter—had meant to me.

I also highlighted my motto in life is "pursue your passion, live your purpose, engage the culture, change the world," and SPU's official slogan was now "engage the culture, change the world."

The previous weekend I had done the Scripture reading in church—it was the Golden Rule, "Do to others as you would have them do to you" (Matthew 7:12, NIV). During his sermon, the pastor said that while other religions had similar statements, there is a crucial difference between Christianity and all the other religions. As this verse states, Christianity talks about doing. Other religions talk about what you shouldn't do, i.e., don't hurt someone, but they don't talk about doing things for others.

So many people go through life without a purpose, just being, not doing. Our Christian faith calls us to be doers, to reach out to others, to engage our culture, and to change the world. We do it for the personal satisfaction of knowing we are living out that calling, not with any expectation that we will reap a reward here on earth. As Matthew 25:40 (NIV) says, "Truly I tell you, whatever you did for one of the least of these brothers and sisters of mine, you did for me."

Then I summarized the highlights of my life and career since graduating from SPU. So many times, I realized I had been placed in a specific position at that particular time for a special purpose.

When Esther's people, the Jews, were threatened with extinction and she had a chance to save them given her relationship with the king, her uncle Mordecai said, "And who knows but that you have come to your royal position for a time such as this?" (Esther 4:14, NIV).

My closing remarks were: "It's been an amazing ride—more like a roller coaster than cruising along the beach with the top down—but I wouldn't change it, for those experiences have shaped me and made me who I am today. I believe that I have been where I was meant to be at any given time so God could use me—just like he used Joseph and Esther—when my countrymen and others needed help. No, engaging the culture and changing the world is not the easy path—it is the path less followed—but, to paraphrase Robert Frost, taking the road less traveled has made all the difference."

I closed with a favorite quote:

> *Never doubt that a small group of committed citizens can change the world. In fact, it is the only thing that ever has.*
> ~Margaret Mead

Following the Medallion Award ceremony, SPU interviewed me for the spring edition of their *Response* magazine. The headline read "Innovation Evangelist: Alumna Leads High-Tech Government Partnerships." A quote they pulled from that interview is as follows:

> I'm a purpose-driven person. What's most important for me is knowing I'm in the right place at the right time to make the most difference. I believe that's how you find and track God's purpose for your life. My faith gives me the strength to have the courage of my convictions and to speak truth to power, even at personal cost, because I feel that is why God put me on this earth, gave me the talents I have, and put me in the places in which I've served.
>
> Service to others is the pathway to a life of significance.

Service to others is the pathway to a life of significance.

Speakers Bureau

Google has a speaker's bureau. One of my roles was representing Google as a keynote speaker and panelist at events worldwide. In my time at Google, I had over one hundred speaking engagements, which allowed me to meet many people from different backgrounds, encourage and inspire, and expand my network of like-minded, make-it-happen people. I'll highlight a few of these experiences.

One such opportunity was in June 2013 at the first-ever NERVE Disruptive Technology Conference held in Cambridge, England. There was a fantastic lineup of speakers.

The day I spoke, I was the second speaker in the lineup. The man before me talked about the NASA WARP drive (á la *Star Trek*), and the man who followed me spoke about a hovercraft he was building and testing in the California desert (á la *Star Wars*). We loved each other's presentations—it was like a mutual admiration society. We had a great time hanging out together and talking during the rest of the event.

Michele speaking at the NERVE Disruptive Technology Conference in Cambridge, England (2013)

In September 2013, I spoke at Startup Phenomenon Women in Boulder, Colorado. They had a packed lineup of speakers, and I only had ten minutes to talk, so I shared highlights of insights from my career, including innovation best practices.

The editor of *Entrepreneur* magazine was in the audience and was impressed. Later, *Entrepreneur* interviewed me, and I was featured as "One of the 7 Most Powerful Women to Watch" in their January 2014 issue.

In March 2014, I had a speaking engagement at the US Consulate in Juarez, Mexico. I would fly into El Paso, Texas, the day before and be picked up early the next morning for the trip to Juarez.

Having lived in Las Cruces, New Mexico, for his first IC assignment, Chris knew how dangerous Juarez was. He did not want me to go there unless he accompanied me "packing heat," which meant carrying a gun. The organizers later informed me I would be picked up in an armored vehicle in El Paso and driven to the consulate in Juarez by people packing heat, which gave us peace of mind.

The consulate was having a Women's Day event, and I was one of four guest speakers. The commanding general of White Sands Missile Range, a woman, was also a speaker. Her young female executive officer accompanied her.

The entire event was just a few hours long, so we all had less than thirty minutes to speak and take questions. I summarized key insights from my life and career and concluded with my philosophy on life.

During the Q&A session, the general's exec raised her hand. When I called on her, she said, "You're different. What makes you different?" I knew what she was getting at without her coming out and saying it, and I had a split-second decision.

Recognizing that we had an international audience, I prefaced my response with this. "I recognize this room is full of people from diverse backgrounds and beliefs. I am a Christian, and my faith informs and guides everything I do." The general's exec got a big grin on her face. I proceeded to say, "I believe every one of us is uniquely and wonderfully made by our creator God and put on this earth for a purpose with the talents and interests to fulfill that purpose. It may not be easy, but we can do it with God's help."

Every one of us is uniquely and wonderfully made by our creator God and put on this earth for a purpose with the talents and interests to fulfill that purpose.

When I finished my response, the general's exec had an even bigger smile on her face and started the applause. I had taken a calculated risk, though it was minimal in the scheme of things, especially compared with risks people must take in combat zones. I had to be true to myself and fully honest in responding to her question. She was asking what made me different, and I told her. Frankly, she was not the first nor the last person to make the observation or ask me such a question.

My very first officemate made that observation and asked the associated question. He admired how I conducted myself and recognized it was not the norm. While I will be the first to admit that I am flawed—we all are—I make a sincere effort every day to live my faith, have the courage of my convictions, and fulfill whatever purpose God has for me at that place and time.

Despite what anyone will tell you, how we live each day is a testimony to everyone who observes us—family, friends, coworkers, associates, and passersby. May it be a good one, and may we never shrink from sharing hope and light with others in this world.

In mid-to-late August of 2014, I keynoted at Innovation for the Nation events hosted by the Google teams in Australia and New Zealand. This was my fourth trip to Australia and my second to New Zealand.

Coincidentally, my previous three trips Down Under were in March 2003, 2004, and 2005. While March is the time of the transition from winter to spring in the northern hemisphere, it is the transition from summer to autumn in the Southern Hemisphere, and the weather was always relatively warm where I was visiting.

Unfortunately, I packed with my past weather experience in mind and didn't note that August was when their weather was transitioning from winter to spring and could be rather cold and wet. It rained most of the time I was in Australia, and it was sleeting sideways in New Zealand. I seemed to be perpetually shivering! I was not dressed for the weather in my light jacket, dress, and strappy sandals.

One evening in Sydney, when it wasn't raining, I walked from Circular Quay to Darling Harbor and bought some boots—my first pair of UGGs. My freezing wet feet thanked me. Then I made a mental note to myself—next time, pay more careful attention to the weather Down Under when you pack.

There was a special moment for me in New Zealand. My reputation preceded me from my US IC DCIO days. They were happy to see me because they knew I was the one who ensured that the imagery-sharing problem with New Zealand finally got fixed. They now benefited from access to US satellite imagery, and NGA and NSA could more easily collaborate because the sharing was five-eyes across both agencies, as it should be!

In early March 2015, I traveled to Vienna, Austria, to speak at the Front End of Innovation conference. The person who preceded me was Chris Chapman of Disney Imagineering. I liked everything he had to say. When I finished my presentation, we had a chance to talk. It was another case of the mutual admiration society—he liked everything I had to say too. We realized that, in reality, we had both effectively said the same things but in our own ways with a Disney and Google twist, respectively. Chris and I became fast friends and would have opportunities to collaborate again.

The following week I traveled to Austin, Texas, to speak at dProgram, produced by Emergent Order as part of South by Southwest. I spoke about creating a culture of innovation based on my career experience and personal insights.

One of the other speakers in the dProgram lineup was John Mackey, cofounder and co-CEO of Whole Foods. Based on what he shared in his presentation and our conversation afterward, I realized we were like-minded and both vegetarians.

Michele with John Mackey, author of Conscious Capitalism *and cofounder and co-CEO of Whole Foods Market, following their talks at dProgram SXSW (2015)* | *Michele with US Senator Rand Paul, MD., at his office in Washington, DC (2015)*

We both agreed that purpose-driven, values-based capitalism is the most powerful system for uplifting humankind to higher levels of peace, prosperity, and happiness. John signed a copy of his book, *Conscious Capitalism,* for me and wrote, "To Michele, Stay conscious and liberate your heroic spirit. John."

Dr. Rand Paul, US Senator from Kentucky, asked to meet with me later that month. I appreciated Senator Paul's common-sense approach and willingness to speak the truth and hold people accountable. He was the type of person you wanted in public office.

We discussed various topics, including opportunities for innovation in the government. During our meeting, Senator Paul asked me to serve on his tech council, and I agreed. He announced his tech council members, including Patrick Byrne, CEO of Overstock.com, via Twitter on 9 May 2015.

In June 2015, I headed to Denver, Colorado, to be the opening keynote speaker for the first-ever GlobalMindEd Conference. Many notable people were there, and I was honored to kick off the event.

It was exciting to be a part of this gathering, which focused on enhancing the educational experience for students. It was particularly gratifying to have the opportunity to inspire first-generation college students, and twenty such students had received an all-expenses-paid sponsorship to attend.

While I had been booked for the event a year in advance, two weeks before the event on a call with the coordinator, Carol Carter, I learned one of their primary objectives was outreach to first-gen college students. I remarked, "I'm a first-gen college student."

She said, "What? You must tell your story!"

I replied that I had never told that part of my story before. It was very personal, and I'd have to think about how to go about weaving that in, especially given the rest of my presentation was already complete. I discussed this request with Chris that evening, and he helped me formulate a few slides to insert at the beginning of my presentation to set the stage.

After my keynote, many people wanted to talk with me. They included leaders in education like the head of George Lucas's (of *Star Wars* fame) Educational Foundation.

There were also first-gen college students. Some were in tears, and others hugged me, but all of them said they could identify with my opening remarks regarding a disadvantaged start and the statistics that go with it. Then when they realized that the person I was talking about was me, they were in shock. Then they thought, "If she can do this, so can I!"

Throughout my time at that two-day conference, every one of the sponsored first-gen college students approached me and told me what an amazingly positive impact my message had on them. They saw how I overcame obstacles, and it encouraged them that they could too. As someone whose best days are the ones where I know I've made a positive difference in someone's life, that was a personal highlight for me.

During the conference, Clifton Taulbert, a successful man from humble beginnings like me who heard my keynote, came up to me and said, "You must write a book, Michele. You owe it to everyone who cannot travel to hear you speak in person. They need to hear your story and be inspired as we were."

While people over the years had told me I needed to write a book, the feedback I received from people who heard my keynote at this conference was tremendous. This feedback ultimately drove me to commit to writing this memoir to inspire the next generation.

Upon returning home, I shared this with Chris. We agreed that a good time to start writing was early in the new year following my transition to self-employment and his retirement from the military.

When I joined Google, I wondered what would motivate people to leave, given the innovative work environment and good benefits. The common theme was the opportunity to start their own business. With Chris's retirement imminent, now was my chance.

CHAPTER 33

Transition

After I returned home from Colorado, I tendered my resignation from Google. My last official day with Google was 1 July 2015.Following a Weslander family reunion in Santa Barbara at the end of June, Chris and I traveled to Grand Tetons National Park for a special invitation-only event hosted over the Independence Day weekend at the lodge. It was the first such event we had attended, and we did not know what to expect, but to Chris's adage that "networking *is* working," we figured it would be an opportunity to meet new people and build our network.

The hosts advertised the event as follows: "Transforming ideas and relationships. An incredible mix of preeminent leaders, passionate change-makers, and rising stars of all ages. More than a conference: invitation-only, off-the-record. Nonpartisan: All participants heard, all opinions welcome." That sounded good to us.

Upon our arrival, we learned that the speakers for all sessions, whether plenary or breakout sessions, were the attendees, which meant we all had a part to play in the event. We received our speaking assignments and started thinking about what we would share based on the topics.

One speaking assignment I received was for a lunchtime plenary session. The instructions were, "What advice would you give the president of the United States? Keep your remarks nonpartisan." I had less than five minutes to speak. There were many things I would like to discuss with the president at the time, Barack Obama, but I had to get to the crux of the matter given such a short time constraint.

Chris and I brainstormed. He had a lot of ideas regarding what he would say. In the context of keeping it apolitical, we both agreed that all the issues we saw essentially boiled down to the definition of the role of the government—specifically, the role of the president as defined in the Declaration of Independence and US Constitution.

I worked to tailor my remarks accordingly. Below I have included the full text of the remarks I gave—copied and pasted from the document I created on 5 July 2015—unrevised, for your review and contemplation.

There is not time to talk in detail, so I want to take us back to the principles upon which this great nation was founded, for if we look at our current situation in that context, we will see where we have gone off track, and if we make decisions and take actions with these core tenets in mind, we can get back on track.

239 years ago, on the 4th of July 1776, our founding fathers wrote the Declaration of Independence which states, We hold these truths to be self-evident, that all men are created equal, that they are endowed by their Creator with certain unalienable Rights, that among these are Life, Liberty and the pursuit of Happiness.– That to secure these rights, Governments are instituted among Men, deriving their just powers from the consent of the governed,

Key Points

- We are created equal. This equality was not given to us by the government.
- We are imbued by our Creator with inalienable rights (just because we breathe). These were granted by God, not the government.
- #1: **Life**: the right to live; recognizing that all life is precious, we must defend the lives of those who cannot defend themselves.
- #2: **Liberty**: the right to be free.
- #3: **The Pursuit of Happiness**: this is the right to the fruit of your own labors; you are entitled to keep what you earn.
- The whole purpose of government is to *secure* the inalienable rights and to ensure that no one and nothing infringes on your rights.

- Big Government does not equal Big Freedom.
- The **US Constitution** gives us Big Freedom.

US Constitution (17 September 1787)

Preamble: states that the Federal Government was created in order to form a more perfect Union, establish Justice, insure domestic Tranquility, provide for the common defence, promote the general Welfare, and secure the Blessings of Liberty to ourselves and our Posterity.

Article II Section 1: States that the elected President, before entering the Office, shall take an Oath to faithfully execute the Office of President of the United States, and preserve, protect and defend the Constitution of the United States.

The US Constitution clearly states the president is to uphold all the Constitution, not selective parts of it.

The role of the president is to be a servant leader and, along with the rest of the government, to empower the people to govern themselves, to be free to "pursue happiness," and enable current and future generations to realize the American dream.

The federal government today has grown well beyond the role defined by the US Constitution, encroaching on individual rights.

To quote The Great Communicator, *"Our Government has no power except that granted it by the people. It is time to check and reverse the growth of government, which shows signs of having grown beyond the consent of the governed. Government is not the solution to our problem; government is the problem... From time to time we've been tempted to believe that society has become too complex to be managed by self-rule, that government by an elite group is superior to government for, by, and of the people. But if no one among us is capable of governing himself, then who among us has the capacity to govern someone else?"*

We are a proud and resourceful people. We long to be independent. When a free people are made dependent, it crushes the human spirit.

Defending the welfare of America includes economics, because economics matter. When you are a powerhouse economically, you have security and influence.

Responsible individuals and families understand that they must live within a budget, spending less than they earn or end up in debt, dependent and beholden to others.

The US government's spending on things well beyond the original scope outlined in the founding documents has resulted in a national debt approaching $18.3 trillion, which translates to over $154,000 per taxpayer, or nearly $57,000 per citizen.

In the past six years, through excessive government spending, we have doubled the debt that our nation had accumulated in the previous 200 years.

In our history, every US generation has worked to make life better for the next generation…until now.

This generation is spending the next generation's future, leading to the high probability that future generations will be worse off than the current generation for the first time in US history.

This is a moral issue.

As stated in the Declaration of Independence, it is the nature of the human spirit to be independent and free. People want a hand up, not a hand out.

We must preserve America as a land of opportunity—not entitlements—for all.

America is the land of the free because we are the home of the brave. Many have made the ultimate sacrifice for the cause of freedom.

To quote the Gettysburg address: *"We resolve that these dead shall not have died in vain—that this nation, under God, shall have a new birth of freedom—and that government of the people, by the people, for the people, shall not perish from the earth."*

As has been said by a famous Brit, *despite its faults, America is still the last, best hope of mankind, because it spells out so vividly the kind of happiness that most people actually want, regardless of what they are told they ought to want.*

In conclusion, I believe it is a great privilege to serve as the president of the United States, and the person who holds that office must do so with honor, integrity, and humility, with respect for the great responsibility to keep America one nation, under God, indivisible, with liberty and justice for all.

Let these core tenets and founding principles guide your actions and decisions.

The Declaration of Independence and the US Constitution are thoughtfully crafted documents that contain the moral tenets upon which our nation was founded and the framework to uphold those tenants, which are timeless. These documents were written by God-fearing men who understood humans had inalienable rights because they were made in the image of God. They also understood the sinful nature of man. While they had different points of view, they debated them long and hard and worked to arrive at a framework they believed was best for the nation and would uphold those moral tenets for all time. To safeguard those documents is patriotic, not political.

However, almost everyone at the head table, which included the event founders and organizers, was looking daggers at me, so I gathered that not everyone saw it that way. Of the dozen people selected to give remarks during that plenary session, many made comments that were not remotely nonpartisan; of those that were partisan, they were very left-leaning politically.

Shortly after our arrival and participation in the opening session, we learned that the founders of this event were very left-leaning progressives, as were the majority of the participants. However, they invited a few people from the right side of the aisle so that they could call the event nonpartisan.

Later I would learn that progressivism is essentially American Marxism. Progressives do not believe in America's founding principles, and they do not support America's founding documents.

Chris and I were constitutionalists. We believed in America's founding principles and cherished America's founding documents, which were based on Judeo-Christian values and divinely inspired. It became clear there were very few people like us in attendance.

After that plenary session was over, I returned to my table. Chris was smiling and congratulatory—he was very proud of his wife. A couple seated at the table with us leaned over and quietly said they appreciated my remarks but could sense they were in the minority. I told them I gathered as much observing the looks on people's faces, especially the glares from the head table as I gave my remarks.

For the rest of the day and the weekend, people quietly, almost sheepishly, came up to me and told me they appreciated my remarks, though they realized they were not popular with most attendees. It's interesting how all of us who were not left-leaning picked up on that vibe.

There was a plenary session after dinner that night. One of the founders moderated the panel, which included a Tenth Circuit judge from Colorado. This judge was rarely given the mic compared to the other speakers. However, when he spoke, everything he said was on target. He knew America's founding documents well and diligently worked to uphold the US Constitution.

At the end of the session, Chris and I made our way across the room to where the judge and his wife were standing. There was a line of people wanting to talk with them, and we took our places at the end of the line.

When it was our turn to greet him, the judge looked at me and then over to Chris and said in a jovial tone, "I have a huge crush on your wife."

That caught us both by surprise, and we laughed out loud. The judge and his wife joined us in laughter. He said he really liked my remarks at the luncheon session, and they were on target. I told him I appreciated his comments at the dinner session, which were on target. It was a mutual admiration society once more. That judge was Neil Gorsuch.

He introduced us to his wife and then took us to meet his two daughters. He said he wanted them to have a chance to talk with me. We had the great pleasure of spending the rest of the evening hanging out and developing a friendship with Neil, his wife, and his two daughters.

Neil told me I needed to run for political office. "We need more people like you!" he said. Others had told me that over the years after hearing me speak, but I had not yet felt the calling.

Throughout our careers, Chris and I focused on supporting national security missions. We had now embarked on a new mission to establish a nonprofit called Global Nexus Alliance, taking our expertise and applying it to the humanitarian sector.

Before the conclusion of the evening, Neil wrote his contact information in my event book.

Less than two years later, President Donald Trump nominated Neil Gorsuch to succeed Justice Antonin Scalia on the United States Supreme Court. Neil was confirmed by the US Senate on 7 April 2017; he took the oath of office on 10 April 2017. I was elated, for I knew firsthand what an amazing man he was—a gifted lawyer who was unwaveringly committed to upholding the US Constitution. Neil was good to reply to my congratulatory email: "Thanks so much for the kind message."

After Chris and I returned home, I focused my time and effort on my new endeavors—Sunesis Nexus (for profit, which I founded) and Global Nexus Alliance (nonprofit, which I cofounded with Chris). While I already had some consulting work set up via Sunesis Nexus before I resigned from Google, I had not had the time to do much work on Global Nexus Alliance. So, I turned my attention to establishing our nonprofit and working with legal advisors to apply for 501(c)(3) status. Chris worked with me to refine the mission and vision.

We were excited to be invited to the anniversary celebration of our dear friends Kathleen Reilly and Parry Baer at Chatham Bars Inn in Cape Cod, Massachusetts, on 12 September 2015.

The drive from our home in Virginia on 11 September took us by New York City on the fourteenth anniversary of the terrorist attacks. As we observed the New York City skyline from the road, we had the first opportunity to talk about what happened with Sophia, who would be seven on 14 September; it was naturally an emotional discussion for us. Sophia knew her parents had served their country and worked to keep terrorists from our homeland, and she recognized that day impacted our lives and careers.

Our route from Virginia to Massachusetts took us through Maryland, Delaware, New Jersey, New York, Connecticut, and Rhode Island. I remarked to Sophia that there are only three coastal states out West, but here we would be driving through eight states in one day.

It was nightfall by the time we reached Chatham Bars Inn. We found our room elegantly appointed, with cozy bathrobes, slippers, and a fireplace. Chris and I remarked that we were living like the Howells—the wealthy couple on the show *Gilligan's Island.* I jokingly called him Thurston Howell III, and he called me Lovey. It was fun to be at one of the iconic East Coast resorts.

Kathleen and Parry threw an elegant party, complete with dancing. They had a lovely buffet and a special cake Kathleen had designed based on a conversation with Sophia at our house when she came to share pictures from her Mount Everest base camp trip with us. We marveled at how our creative daughter imagined such a cake—with multiple sections, patterns, and designs—and how amazing it was that Kathleen remembered it and a chef created it. Kathleen was so sweet to acknowledge Sophia's upcoming birthday when everyone toasted to celebrate their anniversary.

We planned a trip to New York City for Sophia's birthday. Upon our arrival on the evening of 13 September, we quickly changed into nice clothes at our hotel and then headed to see *The Lion King* on Broadway. Sophia loved the theater and was a gifted actress; this would be her first Broadway show. She was thrilled and thoroughly enjoyed it.

Chris, Sophia, and Michele celebrating Sophia's birthday at Disney's The Lion King *on Broadway, New York City (2015)*

The following day, we took Sophia to a birthday brunch at Sarabeth's and then treated her to a horse-drawn carriage ride through Central Park. Afterward, we drove to Battery Park at the southern tip of Manhattan to catch the ferry to Ellis Island and the Statue of Liberty. We took the tours and read about people who had come to America through this port seeking liberty and a chance to change their stars.

On the base of the Statue of Liberty is a tablet inscribed with words penned by Emma Lazarus in 1883: "Give me your tired, your poor, Your huddled masses yearning to breathe free, The wretched refuse of your teeming shore. Send these, the homeless, tempest-tossed to me, I lift my lamp beside the golden door!"

America has always accepted as self-evident the truth that all human beings are created equal and that their rights come from God and are, therefore, inalienable. Unlike other countries, America has always welcomed anyone who longed to live in freedom, and pledge allegiance to the new republic and the principles for which it stands, to become an American citizen and a full-fledged member of our society. This is part of what makes America exceptional.

In November 2015, I was invited to be one of the keynote speakers at the Schools of the Future conference in Oahu, Hawaii, hosted by the Hawaii Association of Independent Schools. This was a paid speaking event; they were flying me out in business class. I used part of my fee to fly Chris and Sophia out with me.

Sophia was the only kid in the front of the airplane. The pilot invited her into the cockpit; he had her sit in his seat and make the welcome announcement for the flight. I told her that was a big deal, especially post 9-11-2001, and I took a photo of her.

Sophia was invited by the pilot to sit in his seat and give the announcement prior to takeoff on their flight to Hawaii (2015) |
Chris, Michele, and Sophia at Disney's Aulani resort in Hawaii (2015)

We flew out a few days before the conference and arrived on 30 October 2015. We stayed at Disney's Aulani Resort using our DVC points, and Sophia dressed up and did trick-or-treat at the resort the next day. We had a great time there, enjoying the nice room, fun waterslides, private beach, kids' club, and character meet and greet.

The conference was held in a huge event center in Honolulu. My keynote on innovation and education received great feedback from the attendees.

I was asked to speak to a group of Omidyar Fellows while I was there. So, I tailored my presentation to that group focused on leadership.

Keynotes were one of the services I offered through my company, Sunesis Nexus, and these were my first two paid speaking events since leaving Google. It was fulfilling to impact people's lives positively in this way.

Following the conference, we spent some time in Maui. It was good to take a break from life in the fast lane in Washington, DC, and spend some time relaxing, exploring, and enjoying each other's company. You must disconnect every once in a while for your health!

We felt blessed to take this trip because Chris had surprisingly suffered a severe medical event on 23 October 2015, leaving him unconscious and struggling to speak. He was transported via ambulance to the emergency room and ended up in the hospital. Chris was discharged a few days later after the doctors said he had made a miraculous recovery.

At the time, I had thought there was no way we could make this trip, just a week away. We were thrilled to be able to go and take some time off together on the islands of Oahu and Maui in the beautiful state of Hawaii.

CHAPTER 34

New Beginnings

As 2015 was coming to a close, Chris became more preoccupied with his upcoming retirement from the military after over twenty-two years of honorable service. That is a significant life event. Retirement required a lot of out-processing, including appointments and paperwork.

Chris had a stellar reputation and a well-established network in the national security community. Many people from the private sector were already trying to recruit him; as soon as he officially retired, they wanted to interview him for positions in their companies.

We had a few "dining for our country" events before he retired, so he had a few more occasions to wear his mess dress. Sophia had become accustomed to her parents dressing up for formal events by this time. Before we departed for an event in mid-November, she wanted to take our picture on the deck overlooking our backyard.

In December, we held a retirement ceremony for Chris in the walk-out basement of our house. Col. Regis Baldauff, USAF retired, was the master of ceremonies.

We cleared an area and set up fifty folding chairs facing the TV in our entertainment room. An American flag hung on a pole to one side. On the other side, the Jolly Roger hung on a pole in tribute to The Rebel Outpost, where Chris and Regis first worked together. The NRO's fortieth-anniversary poster titled "Freedom's Sentinel in Space" was framed and leaning against the wall below the TV.

Michele and Maj. Chris Quaid, USAF, at their first formal event as a married couple (2007) | Michele and Lt. Col. Chris Quaid, USAF, heading to their last formal event prior to his military retirement (2015)

After a career of being a "PowerPoint warrior extraordinaire," Chris had a retirement slideshow he wanted to give as part of his remarks. We used the TV as a display, and I set up a camera on a tripod to record the event.

As he started his remarks, Chris called out our good friend, MGen Mike Ennis, USMC retired, and said, "Just to let you know, for the people who weren't brought up in the Air Force—General Ennis, you don't know what this is about—but in the Air Force there is one thing we know how to do, it's PowerPoint." Then he added, "Oh, by the way, we are using Google, not PowerPoint, so this is on the cloud somewhere."

Then Chris called out people who had meant a lot to him in his career, including Regis and his wife, Lynda, who traveled from Colorado to be there. He said, "People who work with me every day know one of the themes throughout my career is that I surround myself with people better than myself. That's how I do it. That's how the magic happens." This was so characteristic of Chris—always looking to give credit where it was due. It was not about him; it was about the great team. Then he gave thanks all around.

Lt. Col. Chris Quaid, USAF, speaking at his retirement ceremony [left] and standing at attention with Col. Regis Baldauff, USAF (retired), who officiated [right] (2015)

Chris read the next slide, "Why are we wearing these uniforms?" We all noted that he and Regis were in flight suits, which is not the usual attire for a retirement. He then said, "There are a couple of reasons why. First, the serious one, and then the one which I still think is really cool."

He continued, "People are downrange right now every day. They are accepting extensions of service. They are taking the oath again. They are not taking it in their Class A Uniform. They are taking it in their combat uniforms. Sometimes they may get some kind of stipend, but a lot of times they're not. They are not doing it for the money, and they are not bartering with their bosses for what else they could have to stay in service. They are doing it for the love of their country."

Having been downrange himself, Chris added, "When we get back here to headquarters, it is alienating when you are observing that people seem to think they have all the time in the world to make a decision. In the back of your mind, you're freaking out because you realize that every minute we're waiting to do something is another opportunity for one of your guys downrange to take a bullet. That's what it's really all about. The advantage I have is that I'm a very simple person. I'm a space operator. You see a problem, you fix the problem. It's the same thing with folks downrange in the war. See a person getting shot at; do something to help them quit getting shot at. That's how our team operates. That's been our MO since I met you [Col. Baldauff] in 1998."

He added, "So we are wearing these [combat] uniforms because coming back to headquarters I loathed the idea of wearing Class A uniforms. I also thought it was civilian organizations trying to control what I wear, and that made me mad. So, in that sense, I want to wear the uniform that best represents the man in the fight, even if we're not physically in the fight, because sometimes you feel like at headquarters it's more of a fight than being downrange."

Then Chris got a twinkle in his eye and said, "The other reason is a little more interesting. Michele has been an avid supporter. She is the patron saint of all NRO space operators." He looked at the former DNRO, Jeff Harris, who was in the audience, and said, "Sir, you may not know that, but she is."

Then he returned to his story. "When she was in government and sitting on blue-ribbon panels, she'd sit by [someone of high position] such as the head of HR of the Air Force, and she'll tell them what we are thinking [like let space operators stay in the NRO], and what are they going to do to her? They respect her opinion. So, sitting next to General Chili Chilton, she informed him what a horrible decision he made by putting us into non-flight suits. His response was, 'Well, so what? Tell him to retire in a flight suit. I don't care.' So here we are."

Chris finished with his characteristic grin. Then he said to me, "Thank you, honey, for doing that, on behalf of space operators everywhere." Then he finished, "So that's why we're wearing these today."

He continued with a "Long Note of Thanks." He said, "It's all about the Mission and People. A mission is something beyond a career and beyond a job. It is a sense of purpose. So, it's all about the mission, and without the people, you can't do the mission."

A mission is something beyond a career and beyond a job.
It is a sense of purpose.

Chris said that before he was in the military, "We had these really unique problems. We had trouble with China, Russia, and the Middle East." Then he added jokingly, "I'm glad we fixed all that."

He talked about watching the news with his parents when he was growing up and hearing about things like the American hostages in Iran, and his dad would always say, "Son, what are we going to do about that?" That gave him a sense of ownership of the problem and a purpose in finding a solution. That became a theme throughout his career. When Chris saw something that needed to be done, he did it.

Then Chris put up a slide with the poem "Sea Fever" by John Masefield and quoted the excerpt, "All I ask is a tall ship and a star to steer her by." Then he provided context.

Pointing out friends in the audience, Chris said, "Col. Sparky Olsen can tell you, and so can Col. Ted Cope, that there was a contractor who could come in the room, and she could make everyone in the government have a sense of conviction that they forgot... By year four you can get so focused on your career and your next promotion and what your annual reports say and are you going to the right school after this... So much junk that you forget why you joined the Air Force in the first place and why you were here. What was it all about? What am I doing here?"

He added, "That one person could come in, and she would polarize the room." Then he said, "To quote Sparky Olsen, 'She could see BS coming a mile away,' and she would call it out."

Chris explained, "That was very important for me because when I heard her talking I thought, 'Yes, that's what I'm here to do!'" He added, "And I really appreciate that she's been doing that forever. As a polarizer in the room, when I see a person that doesn't get what she's saying, I don't want anything to do with that person because I get that they either don't want to understand, or they don't like what she has to say, or they're indignant that they're being called on the carpet for that."

Chris thought for a moment and then said, "This goes back to the 1999 timeframe... I saw that person—the patron saint of Air Force operators and operations everywhere—doing that with a mission." Then he stopped and said, "By the way, I'm talking about my wife, Michele." Everyone laughed.

"First she was industry, then she goes on to be government—one of the youngest SES, General/Flag Officer equivalents of all time—then she decides they're not getting with the program and goes to Google to fix it that way, and then decides she can do it better on her own." Here he did a plug for my new business. "Sunesis Nexus—if anyone needs some help, she's sitting right here, so just let me know." Everyone laughed again.

Then Chris got serious, looked at me and said, "Honey, I sincerely appreciate the conviction that you gave me." He pointed to the poem on the screen and said, "A star." Chris said, "Thank you for everything." Then he presented me with a bouquet of red roses and a diamond bracelet and added, "Don't forget this day." I haven't. His words were so edifying to me, and I treasure those memories.

Chris shared some favorite quotes during his presentation. His favorite slogan was "*Molon Labe*," which is Latin and means "Come and Take Them." He had picked up that line while working with Task Force Spartan and after watching the movie *300*.

He also shared one of our favorite quotes:

Freedom is never more than one generation away from extinction.
We didn't pass it to our children in the bloodstream.
It must be fought for, protected, and handed on
for them to do the same.
~ Ronald Reagan

That is so true. So many sacrificed so much over our nation's history to preserve our liberty—some paying the ultimate price with their lives. The least we can do to honor their sacrifice is to be vigilant in defending freedom and preserving it for future generations.

Speaking of future generations, Chris honored Sophia during the ceremony. She had been riding in the car with him when he had his severe medical event in October. He cited her bravery and how much he appreciated her love and support. Then he gave her a Red Ryder BB gun.

Chris concluded by reading the poem "Invictus" by William Ernest Henley, which ends with the words, "I am the master of my fate, I am the captain of my soul."

It seemed fitting, for he had served his country honorably and did it his way. Chris was a doer and did what was required even if others thought it was impossible or attacked him for doing it. Through his military service and the innovative capabilities he implemented, Chris saved countless lives and led others with honesty and integrity. I was so proud of him—my husband and soulmate.

As this special celebration concluded and we said goodnight to family and friends, we felt hopeful and blessed. Chris and I had such a happy family and thoroughly enjoyed sharing life with our delightful and beautiful daughter, Sophia. We had good health and a lovely home that was our oasis from the hustle and bustle of the Washington, DC, area.

Chris was wrapping up an impactful military career and had a promising future in the private sector. I was continuing to build my business. We had our shared passion project—our nonprofit startup—that would enable us to apply our national security expertise to the humanitarian sector, building on the good we had done for the country and doing good for the world.

John Quaid, Michele, Chris, Martha Quaid, Shirley Weslander, and Sophia following Chris's retirement ceremony (2015)

That was one of the happiest moments of my life—celebrating Chris, and in his characteristic way, him celebrating me and all we had done together. Our collaboration was so fulfilling. I thanked God for giving me such a wonderful life partner who I loved very much.

Chris and I could have never imagined our respective life journeys would bring us to this moment. God had blessed us so much and given us the desires of our hearts. We had each other and our beautiful daughter; we were a very happy family.

We would celebrate our wedding anniversary on the thirty-first, and the next day would start a new year. As Col. Ted Cope would say, "The future's so bright, you have to wear shades."

EPILOGUE

Choices are the hinges of destiny.
~ Pythagoras, philosopher

Everything in life is a choice, and our choices matter. None of us can control the circumstances we face in life, but we can control our attitudes and responses. The choices we make—big or small—impact our lives, the paths we take, the people we meet, and how we fulfill our destinies. Choose wisely.

Happiness is a choice that begins with gratitude. There is always something to be thankful for, even if it's simply a new day with no mistakes in it. Cultivate and maintain an attitude of gratitude, no matter your circumstances; this will change your outlook on life.

A few years ago, I read a sign that said, "What if you woke up today with only the things that you thanked God for yesterday?" By thinking about what you are thankful for, you will be reminded of your blessings no matter what you go through at any time in your life. And, if you live in America, the land of liberty and opportunity, you are more blessed than most of the world's population.

Character is destiny.
~ Heraclitus, philosopher

Your character determines your destiny. It takes more than intelligence to be successful; it takes grit, determination, innovation, and intelligent risk-taking.

Though my career path was not as I had expected, God gave me the desires of my heart and the opportunity to positively impact my fellow citizens, my country, and the world.

Integrity matters. Always do what is right, regardless of the personal cost. Be trustworthy, and trust your gut instinct. Stay true to yourself and your convictions.

Be courageous. Live boldly, even if others think you are crazy. It takes courage to stand for what you believe in, and there are rewards for doing so. Know that whatever you face in life, you will never face it alone—God is always with you.

Be genuine. My colleagues and I did not see eye to eye on all matters; still, they knew where I stood and that I was committed to hearing all inputs and considering all the information and options available before making a decision. They also recognized that once I made the decision, I owned it and took responsibility for the outcomes.

My colleagues also knew I was open to new information as it became available and would make changes as necessary, if possible. People respected me for that. They also knew my word was my bond; they could trust me to honor my commitments. So when I asked them to take risks with me that could benefit the mission, they were willing to do so. The bond of trust enabled us to do great things together—even things others considered impossible.

Life is precious. You are God's masterpiece, created for a purpose, and you are here for a time such as this. No one is here by accident, even if your parents say you were a mistake. No matter your circumstances, God loves you unconditionally the way you are, and nothing you've done in the past or could do in the future will change that. Nothing can separate you from God's love.

Don't compare yourself to anyone else. What is your value? You are priceless. God has a plan and a purpose for you. Why are you here? God has given you unique gifts and talents and put you here at this time and place to uniquely impact the world. "And we know that in all things God works for the good of those who love him, who have been called according to his purpose" (Romans 8:28, NIV).

We were created to have a relationship with God and relationships with others. Healthy relationships strengthen us and bring us joy. If you look for ways to bless and honor others, God will bless you in return. True love is selfless.

Hold on to hope. Embracing hope on purpose can influence our thoughts, attitudes, and outlook. Hope can be developed over time until it becomes a habit. When we have hope, it releases joy, and "the joy of the Lord" becomes our source of strength even in difficult situations. Jesus said, "I have told you these things, so that in me you may have peace. In this world you will have trouble. But take heart! I have overcome the world" (John 16:33, NIV).

Change can be frightening, but it affords growth opportunities. God works through all your life experiences to shape and mold you into the person you are meant to be. Throughout my life, I faced challenges. I had to think on my feet and problem-solve in real time. Remember, diamonds are created under pressure, and gold is refined through fire.

Though I sometimes did not understand the closed doors and detours in my life, looking back later, I saw the purpose. God directed my path. Even if you think the direction God is leading you in seems impossible, remember the words of Jesus: "With man this is impossible, but with God all things are possible" (Matthew 19:26, NIV).

You will never experience more joy than in fulfilling God's purpose for your life.

You will never experience more joy than in fulfilling God's purpose for your life. We can have peace knowing that God's plan for our lives is always better than our own. He created us; he understands our hopes, dreams, and desires. If we surrender our will and let God guide us, we won't stress trying to make everything work. We will do our best to honor God's calling and trust his perfect will and timing.

God created you, wants what is best for you, and wants to bless you. God will work in and through you to do amazing things if you are willing to be used by God.

Watch your thoughts, they become your words; watch your words, they become your actions; watch your actions, they become your habits; watch your habits, they become your character; watch your character, it becomes your destiny.

~ Lao Tzu, philosopher

The future is "to be determined"—it is yours to define! Your past does not determine your future. Don't accept things as they are today. Imagine how they could be and make it so. We must be the change we want to see in the world.

Take some time to consider what is your higher calling. What are your superpowers? What is your mission in life? Then find like-minded people and leaders who share your core values. Great leaders inspire a shared vision and enable individuals to discover their talents, hone their skills, follow their passion, and fulfill their purpose.

What you regret most are the things you didn't do in life, the risks you didn't take, and the "what ifs." So, go for it! What will be your impact? What will be your legacy? Whatever your answers are, live valiantly! Have faith, and be courageous! Remember, "I can do all things through him who strengthens me" (Philippians 4:13, ESV).

Take some time to think about your dreams for the future and write them down. Ask God to give you hope for the great plans he has for you. Remember, God is always with you, and God is always faithful. "For I know the plans I have for you," declares the Lord, "plans to prosper you and not to harm you, plans to give you a hope and a future" (Jeremiah 29:11, NIV).

"For I know the plans I have for you," declares the Lord, "plans to prosper you and not to harm you, plans to give you a hope and a future."

Walk in faith, act in love, and endure in hope! May my story inspire you to **change your stars, live your purpose, and achieve your dreams**!

GLOSSARY

Four-eyes: an alliance comprising Canada, Australia, the United Kingdom, and the United States

Five-eyes: an alliance comprising Canada, Australia, New Zealand, the United Kingdom, and the United States

ADF-C: Aerospace Data Facility–Colorado

ADF-E: Aerospace Data Facility–East

ADF-SW: Aerospace Data Facility–South West

AFRICOM: Africa Command

AMC: Air Mobility Command

ANG: Air National Guard

AOR: Area of Responsibility

AVID: Advancement Via Individual Determination

BHS: Bothell High School

BIAP: Baghdad International Airport

Blue Angels: United States Navy flight demonstration squadron

C&A: Certification and Accreditation

CAC: Common Access Card

CDA: Congressionally Directed Action

CENTCOM: Central Command

CIA: Central Intelligence Agency

CIO: Chief Information Officer

CJCS: Chairman of the Joint Chiefs of Staff

CJTF: Combined Joint Task Force

CMS: Community Management Staff

CNAF: Commander Naval Air Forces

COIN: Counter-Insurgency

CONOPS: Concept of Operations

CONUS: Continental United States

COTR: Contracting Officer Technical Representative; "co-tar"

CPA: Coalition Provisional Authority

CTO: Chief Technology Officer

CVW: Collaborative Virtual Workspace

DAU: Defense Acquisition University

DCI: Director of Central Intelligence

DCID: Director of Central Intelligence Directive; "d-skid"

DCIO: Deputy Chief Information Officer

DHS: Department of Homeland Security

DIA: Defense Intelligence Agency

DIRNSA: Director of the National Security Agency; "dirn-sa"

DISA: Defense Information Systems Agency

DMA: Defense Mapping Agency

DNI: Director of National Intelligence

DNIMA: Director of the National Imagery and Mapping Agency

DoD: Department of Defense

DOP: Desktop Optimization Pilot

DRNO: Director of the National Reconnaissance Office

DV: Distinguished Visitor

DVC: Disney Vacation Club

EE: Electrical Engineering

EEO: Equal Employment Opportunity

ER: Emergency Room

ESOP: Employee Stock Ownership Program

ESR: Engineering Study Report

EUCOM: European Command

EW: Electronic Warfare

EWI: Education With Industry; "e-we"

EWO: Electronic Warfare Officer; "e-wo"

EXCOM: Executive Committee

EXEs: Exploitation Engineers

FCPS: Fairfax County Public Schools

FDNY: Fire Department of the City of New York

FFRDC: Federally Funded Research and Development Center

FOB: Forward Operating Base

FY: Fiscal Year

GC: General Council

GEMS: Girls Excelling in Math and Science

GEOINT: Geospatial Intelligence

GMT: Greenwich Mean Time

GPA: Grade Point Average

GWOT: Global War on Terrorism; "g-wot"

HMMWV: High Mobility Multipurpose Wheeled Vehicle; "hum-vee"

HOOAH!: Army battle cry

HPSCI: House Permanent Select Committee on Intelligence; "hip-c"

HUMINT: Human Intelligence

HVT: High-Value Target

IC: Intelligence Community

ICA: Image Chain Analysis

IDEX: Image Data Exploitation softcopy imagery workstation; IDEX II

IED: Improvised Explosive Device

IG: Inspector General

IMINT: Imagery Intelligence; "m-int"

INTELINK: a set of web-based services, tools, and technologies hosted for the benefit of the intelligence community, with the purpose to share intelligence and related information across the national security enterprise; services are provided at the unclassified (U), Secret (S), and Top Secret (TS/SCI) levels

IR: infrared

ISAF: International Security Assistance Force; "i-saf"

ISR: Intelligence, Surveillance, and Reconnaissance

IT: Information Technology

J2: Chief of Intelligence for a Joint Military Command

JCC: Joint Collaboration Cell

JFCOM: Joint Forces Command

JIATF: Joint Inter-Agency Task Force; "ji-at-if"

JSOC: Joint Special Operations Command

JVB: Joint Visitors Bureau

JWICS: Joint Worldwide Intelligence Communication System; "j-wix"

KSG: Kennedy School of Government, Harvard University

MBA: Master of Business Administration

MCS: Mountlake Christian School

MILAR: Military Aircraft

mIRC: Microsoft Internet Relay Chat; "merk"

MD: Mission Director

MOU: Memorandum of Understanding

MREs: Meals Ready to Eat

MS-DOS: Microsoft Disk Operating System

Multi-INT: Multidiscipline Intelligence

NASA: National Aeronautics and Space Administration

NATO: North Atlantic Treaty Organization; "nay-toe"

NDU: National Defense University

NFA: National Flight Academy

NGA: National Geospatial-Intelligence Agency

NGB: National Guard Bureau

NGO: Non-Governmental Organization

NIMA: National Imagery and Mapping Agency; "nee-mah"

NPIC: National Photographic Interpretation Center; "n-pic"

NPS: National Park Service
NRO: National Reconnaissance Office
NSA: National Security Agency
NTM: National Technical Means
NYPD: New York City Police Department
O&M: Operations and Maintenance
OCIO: Office of the Chief Information Officer
ODNI: Office of the Director of National Intelligence
OEF: Operation Enduring Freedom
OIF: Operation Iraqi Freedom
Ops: Operations
OSO: Operational Support Office
OTEC: Operational Technology Evaluation Capability; "o-tech"
PDDNI: Principal Deputy Director of National Intelligence
PE: Physical Education
PEB: Product Engineering Branch
PM: Program Manager
POTUS: President of the United States
RADAR: radio detection and ranging
ROC drill: Rehearsal of Concept drill
ROTC: Reserve Officers Training Corps; "rot-c"
S: Secret
S&T: Science and Technology
SAP: Special Access Program
SBCC: Santa Barbara City College
SCIF: Secret Compartmented Information Facility; "skif"
SecDef: Secretary of Defense
Semper Gumby: always flexible
SETA: Systems Engineering and Technical Assistance; "see-tah"
SIGINT: Signals Intelligence

SIPRNET: Secret Internet Protocol Router Network; "sip-er-net"

SME: Subject Matter Expert

SOCOM: Special Operations Command

SOF: Special Operations Forces

SOP: Standard Operating Procedure

SSCI: Senate Select Committee on Intelligence; "sis-c"

STEM: Science, Technology, Engineering, and Mathematics

TA: Teaching Assistant

TDY: Temporary Duty

TOPGUN: United States Navy Strike Fighter Tactics Instructor program

TRUEX: Training in Urban Environment Exercise

TS: Top Secret

TS/SCI: Top Secret/Secret Compartmented Information

TX: Technical Executive

U of R: University of Rochester

UK: United Kingdom

US: United States

USA: United States of America

USAF: United States Air Force

USDI: Undersecretary of Defense for Intelligence

USO: United Services Organization

UTC: Coordinated Universal Time

VAP: Virtual Archive Portal

VTC: Video Teleconferencing

WWF: World Wrestling Federation

WYSIWYG: What You See Is What You Get; "whiz-e-wig"

Zulu time: the time at the Zero Meridian, more commonly known as Greenwich Mean Time

ACKNOWLEDGMENTS

To God be the glory. Though I never met my earthly father, I know that I am a daughter of the King, and God created me for a time such as this. It has been my prayer that God would work through my story to touch the lives of others.

I am grateful to my mother, Shirley, for telling me I could do whatever I set my mind to and achieve it. She started me down the path of believing in myself and pursuing my dreams.

My grandparents, Glenn and Ruth, were the prayer warriors in my life. God heard their prayers for wisdom, discernment, favor, and protection. I have felt God's presence and blessing in my life and career.

There has been no greater cheerleader in my life than my beloved Chris. No one could ask for a more loyal and trustworthy friend, loving husband and soulmate, and stalwart protector and defender. He was such an affectionate and doting father to Sophia and kept us laughing and in good spirits. Sharing life together was such a joy.

Chris was very excited for me to write this memoir and planned to help me after he retired from the military in December 2015, which I greatly appreciated as we had so many shared career experiences.

Instead, in January 2016, we found ourselves battling for his life, which turned our world upside down. Held in Sophia's and my arms, Chris passed from this life to eternal life with Jesus on 16 December 2017. That journey is a whole other story. Even through the pain and heartache, we know God was with us and that someday we will be reunited with Chris in heaven.

It was challenging to write this memoir without Chris, and I hope to have honored him in writing it. There's a saying, "It's not the years in your life that count, but the life in your years." Chris lived life to the fullest, loved with passion, led with honor, and did so much good in his forty-seven years on earth. He is deeply loved and sorely missed.

Our darling Sophia is the greatest gift in my life. It is an honor, joy, and privilege to be her mother. True to her name, Sophia has demonstrated wisdom beyond her years, and I know God has a special plan for her life. Her loving encouragement has meant so much to me. I appreciated Sophia reading my draft manuscript before I sent it to the publisher. As she grows into the woman God intends for her to be, I believe the stories I recorded will be even more meaningful to her.

Once I finally set my mind to achieve this goal—years in the making but delayed due to extraordinary circumstances—I was blessed to have Michael English by my side through the process. I appreciated his willingness to read parts of the early rough draft to help me determine if I had decrypted "national security speak" enough for those not in the business to understand. Mike was always willing to take time to review sections and provide feedback along the way, and help with photos.

It was providential that Lydia (Belzer) Bagley and I met. She was interested to know more about me and willing to take time during her college break to review the early draft of my manuscript before I sent it to the publisher. Her feedback was invaluable and encouraging.

I appreciated Erica Christiansen's willingness to review the first draft of my manuscript, which I sent to the publisher. She is a dear friend, young professional, and industry partner in the national security community. Erica's feedback was significant and immensely valuable.

Thank you to the Capucia Publishing team for their support during this process!

ABOUT THE AUTHOR

Michele R. Weslander Quaid is a keynote speaker, author, consultant, and educator. She is a certified professional coach specializing in executive leadership and success coaching.

Before founding her company, Sunesis Nexus, in 2015, Michele served as Google Inc.'s Chief Technology Officer for Public Sector, working with partners and clients worldwide.

Following the terrorist attacks of 11 September 2001, Michele was recruited into public service to lead change, innovation, and organizational transformation and became one of the youngest people ever sworn in as a senior executive in the US government. She led the cultural and technical integration of the national security community, establishing and serving in senior leadership positions in the Department of Defense and Intelligence Community, inspiring a shared vision and affecting positive change. Michele was the first deputy Chief Information Officer for the Director of National Intelligence. Her support of the troops at home and abroad earned her the call sign "Warrior Goddess."

Michele earned a BS in Physics and Engineering Science with honors from Seattle Pacific University and an MS in Optics from the University of Rochester. She is a graduate of Harvard University's Kennedy School of Government program for Senior Managers in Government and a Fellow of the Chairman of the Joint Chiefs of Staff CAPSTONE program.

She has received prestigious honors and awards, including the National Geospatial-Intelligence Agency Meritorious Civilian Service Medal. Michele was named one of "DC's Top 50 Women in Tech" by *FedScoop*, in the "Power 100" list of influencers by *Washington Life,* and one of "The 7 Most Powerful Women to Watch" by *Entrepreneur Magazine*.

Michele is a professional member of the National Speakers Association. She is a Certified Professional Coach (CPC) and Energy Leadership Index Master Practitioner (ELI-MP).

Photo credit: Robb Lee, Coffee and Pie Productions